I0816456

LIFE LESSONS, WILD STORIES AND UNEXPECTED EPIPHANIES FROM FORTY YEARS OF FRIENDSHIP WITH THE PRINCE OF DARKNESS

STEPHEN REA

SIMON & SCHUSTER
New York Amsterdam/Antwerp London
Toronto Sydney/Melbourne New Delhi

Simon & Schuster
1230 Avenue of the Americas
New York, NY 10020

First Simon & Schuster hardcover edition November 2025

Interior design by Wendy Blum

Manufactured in the United States of America

1 3 5 7 9 10 8 6 4 2

Library of Congress Control Number has been applied for.

ISBN 978-1-6680-6107-7
ISBN 978-1-6680-6109-1 (ebook)

INTRO TAPE

This book is dedicated to Ozzy and Sharon, Michael and Lynn, my dad, Billy, and mum, Linda, and Elicia and Nicola.

The women win, 5–3.
No need for extra time or penalties.

CONTENTS

FOREWORD

BY JACK OSBOURNE

August 7, 2025

I'M WRITING THIS FOREWORD on a flight back to Los Angeles, having just left my family home in Buckinghamshire, England. Before heading to the airport, I half joked with my mum, "This might be the worst trip home ever."

We had just laid my dad to rest, and the weight of that moment hung heavy in the air. Walking out of the house for the last time on that visit felt surreal. The familiar walls, the quiet rooms, the reality that I would not see my father back in LA, and the faces of people who had come to pay their respects were still fresh in my mind as I stepped outside. Waiting in the driveway was the car that would take me to Heathrow. Behind the wheel was Stephen Rea.

Stephen showed up at the house within hours of my arriving in England the day after my father passed. I'd last seen him only eighteen days earlier at the Back to the Beginning concert in Birmingham, England—my father's final show. On July 5, Stephen was buzzing around with a huge smile on his face, full of life, working. Doing whatever needed doing. This time, it was completely different. The house was full of people crying, flowers were showing up, letters were piling in, the house felt like chaos as we made the preparations for my father's funeral. Stephen was one of a very small circle of people that came to support us. He was in the corner, eyes red from crying, but in true Irish fashion, he never let it show in front of us. He was there to help, to be a friend, to help us hold it together, to serve my family when we needed it most. My mum had lost her husband. My siblings and I had lost our father. The world had lost Ozzy Osbourne. And Stephen had lost his childhood hero turned lifelong friend. We were all hurting differently, but the common thread was love for my dad, who was no longer with us. At one point Stephen said quietly, "Whatever you need, I'm here." That's when you really find out who your people are. When everything falls apart.

I honestly don't remember the first time I met Stephen, because he's just always been there in my life. So when I heard he was writing a book about his relationship with my dad, I never doubted it for a second. I knew it wouldn't be some overblown rock 'n' roll fairy tale or a bunch of recycled headlines. It would be real, because Stephen was there. He lived it. He was backstage, on the buses, in the dressing rooms, across the dinner table, and in our home. He carried these memories not because he had to, but because they mattered to him.

This book is a love letter to a life shared with Ozzy Osbourne—the man, not just the myth. When I first read it, I was struck by how surreal the whole story is. Who takes in a random teenage fan from Northern Ireland and brings him into the heart of a rock 'n' roll family? My mum and dad, that's who. They always had the best instinct for people. This book is full of wild moments, hilarious stories, and plenty of close calls. But at its core, it's about loyalty, friendship, and a bond that fame, chaos, and time couldn't break. Stephen doesn't just write about my father—he writes about knowing him, which is something very different.

Reading Stephen's book hit me hard. Some parts made me laugh out loud, others stopped *me* in my tracks and made me say out loud: "What. The. Fuck." (And that's saying something.) It's strange to see your dad through someone else's eyes, especially during the eighties, a decade my dad famously admitted he barely remembered. Stephen had a front-row seat to the madness, and somehow managed to stay sane while the world around him spun out of control. His book reminds me of everything that made my dad unforgettable: his generosity, his unpredictability, his vulnerability, and his heart. It's all here.

I'm grateful to Stephen for putting it down on paper—for giving people who love my dad, whether they knew him personally or only through the music and persona, a closer look at the man behind the Prince of Darkness. This book is funny, raw, and full of soul. Just like the guy it's about.

It mattered to me to write this foreword because I don't want anyone to think Stephen is trying to profit from my family's loss. This book was always meant to come out in the fall of 2025, scheduled long before my father passed. Stephen and I talked about whether he should still release it, and I told him without a second thought, absolutely yes. My dad would have wanted it that way. He was proud that Stephen wrote a book about their friendship, and he loved that it existed.

So in the words of my father, "ALL ABOARD!" You're in for one hell of a ride.

PROLOGUE

THE PHONE RANG IN MY HOTEL room. A summons to Ozzy Osbourne's penthouse suite.

It was January 1996, a bitingly cold afternoon in New York City and eleven years, almost to the day, since I first met the Prince of Darkness. Back then, in the balmier climate of Rio de Janeiro, I was a fifteen-year-old with a thick Northern Irish accent, a bad mullet, and an even worse wispy adolescent mustache. I'd matured into a clean-shaven twenty-six-year-old with shoulder-length hair and an Americanism-twanged brogue from a decade of international travel. Sprawled on a cushy king-size bed, trawling cable channels, killing time before I left with the band for our next tour stop in Worcester, Massachusetts.

We were holed up in the swanky Essex House Hotel, tucked away in ritzy, glitzy Midtown Manhattan. The doors exhaled a delightful swish gliding shut, the carpet swamped your feet like quicksand, the all-enveloping bathroom robe warm enough for the Antarctic. Two nights running, returning in the wee hours after a late-night bite with Ozzy's management staff at the Carnegie Diner, Liza Minnelli was in the lobby. Both times she was alone and tipsy, clutching a glass of champagne and smiling while shimmying a little dance by the front desk, looking lost in her own world. The hotel oozed class, but it was discreet, less ostentatious than the brash Trump Tower or the boastful

Four Seasons, both nearby. A soothing oasis stuffed with luxurious comforts for global celebrities to escape the Big Apple craziness.

I rapped on Ozzy's door and his assistant answered. "Ahhhhh, our favorite Irishman! Come in, come in. Ozzy has a present for you," he said with a grin. Ozzy had already given me the gift of changing my life forever, but while I never took my luck for granted, I grew accustomed to it. I stepped into the suite.

Its colossal single picture window framed Central Park, battling for attention with the towering skyscrapers. On the gleaming dining room table ringed with high-back cloth chairs Ozzy's artist sketchbook sat open. He frequently doodled with felt-tip pens during downtime, and it was typically a rainbow of psychedelic colors, a surrealist montage of curls and swirls. The smell of coffee draped over me: he called it his "rocket fuel" and drank it so strong and thick it was more solid than liquid. I walked past his Lifecycle, an exercise bike installed in every hotel and dressing room, positioned opposite a TV in the living area. Six heavy-duty black duffel bags and suitcases littered the floor, some zipped open and partially hidden under jumbled clothes—with luggage for a fourteen-month world tour, he was perpetually digging around for something.

Ozzy was on the couch, engrossed in a World War II documentary on the History Channel. Barefoot in his ubiquitous hotel room uniform of black leisure pants and plain black T-shirt, he looked relaxed but tired, as he often did on the road, a concoction of chronic insomnia, a hectic touring schedule, and a bombardment of afternoon media interviews taking its toll. He glanced over his shoulder, smiled, and beckoned me over.

"Steve, these are for you," he said, gesturing to two books on the marble coffee table in front of him, gold bangles jangling on his wrist. "I bought you these. I want you to write things down, stories, just to keep a record, write whatever you want, they're for you."

The words tumbled out in his unique mid-Atlantic voice. He had a move he did all the time, like a shrug crossed with an open-mouth expression, followed by him scooching forward, as if instead of hitching up his trousers, he was hitching up his body. He watched from behind round, blue-tinted glasses, mouth ajar, as I put my hair behind my ears and bent to examine the two fantastically lavish notebooks.

I had never seen books this fine, but I instinctively knew he bought them in the foyer gift shop. Bored and restless in his room, he was prone to turning up in the boutiques and cafés in hotels, desperate to get out for a bit, looking for a change of scenery and to stretch his legs, but not wanting to head onto the streets. That brought hassle: fans demanding autographs, tourists pushing for photos, unsigned musicians thrusting him demo tapes.

Each book measured nine by eleven inches, the size of printer paper, and was a hefty inch and a quarter deep. One was black, the plain white paper embellished with a velvety yellow ribbon bookmark stitched to the top. The other was its nonidentical twin, a majestic navy-blue cover with a white ribbon and lined pages. Inserted in both, elongated cards read "Naturally finished full-grain leather." This was typical of Ozzy, the most generous person I ever met. Unsure whether I preferred lined or unlined, he bought both. Anyone else would have picked one and told me I could exchange it.

I lifted each in turn, tracing my fingertip along the gilt-edged tops, flipping them open, listening to the meaty sound the pages made when flicking through them, like shuffling a new deck of cards. They had that instantly identifiable rich leather smell you find inside a new high-end sedan. A tiny *99.00* was written in pencil in the top right corner of the first page. With tax, he spent $220, probably on a whim, as I guessed it unlikely he went shopping specifically to hunt down something for me to write in. I stuttered and spluttered an incoherent thank-you, but he waved me away, not as a ruler dismissing a courtier, but because he knew I was embarrassed and my gratitude was embarrassing him. Though a legendary rock star, he remained modest and unassuming, always dodging praise and expressions of appreciation.

I heaved them up, grunted another thanks, and said I'd see him later. I didn't ask for instructions or clarifications and returned to my room.

Three decades later, the books sit side by side on a shelf in my home office in New Orleans, not two feet from where I'm typing this. The black one, with the plain pages, I've never written a word in. I wanted to keep it untouched, to preserve his thoughtful present, a symbol of our relationship. It still crackles when opened, the gold bookmark as dazzling as on that day in New York.

But the other, the dark-blue journal with the lines . . . It's battered, the cover scratched, the spine nicked, the pages jam-packed with cursive longhand.

It contains stories experienced firsthand. Sometimes transcribed in real time, in a backstage dressing room or on a tour bus. Sometimes jotted down later, when I returned to my hotel room, often as the sun was rising, determined to recount the night's events no matter how many drinks I'd had. (Usually a lot.)

And it contains stories I didn't experience, stories of Ozzy and his bandmates that occurred before I was born, incredible stories even I—the most obsessive Ozzy Osbourne fan ever—had never heard. Sometimes they were shared as a group of us drank through the night in a hotel bar. Often, though, Ozzy told them to me, sitting at his kitchen island, on his living room couch, on his private jet, sipping hot chocolate and eating cake in his suite.

After leaving I did what Ozzy asked—like I did any time he or his wife and manager, Sharon, requested something, as I always will, so indebted am I for the unexpected way they made my dreams come true.

He asked me to write. So, I wrote.

IT TOOK ME A LONG TIME to crack open that book after filling it in the nineties, around a quarter of a century in fact, but it feels much longer.

Now I'm in my fifties. I've still got shoulder-length hair, but it's streaked with gray. When I go home to Belfast, I'm told I talk like a Yank. Back then

I wore the same blue-tinted round glasses as Ozzy to be like him, but these days, revisiting the pages, I need plain old reading glasses.

When I started writing this, I was three years older than Ozzy that day in Manhattan. He seemed like the elder statesman of rock then, but the Ozzy I knew never lost his childhood exuberance. Much of that is down to Sharon. She handled the grown-up stuff so Ozzy could stay Ozzy—always up for a caper, always ready to play a joke.

That book was this story's source material. Sure, I recounted late-night drunken escapades, but it's also a diary and a journal, the thoughts of a young Irish lad swept up in an adventure alongside his hero, an international rock icon. I trace back my life's important moments to his shows, and marked milestones not by birthdays or holidays but by Ozzy gigs. When he bought me the books, I'd been to around 80 concerts—I finished up seeing 219, culminating with his farewell performance in July 2025. The chapters in this book are numbered for those shows, starting with #1 back in August 1984.

I fell in love with Ozzy's music from a distance, but when I got to know him, he taught me about relationships, family, fatherhood. Enough time has passed for me to dispassionately examine those life lessons. We are both older—and maybe even wiser.

So down from its shelf I take the book—the first draft, really. And I write again.

PART ONE

FAN

#1

MONSTERS OF ROCK FESTIVAL

DONINGTON PARK RACETRACK
CASTLE DONINGTON, ENGLAND

August 18, 1984

WHEN I WAS FOUR, terrorists riddled my grandmother's house with bullets. She escaped death by inches. She was on her couch when gunmen sprayed her living room from the street. I remember visiting the day after and picking at the holes in the wall. It was mistaken identity. She lived in a Lilliputian two-up, two-down terraced house in a staunchly loyalist area often scarred by burned-out vehicles and homemade barricades. The next-door neighbor was a prominent paramilitary and the hit men mixed up the addresses, typical of botched, amateurish attacks then. I was born in Belfast in 1969, months after "the Troubles" began in Northern Ireland, so it was all I knew. Shootings and bombings cloaked my childhood: Ulster is a minuscule county, and everyone was affected by the euphemistic "civil unrest."

My dad owned a small commercial printing business wrecked twice by close-proximity bombs. I was in elementary school when the first detonated two blocks away, and I went to the premises in the aftermath with my parents: my dad, slight with a bushy mustache and not an ounce of fat, in jeans and a dress shirt featuring the huge collar of the seventies; my mum, smaller and rounder with long dark hair and oversize glasses. We cleaned up as best we could, scrabbling to erect temporary window coverings over a carpet of broken glass, razor-sharp shards lying ensnared on machinery and furniture. The Troubles were everywhere, constant, pervasive, intrusive.

Until 1975 we lived one street over from my grandmother, but that year we escaped to the suburbs, with cul-de-sacs and bungalows, garages and gardens, where door-to-door bakers delivered homemade pies. At eleven, I passed an exam to attend an exclusive all-boys school for free. By then I was passionate about music, a love I immersed myself in away from the terrorism, and I pawed through my parents' vinyl albums, seventies mega-sellers by the Eagles and Meat Loaf and Supertramp.

I spent summers with my dad's parents at their vacation home, a trailer in the seaside village of Groomsport, eleven miles away, but it felt like the other side of the world. The day we arrived I met Brian, whose family owned the trailer next door. It was he, and others there, who turned me from pop to punk to heavy rock. My first 7-inch single was "C'mon Everybody" by the Sex Pistols. When I looked it up, I was shocked to discover it came out in June 1979, so I was only nine. Sucked down a rabbit hole, I researched the release dates of others I owned, such as "At the Edge" by Stiff Little Fingers (1980), so I guess by ten I was a full-fledged punk rocker. My parents took my friend Joe and me to see the Boomtown Rats, fronted by future Live Aid organizer Bob Geldof, at the Ulster Hall. There were two ticket prices, and my dad sprang for the more expensive, but when we got in, we discovered those were for floor general admission. A pair of ten-year-olds in that mosh pit at the height of punk would have been disastrous, so he convinced the staff to let us onto the balcony. I was underwhelmed, complaining to Joe afterward, "They played all their good songs in one go at the end." I hadn't yet grasped the concert concept of crescendoing to a climax.

I morphed into a metaller, Brian buying me the AC/DC single "Girls Got Rhythm" for my tenth birthday, my first outright heavy rock record. There was no Sirius, no YouTube, no streaming, and you copied albums onto blank cassettes to pass around. Independent radio stations were rare, and the tyrannical BBC ruled the airwaves like a despotic dictator. The sole national exposure to our genre was Radio 1's *Friday Rock Show*, from 10 p.m. to midnight weekly, a two-hour oasis of hard-edged refreshment in a broadcasting desert of soulless trendy boy bands and mindless disco bollocks. For rockers of my generation, the program was a ritual and the soundtrack of our youth, presented by Tommy Vance with an inimitable baritone voice smoother than a five-hundred-year-old whiskey. (I met him once; he was so courteous and played a request for me.)

At the caravan site, a handful of us, in jeans, black T-shirts, and stone-washed faded denim jackets pocked with patches, would meet at the playground. Someone would have a boom box, though often there was little boom about it. We climbed onto the rickety merry-go-round to listen, the radio in the middle, our skinny legs rubbing against the graffiti-covered splintered wooden boards, huddling for warmth (even in summer), the volume just loud enough to cover the rhythmic squeak from the lolling rusty swing set swaying in the breeze, our fingers tapping along on the flaking blue handrails, tasting the salt of the sea, smelling the beach, the darkness punctuated by the glowing ember of an older teen's cigarette, or the sweep of the lighthouse in Donaghadee.

THE FIRST TIME I ENCOUNTERED OZZY Osbourne was in November 1981 with *Diary of a Madman*, his second solo release. My classmate Neil brought it into school, and I borrowed it to copy onto a C-60 cassette, six songs on one side, two on the other. I can still picture that blue-and-white tape: the scrawled writing in black ballpoint pen; the clacking of the cheap plastic box snapping shut; the peeling identifying sticker with a frayed corner. It was the album that made me a fan, and I played it so many times it groaned in protest during the silence between songs. Ozzy later told me about making it, a story I recorded in my journal:

> "*Diary of a Madman* we wrote in three weeks and recorded it in two. We only had a one-album deal, and the record company didn't even know we'd done it. I mixed that album over the phone. I swear to God, I was on the telephone from truck stops in the States listening to the middle section of 'Little Dolls.' And that, 'Oh no, oh no . . . ' at the start of 'Flying High Again' was a mistake. I started singing late, but once I heard it, I said, 'Stop, leave it as it is, don't touch it.' Randy [Rhoads, his first guitarist] would deliberately do stuff up and down the frets, string noise, just so it didn't sound so clinical."

I adored Ozzy's uniquely identifiable voice and was entranced by the evil churning around his image. The inverted crosses, the black magic undertones, the satanic throne, songs like "Mr. Crowley" about an occultist . . . I knew he wasn't a devil worshipper who led black masses, then slept in a crypt—it was an act, a role he played, like Christopher Lee or Bela Lugosi. He was a hypnotic showman shrouded in a forbidden persona with a sinister sound. I wrote to the embryonic fan club—the Ozzy Osbourne Information Centre—and received a membership packet and ID card. I was official member #90.

While not listening to *DOAM*, I was poring over the biweekly magazine *Kerrang!* Ozzy was in it a lot. I remember a reader's letter published in the Kommunication section: before automated spreadsheets, he had combed every issue to compile a table of the most-featured acts, something like a half point for a short article, two points for a feature, five points for a multipage spread. Ozzy was top, the most written-about artist in the publication's history. They ran a small photo of him in his underwear pretending to masturbate, adding, "Ozzy notches up another half point." How can I have a perfect recollection of a photo caption from over forty years ago, yet nowadays I forget why I walked into the bedroom?

Ozzy's next release was the live recording *Talk of the Devil* (*Speak of the Devil* in the US, a difference I wondered about for years), exclusively containing Black Sabbath songs, no solo material. He was the original singer, fronting the trail-blazing band for a decade before being kicked out in 1979, and this was a one-fingered salute to his acrimonious firing. It went on sale the day I turned thirteen, and I used birthday cash to buy my first Ozzy record. If *DOAM* caused me to fall in love, *TOTD* cemented the relationship. My dad was teaching me to play drums on a practice kit with rubber pads, and for months I placed the album on the turntable, put on the headphones, whacked up the volume, and banged along. By 1983 I was doing odd jobs for family and neighbors for money and saving my allowance as I graduated from fan to fanatic with every version of everything: 7-inches; 12-inches; picture discs; colored vinyl; limited editions.

It was a decade before cell phones, and Belfast was mired in the Troubles, but I was allowed to go with friends to see bands like Whitesnake and Saxon. Concerts had a suffocating security presence. Police milled around, cradling machine guns, their heavy black shoes scraping the pavement, their radios squawking. They traveled in boxy gray Land Rovers, square armor-plated vehicles rattling and echoing as they bounced along. Sometimes it was the British army, or a hybrid patrol of both, but always someone with a rifle: watching, waiting. The acts venturing into our war zone were rapturously received, but not many did—neither Sabbath nor Ozzy had ever made it.

Marooned in that gig-starved wasteland, we resorted to illegal bootlegs captured by fans sneaking in a recorder like a Sony Walkman. Then they had it on cassette, and using a double tape deck they copied it to sell or swap. Sometimes the tapes sounded abysmal. Sabbath performances in the US from 1972, recordings relayed from the original for thirteen years, leaching quality every time, an analog snapshot degrading in each iteration as it circled the globe. But others were spawned from the mixing desk, so crystal you heard the PA hiss between songs, and my collection grew, mainly bought from adverts in *Kerrang!* (each cost around £1.50). The homemade catalogs were typed, then photocopied, and the entries looked like this:

OZZY Memphis, Mid-South Coliseum 28/4/82 C-90 B

Artist, city, venue, date, show length in minutes, and finally, quality (a subjective rating by the owner).

I was also a frenetic trader, and it seems archaic and quaint how much time I spent writing letters.

A Belfast collector wanted to meet for a beer—I was five years from the legal drinking age, so declined—even though they had plenty to occupy them in Ulster, I'm sure the cops wouldn't have turned a blind eye to my scrawny underage ass.

An older Canadian sent letters and photos with the cassettes we traded, and after one bootleg finished his voice kicked in as he recorded me a message—while smoking a bong. The concert quality I don't remember, but the clarity of his rambling, drug-fueled monologue was pristine: sucking, deep draws of breath, smoke gurgling and bubbling through the pipe as he filled his lungs, him coughing and spluttering about a trip to Thunder Bay. I was barely in my teens, living in a suburban bungalow on the edge of Europe, listening to a man on the other side of the world getting high.

I hunted Ozzy bootlegs relentlessly. If a device was secreted into a venue, you can be sure I had the result, and I was ecstatic if I uncovered a new recording. Even now I can recall exact dates, cities, and arenas from concerts in the eighties, etched into my memory forever. As my hoard passed three hundred, I created elaborate covers for the lined index cards in the flimsy plastic boxes. The inlays arrived with a handwritten track listing, but I advanced into custom design, photocopying pictures from *Kerrang!* and cutting and styling them to fit. I bought transfer stencils and rubbed the lettering onto the artwork, always a Gothic font for "Ozzy."

I SAT WITH THE LIGHTS OFF, waiting for 10 p.m., because it was better to concentrate on the music in the dark. I was in my grandparents' front room—"parlor," as they called it—my hand tapping impatiently on the tweed armchair, the thorns on the immense rosebush scraping against the condensation-slathered window, one bar of a buzzing electric fire the only insulation from the dark and windy late-autumn night. Tommy Vance always started the *Friday Rock Show* with two songs back-to-back with no introduction, and I thought for sure he'd feature a track from *Bark at the Moon*, Ozzy's first studio release in two years.

That night, November 25, 1983, he launched the show with album opener "Rock 'n' Roll Rebel," an instant classic in my opinion. Two days later, on my birthday, I got a cake decorated with "Happy 14th Birthday Ozzy Rea." Ozzy was touring Britain, and although I'd loved to have gone, I didn't dare ask my parents to spring for an expensive trip to the mainland. But two weeks before my birthday I floated the idea: Liverpool was the closest venue and accessible by boat, but when my mum called the box office, the only tickets left were at the back. I agonized for a day, but I couldn't justify the travel and expense for crappy seats. Thank God. He fell ill and canceled the gig. I would have been crushed if we went for nothing.

IN APRIL 1984, I PAID TWENTY pence per word (thirty pence for bold type) to place a notice in the Klassifieds section of *Kerrang!* reading "WANTED. OZZY ITEMS. Bootlegs, rarities, videos, anything." It happened to appear in the edition with Ozzy's guitarist Jake E. Lee on the cover under the headline “Ozzy’s New Blood!” and I depleted my meager savings further snapping up the offered memorabilia.

The first time I saw him live—the first and last time I paid for a ticket—was August 1984 at the Monsters of Rock festival at the Donington Park racetrack in England.

Every summer, a crunching one-day bill lured tens of thousands of long-haired, denim-clad, patchouli oil–smelling devotees. The 1984 edition was anchored by AC/DC, Van Halen, and Ozzy, a trio of hard-hitting heavy-weight headliners. My mum was vacationing in Malta with my aunt Carol when my dad agreed to take me. She arrived home and I greeted her at the door with “I’m going to Donington!” not “How was your trip?” My friend Brian from the vacation park—who helped introduce me to Ozzy—came with his sister and her friend, and we squeezed into my dad’s car, drove to Dublin, caught the ferry across the Irish Sea, then headed to Derbyshire.

It was crowded and hot, and we scrimmaged to get close to the front, but surrendered and camped stage right, level with the mixing tower. There was no video screen, so Ozzy was a distant action figure, but I could tell he was on form, reveling in the late-afternoon “underdog” spot, cajoling the crowd, clapping as if he were a seal on acid one minute, prowling like a lunatic serial killer the next. I knew the set list by heart. I’d been listening to bootlegs since the tour started nine months previously, and I predicted the songs he’d drop for his truncated one-hour festival slot. I was blown away. I loved Van Halen and AC/DC—still do—and bought records by both before owning an Ozzy release. But I was so ecstatic at finally seeing my hero, I checked out when he left the stage, emotionally and physically. I eased out of the sweaty, heaving throng and wandered the grounds.

In the decades since, I’ve seen hundreds of concerts—more than two hundred by Ozzy alone—by dozens of artists and many marvelous shows. But this remains my favorite gig ever. The one disappointment was I had not got nearer the stage.

The next time I saw him live, I stood on it.

#2

ROCK IN RIO

CIDADE DO ROCK
RIO DE JANEIRO, BRAZIL

January 13, 1985

AT 6 P.M. ON Thursday, November 1, 1984, the local news played on a ten-inch portable black-and-white TV in our tiny kitchen. More death and destruction in dark, depressing Northern Ireland. I was four weeks away from turning fifteen and sat on a hard wobbly wooden bench at our worn soft-pine table in my school uniform of black sweater, white shirt, black tie, and black trousers, my black-stockinged feet slick on the torn muted-beige laminate floor. I was inhaling the usual dinner of fish sticks, fries, peas, and buttered bread.

Head down, mouth full, I attacked issue 80 of *Kerrang!* Page three had a photo of Ozzy's surprise appearance at a recent Iron Maiden gig, and alongside it a breakout box read:

> A major ten-day rock festival is to take place in Rio de Janeiro (Brazil) between January 11-20 next year. Altogether, 13

> international acts will appear alongside an equal number of Brazilian artists. Among the top names already confirmed to perform are Queen, Rod Stewart, Def Leppard, George Benson, James Taylor, Iron Maiden, AC/DC, Nina Hagen, the B-52's, the Go-Gos, Al Jarreau, Ozzy Osbourne, and the Scorpions. All bands were chosen via a national radio poll conducted to find the most popular names among the Brazil community. A special site is being constructed by the organisers, Artplan Promocoes. It will cover 250,000 metres and accommodate a capacity crowd of 350,000. It will have 30 stores, beer gardens, restaurants, two 1,000-seater video centres, a telephone area, a mini-hospital, and a car park with room for 40,000 vehicles. The daily energy consumption is expected to be enough to light a city of some 30,000 inhabitants, whilst the sound system will deliver 70,000 watts.

I muttered, more to myself than anyone else, "Ozzy is playing a big festival in Rio."

My dad, his attention on the screen, sipping heavily sugared tea, turned away just long enough to say, "Find out about it. I've always wanted to go to Brazil."

My parents weren't wealthy, but they believed in enjoying what money they earned and valued experiences over possessions. When my dad was nineteen, he and a pal tried to hitchhike to see our local amateur soccer club Linfield play in Portugal. They turned around a few days in. Their progress was slow, and they weren't going to make the game. But that experience helped instill in him a love of travel, a love my mom shared. When I was only a few months old, they took me to Majorca in the Balearic Islands, then a run-down backwater ruled by fascist dictator General Franco. They saved all year for our summer vacation: while most Brits went to the Mediterranean, in 1980 and 1981 we flew to Florida, though in 1982 we went to Spain for the soccer

World Cup. Nonetheless, not for a nanosecond did I think I would end up six thousand miles away in Rio. I figured my dad was joking, so I laughed it off and returned to my fish sticks and magazine.

He wasn't joking. His shop was next door to a travel agency. He asked if they knew about Rock in Rio. They rummaged in their files and found a four-page leaflet—a half-assed sliver of a brochure from a London tour operator. On the front and back were the most uninspired photos ever used to advertise one of the planet's most exciting cities: a beach, a palm tree, a lily pond, those souvenir bottles containing scenes made from colored sand. It listed the daily lineup and had a brief description of a thirteen-night tour costing £895 per person (about £3,600, or $4,700, in 2024). It also featured the whimsical caveat: "The price does not include surcharges arising from unavoidable increases in costs due to Government action." As Latin American specialists, they'd seen new administrations seize power and lobby a tourist tax. With connecting flights from Belfast and spending money, it would cost more than $15,000 today.

My mum wrote to the fan club looking for more details, mentioning my early membership status.

The following Thursday, I arrived home from playing soccer. "Ozzy Osbourne's secretary called," my mum said nonchalantly. Technically it was Sharon's assistant, Lynn. She had worked for Sharon for a year, and one of her many jobs was overseeing the fan club. No doubt she was permanently swamped and answering mothers of teenage fans was low on her priorities. She could have ignored it or sent back a form letter referring us to a travel agency. Instead, she got our number from information and rang.

My mum had scribbled notes on the back of a torn envelope: the days Ozzy was playing, the hotel they were staying at, their arrival date.

"Lynn told me not to buy tickets to the concert," she said like they were old friends. "If we make it to Rio, they'll get us in for free. She gave me her number and said you should call her. She wants to speak to you herself."

I couldn't believe how casual she was acting. Did she not realize how insane this was? I wasn't really going to fly to South America to see Ozzy, right? I went to bed bewildered and lay awake for hours.

LYNN AND I WERE IN CONSTANT contact that November and December. She regularly checked in on our trip planning, every conversation elongated by barrages of interruptions as her other line rang nonstop, her putting me on hold while she dealt with the important stuff she was getting paid for. We connected instantly. I had no idea why she was so patient with me—I guess it was her genuine personality: warm, helpful. She was a twentysomething English secretary who had worked in the music business since leaving school, while I was a fifteen-year-old Irish youngster, but we chatted easily. The first time we spoke she told me about an embarrassing incident when Rod Stewart approached her table in a pub, adding, "Not even Ozzy and Sharon know that story!"

Right from the off, though, I knew my school, Campbell College, would be a problem. The festival was January 11 to 20, in the heart of the academic year. Unless they agreed to give me two weeks off, I couldn't go. It was a traditional all-boys British boarding school (though it also had day students like me), an institution superglued to its history, where our exams were set by Oxford and Cambridge. We wore a cap and shorts until we were thirteen—even in snow and sleet—and when an adult entered the classroom, we stood. At recess, the candy store was staffed by the principal's wife, and the most you were allowed to spend was fifteen pence. We queued to wait our turn, and if she heard a noise—a whisper, a laugh, anything—she slammed the hatch closed, and it stayed shut until there was absolute silence.

The worst part was the six-day week. We had classes every Saturday.

It was enriching and challenging, but occasionally like living in a Dickens novel, antiquated and conservative beyond belief. And not the type of educational establishment to grant students an extended absence to attend an Ozzy Osbourne gig. I begged my mum to write another letter, and I delivered it to the headmaster's Victorian study, pleading the case I'd rehearsed eighty times. He kept me waiting until the following week, when I came home and spotted an envelope on the floor, underneath the telephone seat, where it nestled after being aggressively projectiled through the letter box by our mailman. I picked it up, took a second to rub a thumb over the school crest embossed into the crisp white envelope, blew out my cheeks, and opened it.

There was a preamble about the request being most unsatisfactory . . . highly irregular . . . not wanting to set a precedent . . . but he had consulted with my housemaster, who described me as "pure gold," and added, "A trip to Brazil has to have some academic value." Finally, the crucial sentence I can still recite: "I acquiesce, under protest, and ask that it does not happen again." The reason I recall it is because I didn't know what "acquiesce" meant. I dived into my schoolbag and riffled through my dog-eared pocket dictionary. Elated, I couldn't wait to tell my parents in person, and rang them at work. It was on.

I PACKED AND REPACKED DURING THE Christmas school break as I fought to figure out which heavy metal T-shirts to take alongside my soccer shorts and one pair of jeans. We flew to Heathrow in the morning, and before the evening flight to Rio, we stopped at Lynn's office, two basement rooms on Gloucester Place. She was a chain-smoking petite attractive blonde, with a cackling infectious laugh belying her size. We spent the afternoon talking, and she said she told *Kerrang!* we were going to Brazil. She brought in all the photographs she took on the US legs of the *BATM* tour to show me, and I peppered her with questions about band members and set lists and being on the road. My dad had already bought me a camera for my birthday before Rock in Rio popped up, and I took dozens of photos of gold and platinum discs and framed magazine covers.

That evening at the airport I discovered I forgot to load the film. I rang her begging to visit again on the way back. (Writing this book, I asked Lynn for her memories of that visit. She told me, "Sharon was amazed someone would go to so much trouble and cost to get to the show in Rio from Belfast, and she asked me to arrange to meet you there so you could meet Ozzy. This was never mentioned in the conversations you and I had at that time, although I had secretly told your mum it might be a possibility, but not to count on it! I thought it was important that I meet you before we got there, so first of all I would recognize you, and secondly to check that you were the genuine article and not someone messing about.")

The three of us were among the last to board the plane, and we turned the corner into the jetway and, Jesus Christ! It was AC/DC! Three of them anyway . . . singer Brian Johnson, guitarist Malcolm Young, drummer Simon Wright. They had a hulking bodyguard, but were friendly and indulgent. Their minder took a couple of photos of me with them, but when I babbled, "Keep taking pictures!" he shot me a look saying, "Now, son, don't push it."

Eight other music fans had festival tickets and were making the pilgrimage (they were in their twenties and thirties and not with their parents), and on board we heard *Kerrang!* photographer Ross Halfin ask the row behind us, "Have you seen the kid from Belfast?"

My mum turned around and said, "The kid from Belfast is here." He said they might feature me in *Kerrang!* and introduced me to his colleague, writer Mick Wall, who said to call him in Rio. Rod Stewart was on our plane, too, and queued ahead of us at immigration. But that was just the start.

THE FESTIVAL OPENED ON FRIDAY, JANUARY 11, 1985, and at lunchtime we were bused twenty miles to the City of Rock, a sprawling purpose-built complex featuring the world's biggest McDonald's, the stage towering in the distance like a prelaunch rocket ship. I've read that the site covered 2.7 million square feet and 1.4 million fans attended the ten-day event, while the folklore is 350,000 fans saw Queen on opening night, illustrating the overall monstrosity. The first act was pregnant singer Baby Consuelo (her stage wear had a hole exposing her bulging belly); next were Whitesnake, Iron Maiden, then Queen with Freddie Mercury, the year before his final show.

The following day I called Mick, who was working on a backstage pass for me. If he was successful, I needed a passport photo. We went foraging for one. No easy task, and it took hours tracking down someone capable of producing an instant print. After trying every likely store, we eventually found a one-man operation on the sidewalk with an ancient boxy camera. The black-and-white image was created with a developing technique so rudimentary the edges were blurred.

Mick wrangled my dad and me tickets to a VIP party that night thrown by EMI Music at the Copacabana Palace Hotel. As we got ready, my dad looked at what I was wearing—green Adidas soccer shorts and an Ozzy shirt.

"Umm, Stevo, is what you've chosen maybe a wee bit too casual?" he asked.

"You think? But it's a party for rock bands. Will they not all be wearing denim and leather?" I asked. I should have fired out and bought a button-up, but I was so naive I simply picked my least aggressive heavy metal T-shirt, gray rather than black, and put on jeans. It says a lot about me that I deemed that suitable for a glittering star-studded bash in a five-star hotel on Copacabana Beach.

An hour later we were mingling with rock stars: taking photos with Queen; eavesdropping on Rod Stewart and Steve Hackett from Genesis; getting my Rock in Rio itinerary autographed by Whitesnake and the Scorpions. They weren't ringed by security guards or in a roped-off section; they were circulating, drinking champagne, and we chatted with Whitesnake drummer Cozy Powell and bassist Neil Murray.

"How do I get him to stop worshipping guys like you?" my dad asked them, hooking his thumb at me.

Neil shrugged. "I hope he doesn't think we're perfect," he said, and my dad chuckled politely, he and the Whitesnake bassist discussing me as if I wasn't there.

Decades before cut-price intercontinental flights and airline flash sales, everyone was amazed we traveled from Belfast. An unforgettable evening hanging with famous musicians in a luxury hotel overlooking the world's most quintessential beach—when I should have been in Northern Ireland studying biology.

Most of the acts stayed there, and for all ten days, a crowd of locals rammed the entrance, hoping to see a star. We walked back through it to our place, the cut-price Excelsior, only two buildings away. Although it was patently downmarket, groups clung to our front door, too: the eight other festival-going Brits who flew out with us were mostly young, long-haired gringos, so it wasn't a stretch to surmise they were in bands. Some of them signed more autographs than the artists, stopped in the street, babies thrust at them in restaurants for photographs.

I THOUGHT OZZY WAS CHECKING INTO the Copacabana Palace on Sunday, and wired despite the jet lag, I jumped out of bed before 8 a.m. and camped at the entrance, hoping to see him arrive. I waited three hours, until my parents got up and wandered over to find me—they explained Lynn gave us the date his overnight flight left, not arrived. We headed back to our hotel for breakfast, and an older Canadian tourist at the next table heard our accents and introduced himself—unbelievably, he was stationed in Belfast during World War II and dated my grandmother's friend.

Undaunted, I returned to the Copacabana the same time Monday. I knew Lynn, and Mick was working on a backstage pass for me, yet I still spent hours skulking on the sidewalk to catch a glimpse of Ozzy. An hour into the vigil, a car shrieked up, and bassist Bob Daisley and guitarist Jake—from the *Kerrang!* cover when I placed my Klassified for Ozzy stuff—dived into the lobby. Twenty minutes later, Lynn came out after spotting my Union Jack T-shirt in the mob. Ozzy had been spirited through a back door and was fast asleep.

That evening we were in the hotel bar, figuring where to go for dinner, when the Canadian walked in. "Hey, buddy, you're an Ozzy fan, right?" he said. "I was having a beer in the bar at the Copacabana Palace, and he walked in. I just left two minutes ago, he's there right now."

"Let's go," said my mum.

"No, we can't just walk in there," I replied. "We should wait to hear from Lynn."

"It'll be fine, c'mon," she said, and she and my dad marched off, me trailing anxiously in their wake. With us looking like a vacationing family rather than stalkers, the zealous doormen let us in.

We slid into seats in the corner, ordered drinks, and I glanced across the room. Ozzy and Sharon sat at a table on the far side. I recognized drummer Tommy Aldridge as well. Ozzy had his back to us, but he was loud, animated, talking with his hands, Sharon bellowing. My mum swiveled to look, and I hissed at her for gawking, my dad laughing at me. A few minutes later Lynn arrived, saw us, and came over, giggling.

"You little sneak!" she said, waving her finger. We chatted briefly and she went to join her boss.

Out of the corner of my eye I noticed Ozzy push back his chair, stand, and turn around to face us. He walked to our table, stuck out his hand, and said, "How ya doing?"

I sat, immobilized, staring at him open-mouthed like a catatonic guppy fish.

"How was your flight?" he asked.

I strangled out a garbled whine, struck dumb. I couldn't manage a single word.

He waited a beat, muttered something, then bounded away, probably convinced I was the rudest kid he'd ever met. Lynn reappeared, laughing.

"You let me down!" she joked. She said when he got back, he "freaked out" because I was so starstruck I couldn't even manage a hello.

My parents gave me a good-natured ribbing. But all of Team Ozzy were so friendly, I eventually relaxed. Ozzy's assistant had a beer with us, and Lynn introduced me to drummer Tommy and bassist Bob, though I still felt stupid, and continually snatched furtive looks at Ozzy. He walked past on his way to order at the bar, and my mum said, “Want to ask if you can have a photo together?” I thought about it for a second, decided to risk it, and answered with a tight nod. I hovered beside him, then asked if it was okay.

“ ’Course it is, son, come here,” he said. He put his arm around me, smiled, and tilted his head toward mine. My mum snapped the first picture I have with Ozzy, January 14, 1985. I met Ozzy. Spoke to him. I had a grin wider than the outstretched arms of the Christ statue at Corcovado.

In the lobby the following day I bumped into a music press photographer staying in our hotel.

“Ozzy’s doing a press conference at the Rio Palace Hotel. I’m gonna jump in a taxi up there—wanna come?” he asked, and I tagged along. In a second-floor ballroom, Ozzy sat up front with a translator answering questions from the local press. I stood at the back, too intimidated to sit, baffled at the stream of inquiries about devil worshipping like “Are you a demon?”

When it was over and the place emptied, Lynn saw me and said to come with her. She led me to a door behind the stage, opened it—and there was Ozzy. He shook my hand and smiled, then said, “And how are you today?”

“Better—I’m able to speak to you,” I replied, and smiled back, delighted. I’d completed a full, coherent sentence.

WE SPENT THE NEXT AFTERNOON SIGHTSEEING, included as part of the tour package. A dozen passengers spread out in our coach—a guide, the three of us, and the British music fans—as we took a city tour and rode the cable car up Sugarloaf Mountain. But as spectacular as the scenery was, I couldn’t wait for Wednesday, day six, Ozzy’s first appearance, on the bill with Rod Stewart.

Lynn called and said she’d arranged for me to travel with the VIPs to the site. I told my parents what I was doing rather than asking permission—only my second Ozzy show, and I abandoned them and my fellow festivalgoers to their regular boring bus and watching from the crowd out front, the viewing area drenched by overnight rain. I met Lynn, Mick, Ross, and the others in their lobby and she handed me a backstage pass, a cardboard rectangle with a handwritten male name I didn't recognize. I asked who he was.

"Don't worry about him, he's a ligger," said Mick, a term *Kerrang!* used for a hanger-on who posed about backstage without working. So, perfect for me, then. Lynn told me the guy didn't need it, but later he found me: he was using someone else's pass and wanted his proper accreditation. We swapped, and my new one read "Mark Weiss—photographer." Unease bubbled up and festered within me. If Mark's pass also had his name, and security noticed two of us had passes with the same name, it would be me, the impostor, who was thrown out. Eventually I couldn't take it and shared my concern with Lynn: she scrawled "-ener" at the end of the name to change it. No one paid even cursory attention to Mark Weissener, but those things preyed on your mind when you were a youngster in possession of his first backstage pass.

I sat with Mick to ride the bus to the inner sanctum behind a stage that reportedly cost $10 million. My first time entering the adult fairyland, accessible only to those with contacts in high places.

What I didn't realize then, but know now after decades of backstage access at outdoor festivals, was that it was a first-rate setup. The structure housed dressing rooms, production offices, and a hospitality area for liggers like me, all under one roof. Tan walls decorated with watercolors and prints were erected to carve out a space underneath the stage: a pine corner unit cradled a TV showing the performances, a fridge stocked with drinks guarded the entrance, a gray carpet muffled the din of the gig above, and the greenroom was liberally sprinkled with lime couches. Both nights Ozzy played I spent most of my time there, content to hang out near his dressing room with other privileged guests. No slopping through pungent puddles among the proletariat for me.

From there, stairs climbed to the behemoth of a three-hundred-foot stage, and behind it, crews worked on equipment in a capacious expanse resembling an aircraft carrier belowdecks. They had a groundbreaking innovation for festivals, with multiple acts powering through shortened shows: a section of the stage rotated, so while one artist played, roadies prepped for the next. When the set ended, the circle pivoted, and the gear was assembled and ready. In all my gig-going since, I've never experienced anything close to the scale of that setup.

Forty-five minutes before Ozzy's set, Lynn appeared and said, "You've been summoned, Stephen. Come with me." I followed her to the dressing room—Ross wanted photos of me with Ozzy for *Kerrang!*

I was nervous. Fleeting encounters in hotel bars and press conferences were all well and good, but this was a different level. I clung to the wall like a limpet. Ross had created a studio in the bathroom, his instructions echoing off the tiles, Ozzy in sparkly red-and-black stage clothes, snarling and sneering as the bulbs flashed and pinballed around the ceramic. They paused to reset.

Ross yelled at me, "Pull that lead, will you?" A vipers' box of yellow cables snaked at my feet, slithering back and forth along the floor, and I stared at them, battling to work out which he meant. His hands full of cameras and lights, exasperated by my inactivity, he shouted, "That one! That one right there!" and nodded. Desperate to break out of my moronic paralyzation, I bent and yanked the nearest cord.

Ozzy's hair dryer flew off the makeup table and smashed onto the floor with, what seemed to me, an earth-shattering boom.

I froze, mortified. It lasted three seconds, but it felt as if a horrible silence descended like the angel of death. Lynn picked the hair dryer up off the floor while I cringed and croaked an apology. Red-faced, I walked over and knelt in front of Ozzy with him pretending to throttle and beat me. "Look frightened, Stephen!" ordered Ross, me ruining his shots by grinning and smiling despite my nerves. In forty-eight hours, I went from being a teenage fan to starring in a photo shoot in my hero's dressing room.

WHEN IT WAS TIME, LYNN WALKED me up to the stage, and I stood at the side beside her and Sharon. After years of collecting bootlegs, I knew what was coming, as Ozzy rarely changed his set list. It was something else that got me. In August I'd been bewitched by a dot at the other end of a field; five months later I watched him sing the same tracks from near enough to touch him. We despair of today's generation filming everything on their phones and not living in the moment, but I was as bad in 1985. I've so many photos, I don't know how I had time to appreciate the experience. Sharon left a few times, and whenever she returned, she always ducked in front of me to avoid blocking my lens. Such thoughtfulness toward a fifteen-year-old nobody.

I was right there at the side of the stage, listening to songs I first heard in a darkened room in my grandmother's house on another continent. I saw Ozzy beckon a roadie onstage to grab his rings, Jake lift a finger to signal the song's end to Tommy, Bob jokingly raise and lower his eyebrows at keyboardist Don Airey—nuances you would never spot from the audience, an unspoken language evolved from years of playing together—and I felt Ozzy's sweat on my face when he brushed past on his mid-set break.

Afterward, Lynn came to take me to the band's bus. On the stairs, a guard was clearing a path and took exception to my pass. Neither of us understood why, so Lynn grabbed my hand and led me a different way—where we collided into Rod Stewart coming up the gangway. On the coach, guitarist Jake sat beside me, and Ross took snaps, my second photo shoot of the night.

He said, "Jake, you've had the cover of *Kerrang!* already, good going."

Jake nodded. "Yeah, number thirty-six."

"No, issue forty," I corrected him, rude twat that I was.

He frowned. "Pretty sure it was thirty-six."

"Nope, it was in April, definitely number forty, I had an advert in it," I insisted.

Ross thought the conversation comical and leaned across the aisle to relay it to Sharon. When Ozzy got on, we drove back in torrential rain. Sharon had the coach detour to a steakhouse they visited, but it was closed, and I was disappointed the magical evening wasn't prolonged. The following day my parents sent flowers to the Osbournes to thank them.

TWO NIGHTS LATER, WITH FOUR DAYS left of our trip, we returned to the Copacabana Palace bar and found Ozzy with Ronnie Biggs. He was the UK's most infamous prison escapee after breaking out of jail following his conviction for his role in the Great Train Robbery in England in 1963, and the Brazilians refused to extradite him because he had a child with a nightclub dancer. As he was leaving, I asked for a photo with him. He had downed a few drinks and was in a jolly mood, imitating my accent.

My parents went to find a restaurant for dinner and I hung out at the bar alone, sipping sodas, trying to ingratiate myself further with musicians, Ozzy staff, and journalists. It worked—Jake, Bob, and Whitesnake guitarist John Sykes headed to the steakhouse, and I was invited. With hundreds of fans eternally camped out front, it needed military precision to run the gauntlet: a car pulled up; security cleared a path through the mob; bouncers held open the doors; we sprinted head-down and leapt inside as the yelling crowd grabbed at our shirts. It was the closest I'll ever get to being in the Beatles. My parents were passing by on their way home and saw the commotion, so my mum grabbed her camera in case it was a celebrity—instead it was her son. She took a picture of us speeding away, me off to dinner sandwiched between two metal guitar shredders.

Beforehand, as we waited for our car, Lynn took me aside. "Stephen, listen to me. You can pay for your own meal, but don't pay for anyone else, got it?" I nodded, and knew she was talking about Bob, who had a reputation for being cheap. We rejoined the group, and he walked over and pointed at my white Velcro shoes I'd bought that day.

"I like those. Where'd you get 'em?" he said. I told him, and he asked to try them on, inquired how much they were, then wanted directions to the shop. I started explaining, but thought it was easier to offer to get them. The following day I delivered them to his room, and true to form, he didn't have enough local currency to pay me. He offered a couple of American dollars to make up the difference, but I told him to forget it—after all, what were a few cruzeiros between me and my new rock star friends?

The penultimate day was Ozzy's second festival appearance alongside exclusively hard rock acts. Sharon skipped the helicopter and came onto the bus. I sat behind her and Mick, eavesdropping.

"Ozzy's not old, but he doesn't need a band that's his age," she said. "We want young, hungry guys alongside him, and there are hundreds of musicians out there who look great and sound great." I realized Bob Daisley and Tommy Aldridge wouldn't be around much longer and I never met either again.

At the first conversation lull I poked my head between the seats and blurted, "Sharon, can I ask you some things?" I'd three questions saved for years.

"Of course!" She smiled.

"Why was it *Talk of the Devil* in Britain, but *Speak of the Devil* in the States?"

"Because that's what the Americans say. They use 'speak' instead of 'talk' like us."

"Oh. That's it? Also, why was the song called 'Forever' on the UK album, but 'Centre of Eternity' in the US? On all my bootlegs he introduces it as 'Centre of Eternity' onstage, even in Europe."

"The original title was 'Forever,' then it was changed to 'Centre of Eternity.' But the British record company had already got hold of the name and started the production process, so they went with that."

"Okay. How do you pick where songs come in the set list?"

"It depends on lots of things, there's no one factor. For instance, we have to take into account the order that songs are programmed into Don's keyboards. It's planned around reasons like that."

"I see. Thank you." I sat back. I must have been a pain.

I was only two backstages old, but cocky enough to wander up alone to watch Whitesnake, the band before Ozzy, from stage right. After that, Ozzy's set was even better than his first appearance at the festival. Halfway in, a live chicken was thrown onstage. Did they expect Ozzy to bite its head off like he did with the bat? (The story is true, but accidental: it was hurled onstage in Iowa in 1982; he thought it was a rubber toy and stuck it in his mouth.) How did they get a chicken in? It stood transfixed, then Ozzy scooped it up and ran past us with it. I don't know what happened to it. Maybe it got ejected for not having the proper pass.

I stayed on to watch the Scorpions while the band changed, then Ozzy's assistant called me into the dressing room.

"You want Ozzy's top?" he asked, nodding at a red vest on the floor, wringing wet and drenched in sweat. My mum insisted on washing it when we got home, and I mounted it on black cloth and hung it on my wall. I still have it.

The parking lot had churned to mud under a driving rain, and the odor of the sludge mingled with the exhaust fumes and heat concocted a stink that had us all gagging, forcing us to hold our noses on the slip-slide traverse from backstage to the coach as AC/DC blared behind us. Ozzy bounced aboard, flung open a window, inhaled deeply, and said, "Ahhhhh, lovely smell. Reminds me of Bill Ward."

Ward was Black Sabbath's drummer and the subject of many of the best stories Ozzy told me. Like when they flew the supersonic jet Concorde from London to New York:

> "Bill hated flying and would always get whacked out of his mind on a flight. He turns up at the airport for a two-month American tour with four bottles of cider in two plastic bags. I said, 'Is that your luggage?' and he says, yeah, he'll get some stuff when he gets there.

> "We're flying Concorde for the first time and I'm all excited. But Bill drinks all his booze and takes all his pills, because he's thinking it's going to be a long flight. What he hasn't sussed is that it's only three and a half hours.
>
> "When we land he is still out of his brain, because by his reckoning the flight should be only half over. He doesn't want to know about even getting off the plane. Then yet again it's 'Ozzy—get your mate.'
>
> "So, I drag him into customs and next thing he has gone down like a ton of bricks, and all his pills have gone scattering all over the floor. I'm, 'See ya!' and I'm outta there."

I wasn't on the Concorde that day—though I did fly it in 2003—but my transport felt just as special, as I sat with Martin Birch, the producer famous for his history with the likes of Deep Purple and Fleetwood Mac. I asked what he was working on, and he said he was engineering a live Iron Maiden album. Embarrassingly comfortable with my place in the entourage, I suggested he cut out drum and guitar solos, and he nodded graciously.

At the hotel I helped Ozzy's assistant bring in bags, and he told me to tag along while he delivered them. Ozzy answered, sticking his head around the door. "Oh, it's you, son," he said, opening it wider, and I saw he was dressed only in his underwear. I stuck out my hand and gibbered, "Ozzy, sorry to bother you, but I just wanted to thank you for everything you did for me." He waved us inside. While he grabbed a *Playboy* to show a spread to his assistant, Sharon rolled her eyes and came over. She pointed to a display of flowers, presumably from the hotel or promoter, and said, "Look, Stephen, dead." Then, pointing to those my parents arranged, she said, "Alive." They asked about my flight home, and we made small talk for a few minutes, but I knew I was intruding and made to leave.

Then Ozzy said to ring him in the morning and we would have breakfast together.

I was shocked, unsure I'd heard correctly, but recovered to mumble and bumble, "Really? What time? Should we come here or will we meet you—"

"Call me at ten," he cut me off, and I thanked him and backed toward the door. I walked along the hallway in a daze, the corridor echoing the squeak of my new shoes. The downpour had abated, but the tropical humidity was so heavy it saturated my tongue, and I splashed through the puddles back to our place, oblivious to the grime.

AT TEN THE FOLLOWING MORNING, I rang him on the house phone. He appeared five minutes later, alone, no minders, no handlers, swinging his room key, and we got a table for four in the restaurant. Just me, my mum, my dad, and Ozzy Osbourne. It's my favorite Ozzy memory ever.

"You're from Belfast, right? You know, I really wanna play that gig," he said. (He did, thirteen months later.) "What's it like living over there?"

We discussed the Troubles and how it affected our lives, and that led to him telling us about having a drink with the fugitive bank robber Ronnie Biggs in the hotel bar.

"You know what he told me? When he escaped, he only had fifty grand left outta all that cash. I mean, what's that, like a year's wages?" My parents exchanged a look, and I knew what they were thinking—it was seven times the average annual wage in Ulster.

A woman interrupted us, saying she had an antique shop and wondered if Ozzy was interested in "this little piece"—a two-foot-high statue of a grotesque hunchback. "Maybe you could use it in your stage show?" she suggested. He told her it was very nice and he'd send his wife to see her later, all four of us battling not to laugh in her face.

My dad told him about their lunch the previous day, when a wealthy Brazilian at the next table insisted they try the same local delicacy she was eating. She ordered it for them, then told the waiter to bring a different dish, then another, and another before she left. When their bill came, they discovered the diner had ordered all the food—but told the restaurant to put everything on my parents' tab. Ozzy laughed so hard he had to put down his coffee before it spilled.

It was relaxed and comfortable, just a Northern Irish teenager having Sunday brunch with his idol in Brazil. After an hour Sharon appeared, and I leapt to grab her a chair and bring it to our table.

My dad laughed. "He's not letting you sit beside your husband, Sharon," he said as I placed the chair beside my parents, not between Ozzy and me.

The Osbournes were friendly, thoughtful, and funny. After another half hour, we thanked them and said goodbye. The last thing Sharon said to me was "We'll stay in touch."

Rock in Rio was the greatest, biggest, longest rock festival the world had ever seen. But it wasn't the music blasting from the record-breaking PA that left an indelible mark on this teenage nobody from Belfast. It was when I ate in the rarified atmosphere of the dining room in a five-star hotel on Copacabana Beach, cutting strawberries with weighty silver cutlery chinking against fine china, sipping from a porcelain cup to a background of the hushed chatter of elegant, refined diners. Those I'd met—Ozzy, Sharon, their staff, music journalists—were feeling like people I knew, not just people I knew about from the pages of *Kerrang!* I flew home with pages of addresses and phone numbers.

Rock in Rio changed my life. I don't mean in a spiritual way, but in a tangible sense: it led to bigger and better things. I forged friendships, made connections, and bonded with the people working for the Osbournes. I know I would not be sitting in New Orleans today, certainly not writing a book, if I had not gone. I am sure my life would have played out differently.

Back at our hotel, I asked my mum if she thought Sharon was serious about staying in touch.

"I'm sure they will. She wouldn't have said it if she didn't mean it, right?"

#5

THE ULTIMATE SIN TOUR

AVONIEL LEISURE CENTRE
BELFAST, NORTHERN IRELAND

February 7, 1986

ON THE WAY BACK from Brazil, we stopped in London again to see Lynn. My camera was loaded this time, but I only took a few snaps. Before, I was hypnotized by the shiny discs and awards, but I'd become a ligger who hung backstage and did photo shoots with Ozzy.

After a dip in the rock star whirlpool I returned to my dull-as-dishwater daily drudgery. In my black school uniform, I trudged back to classes, my charcoal scarf wrapped around my bowed head against the chilling hail under dark gray clouds, the color of Copacabana and the sound of samba a taunting memory.

Extra Kerrang! had been launched, a supplement to the regular magazine, and Mick interviewed Ozzy in Rio for a cover story. When issue 4 arrived, I recognized Ozzy's outfit from our session and riffled to the article. Five pages about Brazil, no mention of me. I was so disappointed.

Then *Kerrang!* 89 came out on March 7, 1985, with a full-page color photo of Ozzy and me. The caption read "NO IDOL boast: Ozzy Osbourne beats on the brat, aka Titanic True Fan Stephen Rea, who travelled all the way to Brazil from Belfast to see his hero rock in Rio."

Opposite, Mick wrote: "Seated at another table in the bar is a young man by the name of Stephen Rea. Stephen is 16 years old [*sic*] and has bullied, outsmarted, and persuaded his parents into flying him over 8,000 miles from the family home in Belfast to the Rock in Rio festival. He's an Ozzy fan of the darkest water, and when he's not nailing his soul to an upside-down cross, he's also a very heavy Iron Maiden freak. To be sitting just a few tables from his idol, the mighty Oz, is an experience I'd dearly loved to have been through when I was just 16. . . ."

I bought fifteen copies. We'd cut up rock magazines and plaster pages on our bedroom walls, and two weeks later an older kid at school said he put up my photo, because it was either me or the reverse side with Meat Loaf. I'm still working out whether to be offended.

I remained on the Osbournes' radar, and when I flashed into their orbit it lit up my dreary life with sparks of excitement. The fan club increased the frequency of their mailings, and as Lynn had been with Sharon less than two years, she wasn't a walking Ozzy encyclopedia like me. I became her Google for Ozzy. She called frequently with questions the internet now answers in seconds. She started referring to me as "our consultant." She had me compile competition questions and I fired off seventy. She picked three at random, but they were particularly difficult, and no one got them right. So she sent me the prize, a print of Ozzy by an artist commissioned by Sharon.

I had always enjoyed writing, and from an early age I wrote sprawling narratives from prompts in English class. Aged eleven I was making up my own newspapers with local stories, and by Rock in Rio, I knew I wanted to be a journalist. Mick had given me his address and said to keep in touch. I mailed him stuff I wrote, and I remember a line from one of his notes: "The last thing you sent was the best thing you've written. You'll make it, no problem."

He was compiling Ozzy's official biography, *Diary of a Madman*, and asked for my help with the discography. One fall night I sat cross-legged on the floor in my attic playroom, Ozzy on the turntable low, a rhythmic pounding as the wind and rain lashed my dormer windows in the slanted roof, me shooing away our cats as they padded over, both slipping across the cardboard record covers I had fanned around me like I was a medieval wizard recanting a spell in a protective circle. Mick called and read me the list provided by the publishers, and I checked it against the serial numbers on my records, adding a few special editions and correcting the odd catalog number. He promised me a copy when it was released, and when it turned up, I was shocked to read on the contents page "Discography by Stephen Rea." On Amazon I'm listed as a coauthor. A man with no shame, to this day my resume reads "I wrote a chapter in the official Ozzy Osbourne biography."

SABBATH RE-FORMED FOR LIVE AID, AND Lynn went to their performance in Philadelphia. She sent a T-shirt and a signed Live Aid memo dedicated to me by all four Sabs. When I rang to thank her, she said she forgot to get Ozzy's autograph at the event and so did it in London. When she told him it was for me, he asked how I was doing. He appeared on the BBC's *Desert Island Discs* radio show and mentioned me by name. I was thrilled to the bone by those little moments.

I knew Ozzy was returning to the road, and I squirreled away every spare penny, determined to attend as many gigs as possible. Lynn knew I had an extensive VHS collection and wanted me to copy it so they had everything on hand at the office. She told me to send her a bill for doing it and I declined, too embarrassed to charge the Ozzy camp for duplicating Ozzy TV shows. But she was firm, saying, "Stephen, just do it. You'll need the money for your touring fund."

I would. But not for the first dates: Ozzy's next shows after Rio were in my hometown. A year on from me flying six thousand miles to see Ozzy, he played back-to-back gigs six miles from my house.

In the run-up to the concerts at the Avoniel Leisure Centre, politicians tried to ban him. Because when not shooting or blowing each other up, we were God-fearing folk, and despite daily murderous atrocities (for instance, days before, IRA terrorists detonated a bomb hidden in a trash can, killing two passing policemen), they had nothing more pressing on their plates. Sectarian violence had been with us since the sixties; it was all my generation knew, so normalized and part of the everyday fabric our leaders could ignore it. Instead of saving teenagers from being lured into a life of death and destruction by paramilitaries, they could focus on keeping out Ozzy—the real danger to Belfast youth, apparently.

A week prior, the TV news interviewed irate residents fighting to stop him from playing in their neighborhood, convinced he would be "chewing rats" and biting off the heads of their cats and dogs. The station appealed for viewers' feedback, and I wrote in, relating how well the Osbournes treated me in Brazil. They aired a follow-up piece, and a few days later I received a letter from the presenter—he planned to read it out, but they ran out of time. Probably had to report on an explosion instead.

A DANK WINTER EVENING IN BELFAST, a wind whipping through the parking lot, trash and empty chip bags pirouetting, the hubbub punctuated by the tinny dull thud of drained lager cans as they were kicked over or dropped to the ground, hundreds of fans in no rush to go inside, smoking, drinking. The night of the first show. Walking in, I passed a camera crew interviewing drunk denim-clad rockers, some of whom were engaging the firebrand preacher Reverend Ian Paisley and other protesters picketing the "Satan worshipper" playing our town. I bumped into my classmates, also Ozzy fans, and one, also called Stephen, was interviewed while the rest laughed and shouted behind him. It aired the following night, the lads swilling beer and yelling. Not ideal advertising for an upper-crust stuffy school, they got a dressing-down from teachers, especially as they were two years under the legal drinking limit.

Earlier that day, I was whacked in the face with a soccer ball in PE, leaving a huge ugly speckled-red patch. I looked like a creature from the zombie apocalypse and had my mum dab it with cover-up. In Rio, I had sported an appalling tuft of a mustache in a pathetic attempt to look older, then this inept attempt at makeup camouflage. It was a wonder the Ozzy camp didn't peg me as a lunatic.

I gave my name to the promoter, and he said, "Where've you been? There was a girl standing here waiting for you for ages," and seconds later Lynn ran down the stairs and wrapped me in a giant bear hug. I followed her to the cafeteria doubling as the greenroom. Not exactly Rock in Rio. Instead of that busy backstage, there were only a handful of people around, and no sign of either Ozzy or the band, who were ensconced in their dressing room down the corridor. The TV was tuned to BBC, so I walked over when *Top of the Pops* started, to watch a prerecorded performance of Ozzy's new single, "Shot in the Dark." Aside from Jake, the group was new: keyboardist Don replaced by John Sinclair, and the instrument moved offstage; bassist Bob's post filled by Phil Soussan; while drummer Tommy was gone in favor of Randy Castillo. Randy wandered out of the dressing room and stood beside me to check out the support. He was southwestern swarthy, half-Native American, with long black hair and wearing skintight, jazzy, multicolored leggings. He gazed at the crowd for a minute, revving up, twirling his drumsticks. Even at sixteen I appreciated the juxtaposition—a glamorous American in a converted gymnasium in funereal violence-strewn Northern Ireland.

Ten minutes before the start, Lynn led me to the mixing desk. The concert was better than Brazil. My early Ozzy shows—this was my fourth—still resonate with me decades on.

This had a freshness, a rawness, the debut for a new group of unknowns with something to prove. Ozzy, too, was always better at the beginning of a tour, fit and healthy, rehearsed and refreshed, his singing strong.

I was nervous beforehand, anguished that the Belfast crowd would be as crazy-mad bonkers as usual. Most acts skipped us, the extra cost to transport equipment, band, and crew from mainland Britain prohibitive. Plowing on to Northern Ireland meant going the extra mile—metaphorically and physically. A limited potential audience in a de facto war zone with chronic unemployment and little disposable income—it was a miracle anyone ever came. So, when Ozzy showed up, pent-up frustration and curtailed emotion discharged into an exhaust vent of roaring appreciation.

My classmates, the denim-clad rockers, the neglected Belfast metallers—we all went crazy. It was an incendiary night, for once in Ulster just a figure of speech. Still, after the show, Sharon and Ozzy were obviously intent on hurrying back to the safety of the hotel, only pausing briefly as they walked past to say hello and for Ozzy to shake my hand. But when I caught up with Lynn, she told me Ozzy had asked her, "Is what's-his-name not here, that kid from Brazil?"

The second gig was even better. On the first night Ozzy had cut a track, about an alcoholic drinking himself to death. In the States he was sued by parents claiming it encouraged their kids to use suicide as a solution (doesn't seem a great business model, wanting your fans to kill themselves). This time, two songs in, "They told me not to play this song, but fuck it," he said. (Who "they" were, I don't know.) Jake ripped into the intro of "Suicide Solution." The devil-worshipping image was only a persona, but I was realizing Ozzy truly was an outsider, and it wasn't just a role he played. He didn't give a flying fuck about anybody or anything when onstage.

He and the band were less uptight, while the boozy Friday night crowd was ready to kick off the weekend with two hours of jumping and fist-pumping and moshing and yelling.

I'd listened to his voice endlessly in my room, but live Ozzy was unbeatable, and my journal has something keyboardist John Sinclair told me:

"Most singers from his era had some sort of blues influence—people like Robert Plant or Ian Gillan. But Ozzy's vocal style is

> totally unique. His phrasing is different to anybody else's—and because no one else does it, it's impossible to say it's wrong. Like putting 'Oh yeah baby' into 'Bark at the Moon' before the guitar solo: nobody else could get away with that but Ozzy. There are lots of singers around with a better range than him, but they don't have his emotion. His voice is instantly recognizable, and you know the singer couldn't be anyone but Ozzy. If you think of the real superstars—Elton John, Michael Jackson, etc.—you can tell their voice straight away. Ozzy has the same distinct sound. He would find it hard to get up and jam to some Rolling Stones song because he just doesn't have that background."

Sharon was with Lynn and me on the soundboard, and we watched as a reeling inebriated fan clambered onstage, swaying and gyrating while stripping off his shirt. Rather than kick him off, Ozzy clapped and danced alongside him as he performed the worst *Saturday Night Fever–Full Monty* hybrid routine in history.

Post-show was more relaxed. Lynn introduced me to the tour manager, who walked me to the production office, where they took my photograph and made me a laminated backstage pass. Ozzy came out of the dressing room swigging a bottle of beer in a white-and-black dazzle-camouflage suit and sat with me, just the two of us. He was buzzing and chattering.

We talked about the religious protesters outside the venue, and I said, "All they're doing is drawing attention to the show and giving you free publicity. It's crazy."

"No, it's not," he said, and laughed. He pulled faces for me while I fired off photos, never without my camera—of course.

My mum arrived to get me. Ozzy and Sharon chatted with her for a few minutes then we left. On the way home, I couldn't stop staring at my laminate, reading "The Ultimate Sin World Tour 1986, Access All Areas." My golden ticket to backstage letting me go everywhere, anywhere in the world.

#10

MANCHESTER APOLLO

MANCHESTER, ENGLAND

February 14, 1986

AT SIXTEEN I WENT on tour with Ozzy. This time without the school's permission.

The school-leaving age was sixteen, so legally I didn't have to attend. I simply stopped showing up and no students ratted me out. Occasionally I called my friend Blair to check in. Once, the physics teacher asked a bunch of questions: Did anyone know where I was, what was happening? Blair said there were shrugs, coughs, silence.

God knows how I convinced my parents to let me go. They trusted me and thought me mature and self-reliant—I was motivated, with good grades, and promised to catch up on the studies I missed. I said I'd call every couple of days, and thought I'd be away two weeks, tops, as my money would surely run out by then.

I missed a month.

I'd a hotel booking for the first stop in Dublin and a ferry ticket from there to Wales, then I was winging it, intending to travel by train or bus, finding accommodation when I arrived.

I headed to Dublin with Stephen, my classmate interviewed on TV. I knew the group was at the Blooms Hotel, so we booked in and paid cash. A couple of hours later, when I tried to call Lynn, the receptionist said, “They checked in, then left, because the rooms were too small. They went to the Grafton.” We got our money back and joined them at the Grafton. I got a pass for Stephen, and we strolled to the SFX Hall. My sixth show, and I’d progressed from free tickets to backstage passes to blagging them for friends.

Back at the hotel, we sat in the lobby bar. Ozzy and Sharon shared a couch at the far end, and on his way back from the restroom Ozzy saw us and invited us over.

“This is my friend, another Stephen,” I said.

Ozzy laughed. “Bloody hell—I thought you were a chick! I thought you were his girlfriend!” For years I teased long-haired Stephen that Ozzy had thought he was female. Stephen told him he was on TV defending him.

“Whaddya say about me?” asked Ozzy.

“I told them you didn’t know it was a real bat when you bit its head off.”

Ozzy, fooling around and smiling, grabbed him around the neck and said, “I bloody did know!” He took a swig of Guinness and asked, “You want a drink? What’s the drinking age in Ireland?”

“About thirteen, I bet,” said Sharon. He ordered us beers, and we spent two hours with him, listening to old Sabbath stories, then Stephen returned home the following day.

Ozzy’s support act on the Irish dates was Red Alert. They were from Belfast, and I’d become friendly with them, so after the second Dublin date, I went into their dressing room to say goodbye. “There was a terrible smell up there tonight,” said the singer, and the others agreed. I didn’t mention I had watched them from stage left, and three songs in I sensed someone behind me. I turned to see Ozzy, with a maniacal grin, surreptitiously lobbing stink bombs. It was one of his favorite pastimes, a dedicated drawer in his flight case holding hundreds of the little yellow vials. I loved that, although almost forty and a father of three, he never missed an opportunity to act more like a teenager than this sixteen-year-old.

Back in the lobby bar, the tour manager told me to list the shows I was attending and he'd put me on the guest list for them. I went to my room, wrote every single date on hotel notepaper, and headed back down. Again Ozzy waved me to his table, where he sat with Def Leppard guitarist Phil Collen and drummer Rick Allen, both of whom lived in the city. Sharon had flown home, and this was my first time with the unaccompanied, unsupervised Ozzy, partying free from her moderating influence, and he insisted I join him in downing rounds of whiskey. Five hours in, with four of us left, he called for his special eyebrow-shaving kit bag.

He had a trainer to help keep fit on the road, a Californian martial arts expert who didn't drink alcohol and was quiet and reserved. Ozzy decided to shave his eyebrows off. He bribed the porter for his room key and powered down the corridor, careening off walls as he prowled the hallway on his drunken mission. It was my second night on the road and already I learned a valuable lesson—lock your door and barricade it as well. We were always petrified we would be hit if we retired early, and no matter how late I got in, I ensured the door was locked, then dragged furniture over to block it.

I was to have many evenings like this, some of the best nights of my life, a few of us camped in a hotel bar, sometimes until dawn, Ozzy at ease, telling story after story, us bent double, laughing, snorting beer out of our noses, him on an unfaltering lookout for a victim to wind up.

That night was the first time he offered me a job.

"Steve, you're a helluva guy, come work for me," he said, straightening in his chair, brushing his hair back from his eyes, reaching for his tumbler.

It was an overture repeated every few days amid heavy boozing sessions. It embarrassed me unless we were alone, because I worried it seemed like I was trying to steal someone's position. He never did it sober, but I harbored the hope that some kind of employment would come from our relationship.

"Ozzy, you know more than anything else in the world I'd love to work for you, but what would I do?" I said that first time.

"Odd jobs. Run errands. Bits and bobs, we'd find you something," he answered. The other two at the table fell silent, and in the early-morning deserted lobby there was no one around, the only sound the *glug, glug, glug* as Ozzy poured water into his whiskey, the jug banging onto the wooden table as he drunkenly set it back down. As much as my heart pounded like Randy's drum intro to "Over the Mountain," I knew the offer was alcohol-fueled, sure to be rescinded when he sobered up.

It was my first marathon drinking session with Ozzy. My life's total alcohol consumption to that point amounted to maybe six beers, and the scarring from that night meant I never drank whiskey again.

When I got back to my room (after barricading the door), I dug out my six-inch-by-three-inch notepad. Every night, on the back page, I diligently kept a ledger with a record of my spending. Before the tour, I'd no idea how long my cash would last. My life savings, cobbled together from bootleg sales, the occasional odd job, and my weekly allowance, totaled £600 (worth about £2,200, or $2,800, in 2024), but was in a Northern Irish bank only accessible at limited ATMs, and I couldn't check my balance when making withdrawals.

I then flipped the pad over and scribbled shorthand notes about each day's events. I wanted to create triggers, reminders to look back on and relive staying up until daybreak downing shots with Ozzy. Even as a self-centered teen, exhausted and overwhelmed, I was aware of the special prize I had been handed. I knew I was being treated uniquely, that no other Ozzy fan—no fan of anyone—got the same access and thoughtfulness I was lucky enough to receive.

For instance, the second night in Dublin reads:

> Up sound check–support band–stink–watch p/p–after–midget–story father–aerial W's–job–eyeb's–Phil / Rick Def Lep–515

When I rediscovered the six pages of jottings from that tour thirty-four years later, the brevity was infuriating and frustrating. But I also took hundreds of photographs. Many have been nothing but a waste of storage space, repetitive and out of focus, but I've also got great candids of Ozzy, the band, the crew . . . in the dressing room, backstage, on the bus. With the notes and pictures, I pieced together what I did every day, igniting memories that had hibernated for years in my subconscious, incidents I had not thought about in decades.

AT SOME POINT IN THE EARLY evening, before the scotch-demolishing session, I was invited along on Ozzy's tour bus. It must have been Sharon's idea; only she had the authority to make the call to let a kid hitch a free ride with the artists. Out of nowhere, I was part of the entourage. The following morning, I was reading on the ferry to Wales, and the monitor engineer beckoned the tour manager over.

"Who's the punter?" he asked, nodding at me.

"A fan. Keeps out of the way, doesn't cause any trouble," the tour manager replied and shrugged. I knew even seasoned roadies who had seen it all thought my treatment bizarre.

Sometimes Ozzy and his assistant flew or were chauffeured separately, so there were seven constants: the band (guitarist Jake, drummer Randy, bassist Phil, keyboardist John), Jake's wife, the tour manager, and tour accountant Gary. (Gary had a wooden leg—when Ozzy got drunk, he invariably said, "I'm gonna steal that fucker's leg and hide it before this tour's over.")

We docked and drove north. Randy left the lounge at the back and came up front, where I was gazing at the sleet. He sidled opposite me and stuck out his hand.

"You're on our bus and I haven't even met your ass yet," he said. We were friends from that moment on.

It was late when we pulled into the snow-dusted grounds of Lumley Castle Hotel in Chester-le-Street. A fourteenth-century converted stronghold, its Gothic halls were packed with suits of armor, flickering candles, winding staircases, stone floors and walls echoing footsteps, the wind whistling underneath the heavy wooden doors that clanged shut, the thud of suitcases landing onto plush hall rugs, hissing and spitting open-hearth fires.

We were in isolated stately accommodation, so I thought I needed to taxi to the nearest town to find a cheap place to stay. But when the tour manager checked the party in, he threw me a key. Ozzy and Sharon were picking up the tab—and covering my rooms for the tour.

Around 11 p.m., after a couple of attempts, I negotiated the darkened nooks and crannies to the third-floor snooker room, a game like pool but played on a table twice as large. It had been a long travel day, and everyone but Randy and Phil had retired. I was running on four hours of sleep after our 5:15 a.m. finish, but I didn't want to miss a minute of anything. I hung around snapping photos—no sense of privacy invasion, no thought to ask permission—black-and-white shots of Randy in his leather coat, his cigarette smoke curling up into the light dangling above the table, his fingers spread-eagled on the smooth baize. Phil left and I played Randy, then he turned in, and still pumped with adrenaline, I played a game on my own. Afterward, I clipped downstairs to my room, passing the night porter swinging his lantern as he did his rounds in the snow, locking doors.

I SAW ALL SIXTEEN CONCERTS ON the mainland as well as the four in Ireland, a twenty-date run spanning a month. Before leaving home I'd trepidation about the logistical challenges of accommodation and transport in strange cities in a different country. But thanks to the Osbournes it became insanely easy. I never bought a ticket, I had a backstage pass, I traveled on Ozzy's tour bus, I stayed in his hotels, I ate in catering.

On tour, time was compressed, like living in a sped-up movie montage. Bonds were accelerated, as we were together all day, every day, no going home to the family after work. Spending a month on the road was like a year's relationship under normal conditions, and back then no one disappeared to surf the web or FaceTime relatives.

I became friends with the band, something I would have considered laughable a few months earlier. Jake was the only musician left from Rio, but he usually disappeared to his room with his wife or huddled with her at the back of the bus. I got on well with bassist Phil, but knew his newfound fame from joining Ozzy's band inflated his ego—he spent the month wearing sunglasses and a full-length leather trench coat, the shades less than imperative in the British winter. Keyboardist John meanwhile looked different from his bandmates with his short blond hair and glasses, but was a hard rock stalwart, a droll mimic with an infectious guffaw and a font of entertaining stories.

Randy was easygoing and always up for a good time. He was thirty-five, more than twice my age, and often said to me, "Steve—I'm no spring chicken." (Mötley Crüe drummer Tommy Lee was twenty-three, for comparison.) We often had in-depth discussions on the bus, and these days he'd be termed my mentor. He knew what it was like to struggle financially. He would talk about his upbringing in New Mexico, how he snuck into a Jimi Hendrix show, and how he lost his virginity to his friend's sister camping in his backyard, his friend insisting, "I'm going first. After all, she's my sister!"

Backstage was an alcohol-free zone, but nine gigs in Randy pulled me aside, handed me £20, and asked me to go buy a bottle of liquor. He said to sneak it back, he'd mix it with Coke, no one would be any the wiser. I was torn—I wanted to do it for him, but I knew, even with my negligible road experience, Sharon wouldn't be happy. I found the tour manager and told him. He took the cash and said he'd deal with it.

We had back-to-back dates in Manchester, and we checked into the

Britannia Hotel, along with support act Ratt and both crews. Ozzy's album *The Ultimate Sin* came out the day we left Dublin, but I hadn't seen it. Six months previously, Lynn called to double-check my parents' names, and I didn't ask why.

At the revolving-door entrance, a teen fan waited with a vinyl copy to get autographed, and I asked him to let me look at it. I slipped out the inner sleeve, thinking I might recognize some names—and saw in the credits: "We thank the following people for their love and inspiration . . . Billy, Linda, and Stephen Rea." Wow. I ran straight to a lobby pay phone to call my parents.

The first night, the sound died halfway through the fourth song. Ozzy and the band never left the stage while road crew scampered about like ants mobilizing to defend their home, checking cables, turning knobs, twirling dials. . . . A fan lobbed an envelope onstage, and Phil's bass tech, Barrie, scooped it up and put it on his workspace. I twirled it to read the writing, and he yelled, "Hey! Don't touch my stuff!"

They got power back, and as the equipment didn't need to be loaded out, afterward the roadies were free. Both bands and crews rammed the hotel bar, and I found myself between Barrie and the tour manager. I apologized for earlier, the tour manager asked what happened, we told him, and he said, "Stephen, don't touch his stuff. Barrie, be nice to Stephen." I bought him a Grolsch to say sorry and we went on to be friends, but it was a vital early touring lesson—and one I never lost sight of. The Osbournes and their entourage had welcomed me, I was mates with the band, but it was also important to be accepted by the roadies.

THE SECOND DATE IN MANCHESTER WAS the first time I worked for Ozzy on the road.

The tour manager asked me to video the shows with Ozzy's camera and

I was delighted to have a semiofficial job. From Manchester on, when I was asked what I did on tour—and I got asked a lot—I replied, "I record the gigs." I was rushed through an instructional guide and was terrified I'd balls up that initial concert and let everyone down.

Of course, Ozzy had a trick up his sleeve, with props waiting in the wings: For the Sabbath song "Iron Man," he brought an iron and ironing board onstage, launching into the famous call "I am Iron Man!" and holding up the iron, then miming some ironing.

The next day on the bus to Edinburgh, Ozzy wanted to watch my recording. "Let's see what this fucking dimph managed to get," he said, pointing at me ("dimph" was Ozzy's good-natured term for idiot). When he yelled, "I am Iron Man!" the picture shook, twitching up and down, back and forth. "What the hell were you doing, look at the fucking state of that, you stupid Irish cunt!" he shouted.

"I was laughing so hard I couldn't keep it still! It's your fault!" I said, and it eventually refocused.

It was a rare night off as the band powered through five dates in six nights. Live on TV, Irish boxer Barry McGuigan was defending his world featherweight title against Danilo Cabrera from the Dominican Republic. We gathered in Ozzy's room to watch, and he insisted I back my countryman in a cash bet just to mess with me (thankfully McGuigan won). We went for an Indian meal, and when we returned, the crew was hitting a club called Madogs, and I tagged along.

As soon as I arrived at the rowdy basement pub, rocking at eleven on a Saturday night, stage manager Bobby signaled to the barman to get me a drink. It was the first of many nights I hung with him, and we grew close over the following decades. No one ever had a bad word to say about unremarkable-looking Bobby, average height and weight, balding, usually wearing a patterned sweater, and with a soft Scottish lilt, broad and unmistakable, but without any Celtic harshness.

He joined Ozzy in 1981 and told me about the day in March 1982 when guitarist Randy Rhoads died in a plane crash at only twenty-five: Bobby was on the crew bus, had just opened his first beer of the day, when they heard the news. It was my great regret I never saw Randy live, Ozzy's fabled right-hand man who played on his first two seminal solo albums, and who was credited, along with Sharon, for resurrecting Ozzy's career after he was kicked out of Sabbath.

AFTER THE SECOND SHOW IN MANCHESTER, I felt more like part of the giant rolling family. So, it seemed normal that the night of Edinburgh show, I had lunch with Ozzy before we drove to the Playhouse Theatre, whose labyrinthine backstage—halls and corridors and doors and stairways—inspired the scene in *This Is Spinal Tap* when the band gets lost between the dressing room and the stage. Then we piled onto the bus for the 250-mile ride to Sheffield, the longest of the tour, and Ozzy was fired up, rolling from story to story, and as he often did after a few drinks, reminiscing about Sabbath.

> "We were staying in this place in the Midwest somewhere, I think we were there for a couple of days. I got smashed out of my head–we all did–and there's bottles of booze and pills and fuck-knows-what lying all over my room. I've pulled this Indian chick, and next thing there's this hammering on the door and it's Bill Ward.
>
> "He's out of his mind and he comes stomping into my room yelling and shouting and eventually I get rid of him.
>
> "The next morning we have to leave and there's no sign of Bill. I was really getting pissed off with him by now and I'm in a fucking awful mood. He was never where he was supposed to be and I was always the one getting the blame. So eventually he shows up and I lose it and start punching him.

> "And all the time I'm doing it he is giving a running commentary: 'Nice punch to the head, a body blow, good uppercut with the left.' Then when I stop he asks, 'Are you finished now?' I said, 'Yeah,' so he says, 'Right, let's go then,' and we get on the bus and drive off."

He and I were still awake at 5 a.m. when we arrived in the frost—we slept late, then he invited me to have lunch with him for the second day in a row. It was becoming a habit.

Ozzy was driven home that night after the City Hall gig, and he rang the following morning to tell me that *The Ultimate Sin* rocketed into the charts at number eight (his highest place in the UK album charts for thirty-four years, until *Ordinary Man* in 2020). He woke me, but I was alert enough to offer congratulations. I'm sure he called the whole touring party, but still. He rang me.

London next, where Ozzy did a taxing three successive sold-out shows at the Hammersmith Odeon. I booked into the crew's hotel, within walking distance of the venue, but the band's hotel was in the north of the city, so I'd meet them there, just to ride back and forth with them, my first time in a limo, sitting in the back with the guys, the tour manager up front. I couldn't bear to miss anything, even when it made no geographical sense.

As always at the epochal London venue, it was noisy, flooded with musicians, management, and record company executives talking loudly, raising their voices to be heard above roadies rolling flight cases across the concrete floor. Ross and Mick from *Kerrang!* were there, while Lars Ulrich from Metallica and Motörhead's Lemmy were ligging.

I was holding my breath while I collected the band's pungent black towels, helping Annie, Ozzy's tiny wardrobe girl, with whom I spent a lot of time. She made a joke about the smell of sweat, smiled, and I smiled back. Ozzy, in front of the packed corridor, pointed at me and yelled, "Hey! Are you fucking her?" (Obviously I wasn't; she said she considered me like a younger brother.)

The hallway instantly fell silent, like every VIP was simultaneously taken in the rapture. He had that glint in his eye from wallowing in a windup, stared at me a beat, smirked, then went back into his room. The babble resumed, but I was mortified, a shy lad shot into the glare of backstage attention in the Big Smoke.

In his hometown of Birmingham, Ozzy threw a party to celebrate—I'm still damaged by the memory of Lynn pulling me onto the dance floor, being forced to boogie in front of Ozzy, his band and family, a nightmare for an awkward Irish teenager—and long after it wrapped a few of us sat on with his siblings, though Ozzy was smashed and Sharon dragged him to bed.

The tour was selling out everywhere and extra dates were added, while Ozzy's records were his most successful in years. So we returned to Newcastle for another date and an appearance on *The Tube*, a TV show I watched every Friday. He played live, I stood on an adjoining empty set, and when he ran onstage, the camera caught me slinking among the dry ice. Luckily, none of my teachers were fans.

We sped to the Mayfair Club, the late-night heaving mass of humanity in England's blue-collar heartland drunk and manic. It was Ratt's last show, and I squeezed onstage for their set, smelling hair spray every time they wandered close. (English act Chrome Molly then took their forty-five-minute support slot, but at their first concert they were so nervous they played too fast and tore through it in thirty-five minutes. When I told Ozzy he said, "Yeah, I've done that before.")

I felt an elbow in my side and turned. Ozzy, resplendent in his spandex stage gear, had that mischievous glint in his eye, looking more like a cheeky scamp than a veteran rock star. He rested his left hand on my shoulder and rattled his right fist—opening it to reveal a plethora of stink bombs. He leaned in and whispered, "Watch this. These fuckers won't know what hit them." Cackling like a mad scientist, he launched his fusillade, the silver stones on his black cape glistening like the surf in moonlight, the vials soaring, the bombardment framed against the lighting rig, the glass glinting yellow. The band came over and I snapped photos of them mucking about with him. It reinforced a lesson learned early on the road from the master: enjoy life, and don't take anything too seriously.

Ratt then invaded the stage during his show with lingerie-clad strippers, who covered him with foam and Silly String, presenting a trophy engraved with "World's Sickest Champion." Afterward we swung by their hotel to say farewell, so it was 3 a.m. before we got back to Lumley Castle. I've still got the rooming list from that two-night stay, the first with my name on it, making me feel like I was officially part of the organization. Despite the time, a dozen of us sat down to eat in a private room.

Ozzy and Sharon presided at the top of an immense dark-wood table like a medieval king and queen; flickering fake torches on the walls; us in high-backed chairs like thrones, drinking from ludicrous goblets; the clack of the waiters' shoes on the stone floor; the freezing pitch-black winter night at the windows; the earthy smell of the fire; the eeriness of the empty, echoing chambers when you left to use the bathroom. It was a perfect night, a perfect setting, insulated from reality, cocooned from the outside world. For once I didn't have my camera. I was beside Phil and borrowed his to snap a shot he said he'd send to me, but never did. It doesn't matter, though, the tableau is indelibly engraved in my memory.

Ozzy's agent had flown up, and there was a discussion about if we had enough rooms. I volunteered to sleep on the bus, but Ozzy looked me dead in the eye and said, "Listen, you—never, ever give up your room." He raised a tankard and toasted, thanking everyone for their work on tour. "Even this dimph," he added, pointing at me.

We were due to leave at 1 p.m., and I didn't even wake until 1:45 p.m. I leapt up, threw on a T-shirt, jeans, and sneakers, and ran pell-mell outside into the freezing parking lot. The bus was still there. Everyone else had slept in, too.

The afternoon in Leicester, the penultimate stop, was one of the few times I ever left the hotel with Ozzy. On the road he rarely ventured out, spending his time in his room, the restaurant, or the bar. If you envy rock stars for their money and fame, consider that Ozzy spent his life in near-isolation, decades before COVID-19 made it fashionable. He couldn't hang out in a coffee shop, browse in a store, or wander the streets without being pestered, someone always wanting something. However, that day we took a dander to stretch our legs, with no specific purpose, no destination in mind. We watched a busker for a while, Ozzy gave him a fiver, and he was recognized once as we waited to cross the road, and he signed an autograph. After the show we ate fish and chips in the lobby, then Ozzy brought in the fans who had waited in the freezing cold to get records signed. We sat chatting in the lobby until 2:45 a.m.

Bradford's St. George's Hall, on March 4, 1986, was the end of the line. I boarded the bus for the last time to drive two hundred miles to London. Lynn came in, and I sat with her and Ozzy at the front. At some stage, a titanic promotional display for *The Ultimate Sin* was left at a venue, and I dismantled it and stored it at the back of the bus. I grabbed an album cover and asked Ozzy and the band to sign it to me. Ozzy wrote, "Get your fucking O Levels and get back out here."

We dropped off Ozzy and Lynn, then headed to a Heathrow hotel, where the band was staying before flying to the US the following day. I delivered their bags and said goodbye individually. Randy had part of my advertising cutouts on his bed.

"Hey, that's mine!" I said.

"It's mine now," he replied. I couldn't argue.

Spent and depressed, I checked in, too, and the next morning called my dad to charge the room to his credit card, as I didn't have enough cash to cover it and a plane ticket home.

Around twenty hours after leaving the Ozzy Osbourne tour, I started my day with a double period of history. Two days later, I was writing essays on nationalism in eighteenth-century Europe.

Ozzy went to tour America, and I went back to school.

To this day I'm unsure if my teachers knew where I'd been, and I knuckled down and returned to my studies. But I had glimpsed another world. For a glorious month I was pampered, watching Ozzy from the side of the stage, sharing private lunches and late-night drinking sessions. My diary after the tour is morose and self-pitying, though it has its moments: my favorite entry is about my neighbors, a religious family who protested at the Belfast gig and thought Ozzy was coming to my house. I wrote, "Got the bus into school with the Ozzy-hater from the bottom of the street."

#24

MONSTERS OF ROCK FESTIVAL

DONINGTON PARK RACETRACK
CASTLE DONINGTON, ENGLAND

August 16, 1986

ON A DAY OFF in London on tour, I'd gone with Randy to Abbey Road, as he wanted photos on the famous zebra crossing. Before the show in Nottingham, I got the prints developed, and in catering we looked at them over dinner. Gary, the tour accountant, limped over on his wooden leg to join us, and when Randy left, he had a proposition. He was tour manager for the German band Accept, who was starting a European tour three days after Ozzy's trek finished.

He offered me a job.

I would be a spotlight operator, getting precise instructions in a headset from the lighting director, so it didn't require experience or qualifications. It paid £30 a night, and usually it was done by truck drivers to top up their regular pay. I'd asked them about it earlier on the tour, and they said it was easy money, though more precarious for those clambering high into the lighting truss than for those on the balcony out front. "When Randy's drum platform lifts into the air during his solo you feel the chains grinding across the frame and sense the whole setup straining," one told me over a late-night cup of tea during load-out.

Gary's deal was I'd travel on a truck, not on a bus, and on the days I operated a spotlight, I'd earn the money. I wouldn't receive a weekly wage, but I'd get accommodation, and cash and meals on show days.

He didn't need me to fill a position, as he had drivers to do it; he was offering me a foot in the door, a way into the professional touring world that could lead to more. I was tempted: an opportunity to earn money on the road with a rock band didn't come around every day, and I worried I'd never get another chance. But in three months I was sitting important national exams, and I had studied hard and made the most of my opportunity at a great school. The timing was off.

So I fudged it. I didn't head straight to Germany after the tour, though many of the crew jumped directly from Ozzy to Accept. Accept was playing Belfast, Dublin, and six dates on the mainland that coincided with my Easter school vacation, so I asked Gary if I could join that run to see how it went. He agreed. I went to the Irish concerts, flew to London (I visited Lynn, of course), then rode in a truck to Bristol and on to Birmingham.

We rolled into the Odeon before daybreak, the same place I had been with Ozzy two months previous, and I already knew it wasn't for me.

With Ozzy I was treated like royalty, waltzing in late afternoon on his tour bus, staying in luxury hotels, a world away from a predawn arrival after a night sleeping in a truck cab. I realized being on the road with him was different, unique, how he treated me not just like a roadie but a friend. When Gary arrived at lunchtime, I thanked him but turned it down, and went to the bus station to buy a ticket home, the experience just a three-night flirtation as an intern with the crew.

OZZY WAS SPENDING THE NEXT FOUR months in America, and I tortured myself with the excruciating journaling of an angst-ravaged teenager, complaining I had a difficult French paper to revise on the same day Ozzy was playing Denver. However, Lynn sent me regular postcards and a US tour T-shirt.

The next time I saw him, it was back where I saw him the first time, as that summer he returned to Monsters of Rock at Castle Donington. Two years earlier, he was third on the bill; this time, he was headlining. I had changed, too. Lynn booked me into the crew hotel; I noted in my diary I had to pay for the room. How spoiled I'd become.

On August 13—three days early!—I caught the overnight boat to Liverpool, then the train to Long Eaton. I bumped into stage manager Bobby in the lobby, who offered me a ride to sound check the following day. On-site I met the new wardrobe girl who replaced Annie and hung with her in the dressing room. I ventured onto the stage, but when Def Leppard arrived, I was kicked off, Jake's tech saying, "These guys don't know you, you can't get in the way." This wasn't a club date with Ozzy posing for my photos onstage. It had mushroomed to a monstrous razzamatazz production with new American roadies who had no clue who I was or why I was there.

Ozzy arrived around 4 p.m. He was being ushered to his dressing room, but he spotted me and detoured over for a chat, while Randy squeezed me in a bear hug. Sharon appeared five minutes later. "It's fantastic to see you! You look very smart! And you did great in your exams I hear, I'm so pleased!" and she kissed me and rubbed my arm. Indeed, other than Ozzy's performance, I enjoyed Friday more than Saturday.

I cadged a lift back to the hotel with the crew and met Mick in the bar, who arranged for me to ride to London with the *Kerrang!* contingent (kontigent?)

in their minibus on Sunday—again, I had no prebooked way home, so my ad hoc plan became buying a flight from Heathrow.

Show day I wheedled onto the crew's transport and was at the gig by 8:30 a.m. Why I wanted to be there three and a half hours before the doors even opened, Christ knows. I had an "Access All Areas" pass for *The Ultimate Sin* world tour, but Donington had its own laminates, and I only had a stickie, a lesser pass you stuck to your shirt.

At noon security stopped letting me into the dressing room area, so I marched into the production office and somehow talked the woman manning it into giving me an Ozzy laminate. I tell you what, sixteen-year-old Stephen was a cheeky bugger. Once, I'd dreamed about having a sniff of backstage access, but after four weeks on tour, my sense of entitlement convinced me I deserved the highest-possible credential at the UK's biggest rock festival.

Lynn arrived, and I told her I'd blagged a laminate. "I'm pissed we didn't have enough for our guests," she said. "Who are all these fuckers with them? I've heard there's a bunch of liggers with our laminates in the VIP bar—come with me, I'm going to make a scene." She stomped off and I trailed in her wake, but when we arrived, all the undeserving chancers who bullshitted their way to laminates (like me) had disappeared, though bizarrely, a photo taken there at that moment appeared in *Kerrang!* the following week with us in it.

Two years previously I was constricted in the crowd, craning and straining to see from hundreds of yards away, at my first Ozzy concert. Here I was, back at Monsters of Rock, watching from the side of the stage—thanks to my mum's letter. Sharon threw an aftershow party, then I bummed another ride back with a handful of roadies in their van. As we waited to leave, the photographer Mark Weiss asked to jump in, the guy whose pass I used at Rock in Rio. Though there was space, the guys said no and closed the door. I listened in as they discussed why—it seemed on the US tour, he took photos of them and promised copies, but when they asked about them later, he said they hadn't turned out how he wanted, so he junked them.

They had not forgotten, another lesson in the importance of keeping on the crew's good side.

Nineteen months earlier, I'd used his pass to get backstage. This time, I was on the inside and he was shut out.

On Sunday I clambered aboard the *Kerrang!* minibus for yet another freeloading 150-mile journey, and they dropped me in London, and I rode the Tube to the airport. My diary reads, "**Didn't think I had enough money for a plane ticket but I did, only by a few quid.**" What my backup plan was if I couldn't afford a flight, I've no idea. Full of youthful recklessness, my fly-by-the-seat-of-my-pants skills honed after a month on the road, I was still winging my travel plans in England, obliviously trusting everything would turn out okay.

FOUR MONTHS LATER, FOR THE SECOND time, I chanced upon an article that changed my life. I got a Labrador puppy for my seventeenth birthday and spread newspapers on the floor while we house-trained him. As I dumped them in the trash I spotted a story: *The Sun* tabloid, the highest-selling daily into the English-speaking world, wanted a trainee reporter. I tore it out and applied, which consisted of writing a letter telling them why you wanted the position. They short-listed me from more than six hundred applicants and sent an airline ticket to Manchester for an interview. Lynn had told me to call in the next time I was over—she had a present she couldn't mail. So I cashed in my round-trip ticket to Manchester and booked a one-way ticket there, a train to London, and a flight home from Heathrow.

It was my first-ever interview, so I'd no idea how it went. It was at *The Sun*'s northern office, a few hundred yards from the Brittania Hotel, where I'd stayed with Ozzy earlier that year. I took an article I'd written about Rock in Rio for my local weekly paper, along with copies of pieces Lynn asked me to do for the Ozzy fan club, and stories from the school magazine. When it ended, the interviewers said they'd get me a taxi to the airport, but I told them I'd walk to the train station and explained about my diversion to London.

That was a grueling odyssey. The weather was atrocious, blizzard conditions with three inches of snow on the ground. I was lucky to make it, as many trains were canceled, roads gridlocked, pedestrians trudging through slush.

But the two-hundred-mile detour was worth it. Lynn gave me a platinum disc.

A personalized, framed, spray-painted record, reading "Presented to Stephen Rea to commemorate the sale of more than one million copies of *The Ultimate Sin*." Like you saw in rock stars' homes or waved by musicians at fancy parties. I couldn't believe it. (My diary has five sentences about the potentially life-defining interview with *The Sun*, then half a page about the gift.)

Bassist Phil was in the office, and he showed me his new toy, a mini recording desk, and played me riffs he was working on for the next album. Hypnotized by the sneak peek of future tracks, I stayed until 7 p.m., but ran into delays on the rasping Underground and missed the last flight home.

I was seventeen, it was late, and I was at Heathrow gripping the most precious object I've ever owned, wrapped in brown paper and tied with string like a parcel from a 1950s movie. I had neither the funds nor the inclination to plunge into the freezing dark to find a hotel. I'd flown to Manchester, endured a stressful, rigorous grilling, skidded to the station for the train to London, hopped the Tube to the office, inched back to the Underground at a snail's pace—as I was terrified of slipping and breaking my disc—changed trains twice to get to the airport . . . but though mentally and physically drained, I wouldn't risk sleeping, in case my invaluable cargo was stolen. I bought a 514-page book and settled in to read. I stayed awake for ten hours by alternating between an uncomfortable hard plastic seat and a fabric-covered bench, listening to the drone of a floor-polishing machine, gagging on overpowering disinfectants when cleaners swept through the cavernous hub, shivering every time the wind whipped in as the automatic doors swooshed open. I wrote in my diary, "There aren't half a lot of weirdos about." You think?

Ten days after that, I received a letter from *The Sun* reading they narrowed the short list from thirty to ten, and they would fly me over to be interviewed by editor Kelvin MacKenzie at their Wapping headquarters in London. I got the job. But rather than start right away, they deferred it for a year and a half and told me to finish my education. The dream scenario. I could stay in school, complete my studies, and get my qualifications.

Years later my friend Patrick, who also worked at *The Sun*, rooted through a filing cabinet while bored during the graveyard shift. He stumbled upon my interview notes from that first Manchester meeting. Me changing my ticket and using the opportunity to see Lynn in London impressed them. After bopping around the mainland with Ozzy, improvised travel had become second nature. My mum's letter got me the chance to know Ozzy; knowing Ozzy helped get me a job.

But I'd have missed the original announcement if it hadn't been for random canine urine splatter. Or as Ozzy said, "So the only reason you got your fucking gig then is because of your dog's piss?"

#25–37

UK CLUB TOUR

REPUBLIC OF IRELAND, NORTHERN IRELAND, ENGLAND, SCOTLAND

July 1988

DAWN BROKE OVER BELEAGUERED Belfast. As the first rays of sunlight filtered through the hotel security shutters, Ozzy got that glint in his eye. "I'm gonna find that fucker, you'll see," he promised, and clattering backward, he launched out of his chair and staggered down the hall. In one hand he gripped a razor, in the other photographs he'd asked for from my scrapbooks, six hours into another alcohol endurance session.

There wasn't much to laugh about outside the heavily fortified walls. Hours earlier two civilians died in an explosion, while a terrorist blew himself up when a mortar bomb detonated prematurely. The Troubles were all I'd ever known, and in Ulster, we were desensitized to the "normal" everyday violence. It was the height of the summer, but no foreign tourists were staying in the hotel, though at midnight we fended off annoying drunk guests from a wedding in a function room trying to crash our party.

Mick from *Kerrang!* was over to write a multipage feature on the Dublin and Belfast dates—a big artist playing Belfast rare enough to be newsworthy—with photographer George Bodnar. George took a bunch of shots of Ozzy with me and my high school sweetheart, Sharon, and he later sent them to me for free. Her expression is fabulous: Ozzy, lit, clowning around, the eighteen-year-old Irish lass not knowing what to make of him. Ozzy banned us from calling her Sharon because he kept thinking we were talking about his wife, so we had to use her middle name, Helen. I was an acne-pitted teen with no experience of long-term relationships, but I was figuring out the dynamic between Ozzy and (his) Sharon. They were devoted to each other, but Ozzy was ready to party when she left, and he always felt he had been let off the leash when she wasn't around. I loved being with Sharon—she was generous and kind—but anytime she went home, I relished buckling in for an action-packed all-nighter.

Ozzy had moved on from stink bombs to "doom drops"—quick-acting, heavy-duty sleeping pills. He'd sneak a tablet into a drink, the target slumped into a slumber, then he pounced to shave their eyebrows or dye their hair. We knew to never leave beer unattended, even carrying it to the restroom. One roadie woke to find half his hair buzzed off and quit on the spot, demanding a plane ticket home.

That night, George was the target. Nonsensically, he was getting married in England the following day. His fiancée made Lynn promise he'd get back untouched. Ozzy saw it as a challenge to get him fucked-up, doom-dropping him three times. Ozzy let slip he knew which room he was in, and George was so terrified, he broke into a section of the hotel under renovation and spent the night there. It worked—Ozzy returned from his fruitless manhunt, and we called it a night at 5:30 a.m.

The previous day I'd driven one hundred miles to Dublin for the opening date of the small-scale summer UK club tour set up to give his new guitarist experience. He had fired Jake and hired raw, unknown twenty-one-year-old Zakk Wylde, who had only been onstage with small-time bands in his native New Jersey. He was half Ozzy's age, and Ozzy would say, "Imagine when I started with Sabbath, if you'd shown me a baby in a pram and told me, 'One day he'll be in your band.' Crazy, huh?" He played on the next album, *No Rest for the Wicked*, released two months after the tour. Following that first show, at the dingy venue the Top Hat (Zakk's first public appearance), I sat in the lobby bar sipping coffee, planning on heading home. But as the night wore on and others fell away, Ozzy insisted I stay, so we went to his suite and drank, and I crashed on a roadie's floor.

The day of the Belfast gig I drove Lynn to show her my Ozzy shrine, an attic conversion overflowing with memorabilia like my platinum disc, his framed vest from Rio, and giant concert posters, and I grabbed my scrapbooks to show off. Mick mentioned me and them in his *Kerrang!* article, so I bought six copies. Mick wrote:

> We'd been looking through some scrapbooks that Ozzy's friend, Stephen Rea, had brought over to the hotel—a lot of rare stuff. I asked Ozzy, *Was it a shock looking through those old cuttings Stephen brought over?*
>
> Ozzy nodded. *It was fascinating, actually. There were so many things there that I'd completely forgotten!*

I fell back into my old road routine, but this time there was a complication. I was committed to interrailing around Europe and North Africa with (my) Sharon and a couple of friends. We finagled a compromise: since it was a short tour, they would head to France and I'd go on the road, then join them in Holland. I stayed sober that night to take (my) Sharon home, then off I went for fifteen dates in twenty days.

It would not be the last time I made my partner change vacation plans for an Ozzy concert.

In my diary before the tour, I wrote about checking train timetables and possibly traveling with truck drivers. But Bobby was promoted from stage manager to tour manager and said that, yet again—I'm sure with Sharon's approval—I could ride the tour bus. And I wrangled free accommodation, as I hit it off with Keith, Bobby's new assistant, and most nights I shared his room. We had a journalist from *Kerrang!*'s rival *Metal Hammer* with us for a couple of shows, and he, too, mentioned me in his article:

> Second day on the road and it's off to Bristol, chatting away to Steve Rae [yep, spelled it wrong], possibly, if not probably, the biggest Ozzy fan in the cosmos, who travels with the band whenever possible on tour. Steve holds up a picture of Madonna throwing a punch at an autograph hunter, from a colour Sunday supplement, as a demonstration of how some other bands treat their fans.

Name-checked in both major rock publications within a week, I was turning into a celebrity stalker (as opposed to a stalker of celebrities).

JOHN WAS STILL ON KEYBOARDS, RANDY on drums, while Terry "Geezer" Butler, the original Sabbath bassist, had replaced Phil. Geezer had a mass of flowing dark hair, a trademark distinctive mustache he'd had since the sixties, so full it spanned the width of his face when he smiled, and an impish grin. He was universally known as "Geezer," but for some reason, lost to the mists of time, I called him "Terry" from the day we met. I've an inkling Lynn was the only person besides his wife I ever heard do it, so maybe I followed her lead. He'd been on the road for two decades, and although he liked to drink, he didn't have the same stamina that Ozzy had to stay up until daybreak. He was driven home after shows when possible, and once, after he left, Randy shook his head and said, "I wouldn't feel like I was on tour if I went back to my house every night," which I think was the point.

I saw both sides: I was young and excited enough to be around my heroes every minute, no matter how shattered I was, but I'd seen enough of life on the road to appreciate that, after two decades of it, Geezer preferred to go home to his own bed and his wife and kids.

The night after the show at the Studio in Bristol we were at a stuffy boutique seventeenth-century manor house hotel in the sleepy village of Stroud, raging for hours with the bar to ourselves. I went to order, and Ozzy shouted at me to stop. He got up, walked over, and punched me on the shoulder.

"Don't you ever, never, ever again dare to try to buy a drink in my presence," he ordered. He summoned Bobby and told him to give me £20. Not only was I on the tour for free, I was making money. The following morning, he hammered on the door to get us up so he could treat us to breakfast.

Life on tour, cloistered for days on end and existing in a bubble, was like being a permanent schoolboy. Ozzy was the master and set the tone—he was self-deprecating and quick to poke fun at himself, relishing in relaying idiotic tales, happiest when he made you laugh. He never took himself seriously, the attitude of searching for humor in every situation, something I strove to emulate in later years.

Lynn generously offered me the couch at her place for the London dates, and I turned up at 4 a.m. I was woken a few hours later by a deliveryman. Lynn told Sharon I was staying with her, so Sharon had sent over a mini sofa bed for me. Her thoughtfulness was mind-boggling, and at the venue I tracked her down and thanked and hugged her. Even selfish teenage Stephen appreciated what a lucky boy he was.

After the gig at the Town & Country Club we went to a party thrown by CBS Records, then Sharon invited a few of us to dinner. Lynn realized she'd had too much to drink to drive, so I offered to be the DD and drove us to the Mayflower, the Osbournes' favorite restaurant in the Soho district.

It was 3 a.m. when the conversation turned to me working for *The Sun*. Ozzy lifted his wineglass and pointed it toward me like he was going to toast me. "I know what you'll be doing," he said. "You'll be writing lies. Lies about me!"

The tabloid press had a reputation for sensationalism and half-truths, but I never expected to be put in that situation with Ozzy—with him, the reality was always more outlandish than anything a reporter could make up.

I took a sip of water and shook my head. I put my hand over my heart. I said, "I promise you this here and now, I will *never* write lies about you." More than three decades later, I like to think I've kept my word.

AFTER THE GLAMOR OF LATE-NIGHT MEALS at fancy London restaurants and record label parties, the next show was in Redcar, a coastal resort in North Yorkshire, one of the unlikeliest spots I ever visited with Ozzy. It held only one thousand fans and was next to a chemical plant: the fog rolling in from the sea and enshrouding us, the mist diffusing the spectral glow of the factory lights, the sounds of horns and bells drifting in from the water, the smack of salt on our tongues. I felt like an extra in a horror movie. My diary reads, "Everyone was tired and we were in bed by 2 a.m." That was considered an early night.

We had a rare day off in Darlington, sandwiched between dates in Redcar and Hull. It's hard to imagine three more unfashionable places, all invoking images of dour northern conurbations, barren and uninspiring, devoid of interest or entertainment. Although both band and crew moaned about the location of the free day in the lead-up, it was one of my best days off on any tour, a theme repeated over the years—often the most enjoyment was uncovered in the most unassuming spots.

We were at another medieval country house hotel. (Diary: "It has a golf course and tennis court but we ended up sitting in the bar all day." Shocker.) It was the day before Geezer's thirty-ninth birthday, and I found him and Ozzy in the bar at noon. I sat with them until 4 p.m., when I thought I'd buy Geezer a birthday card, so I walked into town. I returned after a couple of hours and they hadn't moved, and at 8 p.m., after drinking for eight hours, Ozzy called it a night. But Geezer wasn't done, so Keith joined us, and we sauntered to a local boozer, staying until it closed, then stumbling back along a deserted unlighted lane.

Geezer dropped behind, singing soccer songs and yelling, then it went quiet. We went back to investigate, and he had disappeared. Eventually we found him—he fell into a ditch and rolled under a bush. A few weeks previously the closest I'd been to him was swapping cassettes of his performances with Sabbath—that night I celebrated his birthday with him in a quaint English pub then pulled him out of a hedgerow.

We bumbled back, Geezer covered in branches and brambles and leaves and nettles. As I helped brush him down, the receptionist asked, "You're Mr. Rea, right? Stephen Rea, with the Osbourne party?" I said yes, and she said, "We were listening to the radio, and Tommy Vance just read out your request for your girlfriend and dedicated a song to her on the *Friday Rock Show*."

The staff invited us to join them in the bar—not often salubrious Darlington attracted famous musicians I suppose—and off duty, the buxom blond masseuse and her colleagues let rip (a couple disappeared to have sex in the bathroom). I lasted until 3 a.m., but at checkout we discovered we had been a whisker away from being kicked out: Ozzy, hammered, staggered into the lounge area and pissed all over it when he had been unable to find the restroom.

His set contained a new track, "Bloodbath in Paradise," that started with a spoken, spooky, backward-masking intro. It wasn't as evil as it seemed, having been cooked up by Ozzy and John: In *The Exorcist*, the girl, Regan, inhabited by the devil, tells the priest, "Your mother sucks cocks in Hell." Ozzy imitated the line, but changed it to "Your mother sells whelks in Hull," after the edible sea snail that was a local specialty. On the way to the Hull concert, he told John to reverse the intro programmed on his keyboard, so that gig was the only time it was ever played forward—a particularly obscure piece of Ozzy fandom trivia thrilling me no end. I felt like I was being allowed a peek behind the curtain, and those moments on a freeway in Northern England meant more to me than going with (my) Sharon and our friends to see the *Mona Lisa* at the Louvre.

THEN WE HAD ANOTHER NIGHT OFF. But this was unscheduled.

Fifteen minutes before showtime at Nottingham's Rock City, neither Ozzy nor Geezer had appeared. Both had a bug, and at 11 p.m. it was decided to cancel. Only after the band was squirreled out the back door to our nearby hotel did Bobby walk onstage to deliver the bad news.

"Hi, everyone," he began in his soft Scottish brogue. "Unfortunately, tonight's gig is off. Ozzy is sick, Geezer's suffering, too, it's—" A pint glass whistled through the air at him. "Hey! Now, that's not going to help anything. If—" Another, then another. "Fuck this," he muttered, and we bolted backstage.

We locked the wardrobe girl in the dressing room with a security guard, then met in catering. It went south at a lightning pace, the crowd's mood plummeting in seconds. We heard the PA crash onto the floor, banging, yelling, thuds and thumps as gear toppled and projectiles rained onto the stage. The police arrived, they radioed for reinforcements, and there were forty cops by the time the club was cleared.

It was ugly outside, as fans, many of whom had been drinking for hours, hung around and refused to disperse, smashing the box office windows. I ran a nasty gauntlet back to the hotel, which was in lockdown and initially refused to let me in. I bumped into Geezer and his wife, Gloria (also his manager), in the hall coming from Ozzy's room. Ozzy's throat was sore, and Geezer looked terrible, as white as Casper the Ghost.

The rest of us retired to the bar. I never felt threatened—having grown up in Belfast during the Troubles—but it left us with a sour taste. "What's up with people?" said Keith. "If it was me, I'd be thinking, 'I've been out, had a few beers, seen the support band, and I'm gonna get my money back or see Ozzy another time. Canny night.' I wouldn't be smashing up the place." Four fans were arrested, but before we left, Sharon sent Bobby to bail them out, telling the police they wouldn't press charges regarding damaged equipment.

WE WERE IN MANCHESTER THE FOLLOWING night, this time playing the Ritz, a venue so pokey the band changed in a corridor. Both Ozzy and Geezer had recovered enough for another late-night session in the Portland Thistle Hotel. Residents were allowed to keep drinking after the bar closed, but it fell on the night porter to serve guests. Invariably it was an older guy expecting an easy shift, who, instead of putting his feet up and answering the odd call, had to wait on hell-raising rock stars joining the dawn patrol. Tipping was rare in the UK, but Ozzy had a simple tactic to alleviate grumpiness, handing him a £50 bill as we settled in. That always did the trick. The three of us lasted until 4 a.m., polishing off seven bottles of champagne.

The previous summer I spent two weeks interning at *The Sun*'s Manchester office to get a taste of their setup. As we sat in the lobby, at a quarter past midnight, the elevator doors opened, and two reporters I recognized stepped out. I walked over to say hello and discovered they had been at a photographer's retirement party upstairs.

As we chatted, the next elevator arrived, and out came their boss, the northern news editor who first interviewed me for the job. He did a double take and said, "Stephen? What the hell are you doing here?" We were three bottles into the champagne by this stage, but I fought to form a coherent summary of why I was drinking at 1 a.m. with Ozzy Osbourne in the city's best hotel on a Tuesday. He told me to call into the office the following morning for a chat.

It was our last day off. Ozzy had the test pressing of a new T-shirt featuring the *NRFTW* cover, and he gave it to me; we spent a couple of hours in the hotel bar, then went to eat. In the Indian restaurant and drunk, Ozzy again said he wanted me to work for him. Ten hours earlier I'd been in the office where my journalism career began, and here I was being offered an entirely different employment path over beers and balti.

But I knew it was the drink talking, and we never had a serious discussion about it when Ozzy was sober. I think it was a boozed-up extension of him enjoying my company, and indeed I spent all day with him in Leeds: we chatted over tea in the lobby, had a rare walk outside around downtown, then came back and hung out with Geezer. They went back to their rooms, but within minutes, Ozzy was banging on our door to hide from two of Sharon's friends he wanted to avoid.

We were on the fifth floor, and he realized the tour bus was parked directly beneath, the driver going in and out prepping for the next drive. He picked up the fruit bowl and, one by one, threw the contents on top of the bus . . . an apple, an orange, a pear. For years I'd read about rock stars trashing hotel rooms and lobbing objects out windows, and in the annals of scandalous misbehavior it rates dead last, but still, I was delighted to see firsthand him hurling projectiles. Even if it was just fruit.

THE LAST TWO NIGHTS OF THAT tour were the hardest I ever saw Ozzy hit the bottle. He outdrank everyone in epic postconcert sessions, me, Keith, Bobby, and the band along for the ride, laughing at his stories, a nonstop battery of antics. I knew how lucky I was that Ozzy included me, trusting me to be part of the lunacy, aware in the moment I was making special lifelong memories, my stomach aching from howling so hard, us sharing an accelerated bond from being thrown together on the road, the feeling we were different from the stuffy businessmen milling around our bougie hotels, us in jeans and T-shirts, them in suits, the thrill of being with my hero outweighing everything.

The penultimate date had us back at Lumley Castle, the stained glass windows in my room turning the summer sunshine into a kaleidoscope, a secret door disguised as a bookcase leading to the ensuite bathroom. We drank until the sun came up, Ozzy strong-arming Zakk into racing him in downing pints, a rambling, tumultuous drunken saga ending back at the snooker room at 7 a.m. I helped Ozzy to his room, took his key, and returned to check on him later—he was spread-eagled, fully clothed on his bed, and had pulled a metal ice bucket on top of him. (My diary reads: "**We all got up at lunchtime and told Ozzy what he had been doing, but he had a shot from the doctor and felt fine.**")

We wrapped in Glasgow, my thirty-seventh gig, and had an end-of-tour celebration at the Holiday Inn. I sat with Geezer at the bar, and he said in his thick Brummie accent, "So are you gonna stay in touch? You wanna come visit me or what?," asked with such force it sounded more like a threat than an invitation. He gave me his address and number and said to call. I was touched. By 4 a.m. we were down to Randy, Geezer, Ozzy, and me, Randy throwing glasses against the wall and Geezer belting out Irish Catholic rebel tunes, Ozzy joining in though he didn't know them. They riffed a melody and Ozzy said he would write a song and call it after me—that would have gone down well with my Protestant friends and family. Randy bailed when the cleaners appeared, but Geezer and I decamped to Ozzy's room, the pair of them clinging on to each other as they waddled along. I snapped a pic as they passed a maid vacuuming, the three of us laughing so hard we were hyperventilating. Ozzy attacked the minibar and collapsed on the bed; Geezer fell in beside him. After more booze—it was past 6 a.m.—Ozzy passed out and I fought to haul up Geezer.

"C'mon, Terry, time to go," I told him, patting his leg and battling to hoist him up.

"Are those my legs?" he asked, looking down.

"Yes, Terry, they are," I replied, easing him off the bed and walking him to his room.

I had half an hour to pack, then I left at 7 a.m. in a taxi to the airport with Zakk to make sure he caught his flight; while everyone else was staying in Britain, he was going home to the States.

I returned to the hotel, snuck in two hours of sleep, then we all went back to the airport, Ozzy and Geezer still wankered, Ozzy dancing around the terminal, singing at the top of his lungs, Geezer giggling and shaking. I wrote in my diary, "**Said goodbye to them all at the airport and it was terrible, I felt really depressed. Perhaps the worst of my life.**" Poor wee self-pitying Stephen.

The band went to London, and I flew to Amsterdam to meet (my) Sharon for a last vacation before plunging into adulthood and responsibility.

#41

HAMMERSMITH ODEON

LONDON, ENGLAND

May 5, 1989

AFTER A MONTH INTERRAILING around Europe, I had one day at home in August 1988 before flying to Newcastle and starting my new life as a reporter. *The Sun* moved me around: Newcastle; Manchester; Birmingham; back to Manchester; London. They never knew what to do with me—as the first intern-to-journalist in their history, there was no clear career path or training schedule. It made for a nomadic existence, and with a couple of days' notice I was plucked from working in one newspaper office and sent to another on the other side of the country. No Craigslist or Facebook Marketplace back then, and I couldn't afford a car, so I'd arrive at the train station, buy the local newspaper, mark up likely accommodations in the Rooms to Rent section, and schlep around until I found something in my budget.

It was like being on tour—though with less booze and boobs—and I adapted, in part because of my time on the road. The band was sometimes a revolving door of transients, but Ozzy was always nonplussed about it.

When I bemoaned the loss of a musician, the overwrought emotions of youth lamenting a departure, he merely shrugged.

"Steve, it's the business. They get another gig or are offered more dough or whatever. It's happened before, it'll happen again. I don't take it personally. There's always someone else out there and Sharon'll find them."

It was a viewpoint I took from him, accepting whatever my career threw at me, even when it seemed my life had as many changes as his band.

My experiences on Ozzy tours also occasionally transferred to my professional existence. I was posted to *The Sun*'s state-of-the-art Wapping headquarters in London, and Madonna was in town for a concert. The media was in a feeding frenzy fighting to track her down. We had a tip that she was at a certain hotel, and I listened as the useless showbiz editor and his clueless staff got bogged down in an interminable debate about how to get it confirmed. As a rookie reporter I was wary of interrupting, but eventually I could stand it no longer and asked if they had the name of the tour manager. None even knew what that was, so I explained a road crew's structure, and suggested they find out the name. They would not be using an alias, so we could call the hotel and ask for them. If we found the tour manager, we found Madonna. The high-earning team schooled by a youngster, thanks to being an Ozzy road veteran. It didn't surprise me when the whole department was fired soon afterward.

Working at Wapping was cutthroat and demanding, the crushing pressure of daily deadlines a deluge of stress and abuse. Editor Kelvin MacKenzie, who personally picked me for the job, was arguably the most famous leader in tabloid history, responsible for the most famous (and infamous) front pages in history. He stormed around the floor, deputies scrambling in his wake, firing off volleys of insults. I had a meeting with the managing editor in his office, then we walked out into the newsroom, me slouched in his wake. "Oi! Rea, you fucker! Get your fucking hands out of your fucking pockets when you are with the general!" he yelled from the news desk. I just laughed—whether I was on the road with Ozzy or working in a newsroom, fortysomething British men shouted swear words at me.

I WAS DETERMINED TO SEE A gig when Ozzy hit the European mainland and picked the French capital, as he had a day off there after playing Brussels. I waited for them at the airport, then jumped onto their bus to the hotel, claiming a spot on Keith's floor.

Springtime in Paris in the bar of the George V, perhaps the most expensive hotel on the continent. It was awash in elegance and opulence, the fashionable French drinkers sipping exorbitant cocktails and dripping in diamonds, Arab guests swishing past on their way to shop on the Champs-Élysées, a precious stone's throw away. It was early evening, April 1989, and we were drunk and loud. Tutting snobbish staff politely quarantined us behind a string of red leather ropes. Randy insisted I use his video camera to film him messing around in the restroom, then dismantled a three-foot section of the barrier and sat nonchalantly with it protruding from his fly like a giant diseased dick.

Keith and I went sightseeing with Zakk, Randy, and John, but it descended into a pub crawl. I've loads of silly photos—the guys gurning behind each other's backs at the Eiffel Tower or mucking around in front of the Arc de Triomphe—and they stir fabulous memories and make me smile. As the day wore on, we got sloppier, our stops including a sex shop and an impromptu and unintended crashing of a Jewish wedding. We never ate, and by the time we rolled back to the snooty five-star hotel, we were wasted.

After the concert the next night, Geezer asked me to have a beer with him at a nearby Irish pub. I'm sure he regretted the invitation, as I peppered him with questions about his Sabbath lyrics. Today you can find the story behind famous songs in seconds, but back then it was my chance to get the secrets straight from the horse's mouth. But he was patience epitomized with me, then when they kicked us out, he took me to his room to play me his solo demos. Though buzzed I knew they sounded great, and some surfaced on albums by both his own band and Sabbath. I asked for a copy of the cassette and he said no. The balls on me—a teenage fan wanting a famous musician from one of history's foremost rock bands to let me walk out the door with unreleased songs he spent years perfecting. We hit the minibar, and at 4:30 a.m., after also obliterating all its extortionately priced chocolate, I blustered back to Keith's room. I vomited over the floor as soon as my head hit the pillow.

I had a great time, but I spent the weekend getting drunk with the band and barely saw Ozzy—Sharon and the kids joined the tour the same day as me, and he'd been on duty as a father, not a hell-raising rock star.

I hitched a ride the following day to the airport and flew back to England. Again, my diary reads like my suffering was on a par with Anne Frank's: "It felt so bad leaving them—really, really dreadful. I hate it, it's times like these I just want to pack it all in and join up with them. Got back knackered and a bit drunk to an empty house and felt totally depressed."

THE EUROPEAN LEG WRAPPED WITH THREE back-to-backs in Birmingham and London, a trio of dates within one hundred miles of me. The previous summer we had rollicked the length of the country together, drinking all night in remote high-end country houses. After each of these gigs, Ozzy went home, and we only interacted briefly. When we did, he was subdued, not the gregarious hard-drinking, life-and-soul-of-the-party persona from the club tour.

I heard from musicians and crew his alcoholism had soared out of hand on the road, and I knew he was sequestering himself, fighting a private battle to curb his intake. His lifestyle was unsustainable, and as he said numerous times, "I was killing myself on a daily basis."

And he had decades of stories. One of the best I ever heard was from Geezer, about a Sabbath tear through Belgium (he thought) in the seventies.

> "The record company took us out for dinner, and next thing I know, Ozzy is pissing himself at the table. There's piss running down his leg and I'm going, 'Aww, for God's sake Ozzy,' and he says, 'I've got to take a shit.' I'm telling him to please wait until we get back to the hotel, but he's saying that he's desperate to go. We manage to persuade him to hold off and we get back to the hotel. Ozzy gets into the lift, and as the doors start to close, I see him squat down and undo his trousers.
>
> "What he doesn't realize is that the lift is going down, not up. I see on the readout that it's gone down to the basement, and next thing, a group of American tourists walk in and call the lift. The doors open—and there's Ozzy taking a dump in the lift. All the conversation stops and they are just staring straight ahead in dead silence. The doors close and off it goes. I honestly thought I was going to die laughing."

The last two shows before the band shifted to a US leg were at the Hammersmith Odeon. The power went out four songs into the first night at the Hammersmith, but the second was electric, the band on fire, Ozzy's voice strong.

Afterward, I waited in the same drafty corridor outside his dressing room, where three years before he had embarrassed me with Annie, the wardrobe girl. He padded out, smiled, and came to say hello and shake hands.

"Brilliant gig tonight, that was amazing, Ozzy," I said.

He shook his head. "You don't know what you're talking about. It was just okay."

I told Lynn what he said, and she thought it hilarious, him correcting an "expert" like me. I thought it hilarious she thought it hilarious that she thought I knew better than the man himself.

He crossed the Atlantic, and I went home, back to life as a journo. I barely saw him for the following three years. In the summer of 1991 Lynn invited me to the unveiling of *Don't Blame Me*, a documentary tied to his latest album, *No More Tears* (which she'd given me an advance tape of). When I went to meet her, she had kept it a surprise that Ozzy and Sharon were there, too. We went to the theater together and I got another surprise—I was name-checked in the credits.

A few months later, in November, Ozzy rang me. I was at my grandmother's, so he called my home, got the number from my mum, and rang me there. I answered and he said, "It's Ozzy, you cunt. Happy birthday."

#50

THE SUMMIT

HOUSTON, TEXAS

September 23, 1992

THE SUN HONED MY writing skills, teaching me to never waste a word, to produce accurate copy lightning fast, to tell a story clearly and concisely. But London was filthy expensive. Forced to live on the outskirts and use public transport, my commute was one hour, forty-five minutes each way (if everything ran like clockwork), so I returned to Birmingham for a job on the *Daily News*, then moved again to Yeovil, Somerset, to work for the *Western Daily Press*.

I was in charge of a district office, earning good money, with a company car, and dating Fay, a fellow reporter (I'd split with my Sharon after four years together). But when I covered the press launch of the low-budget British movie *Shirley Valentine*, the film's theme struck a chord. It dealt with a middle-aged housewife full of sorrow that she had not explored the world the way she was determined to do when she was young, and I worried I'd have the same regrets. I'd been overseas multiple times but wanted to see more: Africa, Asia, Australia. I always loved traveling and grew up hearing stories about my grandad's overseas postings as he spent twenty-two years in the Royal Air Force, stationed in exotic countries all over the globe.

So in 1992 I left journalism and moved back to Belfast to buy a travel agency.

The store was next door to my dad's business—the same place where he inquired about Rock in Rio. I wrestled with it for weeks. We were still killing each other and blowing things up in Northern Ireland, and after four years in England, staying on the mainland was more sensible. With the UK in an economic slump, travel wasn't a boom industry, while with my unique training and experience I was on an accelerated career path in journalism, years ahead of every other reporter my age.

The Association of British Travel Agents had a dedicated employee to help with agency acquisitions, and I called for advice. "I'm considering buying a travel agency," I started, "and wondered—"

"Why the hell would you do that now? Is there something wrong with you?" interrupted the man whose job it was to help people buy travel agencies.

But I wasn't deterred. If it didn't work out, I'd go back to newspapers. Plus, the ABTA guy wasn't considering an important factor: with unfettered access to flights, I could get to Ozzy shows anywhere.

I was only a few weeks in when Lynn called. Sharon was concerned their record label, Epic, was not pushing *No More Tears* enough in Germany, Europe's biggest market. Pearl Jam's debut, *Ten*, was also out, and she was worried Ozzy's labelmates were hogging the company's attention. She wanted me to fly to Hamburg and Berlin, cities he'd played the previous week, and go to every record store. I was to count how many copies of *NMT* each stocked on the floor, along with what other product was on the racks, and whether any had promotional displays like posters or cutouts. I had to track Pearl Jam's presence as well. Sharon thrived in the vicious male-dominated music business because of thinking like this. The attention to detail, the willingness to sink her own money into checking the label was doing what they promised, the razor-sharp focus ensuring her husband and client was supported.

How could I not answer her SOS after everything she had done for me? Although I was only twenty-two, I was an employer with two staff, so when I left the country I trusted them to run it as normal—and its proximity to my dad's office meant I had someone to keep an eye on things.

I dashed home, threw together a bag, and flew to Hamburg that evening. I traipsed around the shops the following day, caught the last flight to Berlin, and did the same there the next day. I compiled my report and sent it to Lynn.

"YOU'RE A GUEST IN OUR COUNTRY, and I think you're gonna have to go to jail today. I'ma gonna stand over here and think about it. Don't move."

Rays from the blazing sun reflected off the mirrored sunglasses worn by the man-mountain Texas trooper like laser beams.

My schoolmate Gordon had moved to Dallas for flying school, and my friend Patrick and I flew to see him in September 1992. It wasn't just a social visit. In devastating news to superfans like me, Ozzy announced he was retiring from playing live, even calling it the No More Tours tour. Although crushed I'd never hear "Mr. Crowley" and "Crazy Train" onstage again, finally experiencing a full arena–production US show was a fitting way to bow out.

As soon as I got the itinerary from Lynn, I checked airline schedules and prices, researching how far apart dates were, combing hotels for industry deals.

And so as Patrick and I sped to a gig in Houston in a powerful Sunbird convertible we got at a cut-price rate, I was blissfully unaware I'd hit 89 mph in a 55 zone until the cop was kind enough to pull me over and point it out. We had the top down but the windows up as protection from the wind, and he barked at me to lower them, but flustered, I couldn't distinguish between the control for the windows and the electric roof, so it was jerking up and down and he got angrier as I jabbed at the buttons. He demanded my license, which was in my bag in the trunk, so I got out, and maybe he thought I was making a run for it or going for a weapon, and he put his hand on his holster and yelled at me to stop. Ironically, despite growing up in the Troubles, this was the first time I'd been shouted at by someone with a gun, and rattled, I tried to explain, but he couldn't understand me, which only led me to garble quicker.

So I stood by the side of the interstate, my top lip glistening and my hair matted with sweat, straining to hear him over the noise of the vehicles hurtling past, 18-wheelers sending our convertible rocking like a canoe in a typhoon. I bowed my head, trying to look repentant and ashamed. After what felt like a year but was no more than a minute, he strode back, pulled out a pad, and scribbled in silence.

He ripped out a sheet and stared at me. "Take this. And slow down," he said, and slapped a speeding ticket into my palm. I realized I'd been holding my breath, so I exhaled, apologized, and thanked him for letting me go.

My first Ozzy concert in the US was back on.

WHEN WE CHECKED INTO OUR HOTEL I discovered my face was scarlet. Whipping along the freeway I hadn't felt the force of the Texas sun, and wearing neither sunscreen nor a hat, I was burned to a cinder. It was my fiftieth concert, and to mark the special occasion, just like in Rio and Belfast, I had something ridiculously wrong with my face.

Patrick and I arrived at the venue, the Summit basketball arena, picked up passes, and wandered into the backstage maze, where we got lost. By the buses, we happened upon Bobby, who escorted us to the dressing rooms, saying into his walkie-talkie, "Steve's here, I've got him, I'm bringing him back."

"Jesus Christ, it's like you're the pope or a president or something," Patrick muttered to me. We watched the show from the mixer and Ozzy was in superb form, the near-two-hour set the longest I'd ever seen, the scale impressive in a venue dwarfing most UK gigs.

We went in to talk to him afterward, and the first thing he said was, "What the fuck's up with your face?" VIPs received a Polaroid with him and a signed copy of a special limited-edition CD. I didn't want a photo, but Ozzy wouldn't pose with Patrick until I joined them, saying, "C'mon, you Irish dick, I wanna record of this. You look like a cunt."

To mark my fiftieth concert I'd bought an Irish crystal pint tankard and had it engraved to him. He loved it and held it up to the light, saying he could imagine it filled with Guinness. Stupidly, it hadn't even occurred to me that it was an inappropriate present for a recovering alcoholic—in that brief second when desire flashed onto his face, I saw his daily struggle to stay off the booze.

#57

PACIFIC AMPHITHEATRE

COSTA MESA, CALIFORNIA

November 15, 1992

I DROVE LIKE A grandmother back to Dallas and stayed with Gordon. In a bar a gorgeous blonde gave me her number. My last night before leaving for the next gig she invited me over. But that afternoon I fell ill—vomiting so violently it splattered out of the toilet bowl and over the walls—and the walk-in clinic doctor said I had the flu. He could prescribe tablets and let it run its course, or he could give me a shot to clear it up but that would knock me out. On tour Ozzy was always concerned about catching an infection, though Brits thought only cranks worried about that. Everything rode on his shoulders: if he was too sick to perform, he let down thousands of fans and messed up the meticulously planned schedule. I wanted to avoid the needle and go on my hot date, but that meant turning up at the venue looking like crap. I had to choose between Ozzy and the Texan blonde.

I couldn't risk carrying the plague into the Ozzy camp, so I got the injection, slept for sixteen hours, and felt right as rain when I woke.

I had three weeks stateside, but no domestic travel booked. My next destination was Tulsa, and Gordon hired a Cessna to fly me there, my own private Uber Air. The subsequent journey was also straightforward, as Bobby generously invited me to travel on the band's tour bus.

I resumed my position as a parasite on the ten-hour journey to San Antonio for two shows, Ozzy's first there since being banned more than a decade previously for pissing on the Alamo. It was my introduction to American buses, more elaborate and tricked-out than their British counterparts. Up front was a table, seating, TV, microwave, stereo, fridge, and toilet. The middle, sectioned off with sliding doors, contained bunks, while the rear was the lounge with another TV, video games, VCR, and a wraparound couch. We all started at the back playing video games, then moved up front to watch a movie. The rest crawled into bed, but Ozzy's latest bassist, Mike Inez, and I drank beers and watched stand-up tapes, talking until dawn.

I first met him in January 1991. "Hey, brother, great to meet ya. I hear they call you the Oracle because you know everything about Ozzy. I'm Mike," he said, thrusting out his hand when Zakk introduced us in a Dublin hotel. He was twenty-four then and radiated Californian sunshine, his personality clashing with the freezing Irish weather outside, and I instantly warmed to him—personable with a smile for everyone so wide it creased his face in half, a tangle of long black hair churning when he tilted his head back to laugh. He replaced Geezer, who had rejoined Sabbath.

It was 7 a.m. before the two of us hit the hay, and I paused for a moment to gaze at the rising sun, the flat Texas scrubland stretching as far as the eye could see, the *clump, clump, clump* of the wheels' metrical pattern along the highway, the smell of the driver's coffee. I'd been back on the road for only a few hours, speeding along a vast prairie on the other side of the world from my cramped office, but the recalibration was seamless.

I WAS SITTING IN THE BAND'S dressing room talking to Randy after the first San Antonio show when Sharon walked in.

"Stephen, you're still planning to come to LA, right?" I nodded. I'd nothing concrete arranged, no hotels or flights booked, but having made it to Texas, I wanted to push on and visit California. "Then stay with us—we've plenty of room."

The good news. But then there was bad news.

She was in to tell the band that at Ozzy's final two concerts before retiring, scheduled the following month in Costa Mesa, the support act would be Sabbath, touring with Ronnie James Dio singing. And the plan was for the four original members to reunite for a short set. The issue was that Fay and I had booked a vacation in Barbados the same week. It was especially problematic, as she was still a reporter in Bristol, while I had obviously moved back home, so we only saw each other once a month. I'd miss Ozzy singing with Sabbath for the first time (bar Live Aid) in fourteen years. I called Lynn and left a maudlin message. She must have thought I was planning to top myself and rang back to try to cheer me up. My diary reads, "Got mega depressed."

I jumped onto the bus for the five-hour ride to Dallas, again sitting up with Mike, and when we arrived at 6 a.m., I called Fay. In an unexpected turn of events, she was furious I wanted to cancel our romantic beach trip four weeks out. She was generally a laid-back partner—after all, we spent the vast majority of our relationship in different countries. She was a diver and a skydiver and was often away with groups, while it wasn't unusual for me to travel abroad with Patrick or other friends. I knew this request would strain even her patience, but she said she knew how important Ozzy was to me, so she'd consider it.

I slept for a few hours, then called my office to have them price flights from DFW to LA. The last-minute one-way was $250, but then I met Bobby in the lobby and he asked, "Stephen, how are you planning on getting from Texas to California?" I said I was about to buy a flight. He said, "As it happens, we may be able to help you out. Don't do anything just yet. Leave it with me."

The next morning, he told me to pack a small overnight bag and leave the rest of my luggage at the hotel. It would be sent separately—I was flying on Ozzy's private jet.

It still boggles my mind. It was one thing for Ozzy to pay for my room, another to let me ride the tour bus. This was a seat on a $9 million chartered Learjet hired for $12,000, equivalent to about $28,000 in 2024. There were undoubtedly dozens more deserving of a spot. I was knocked out and asked Mike how long the trip was. The band had been on it a few times and he said it was faster than flying commercial; I was hoping it would last all night.

After the show our van drove right to the plane door at a private airfield, and we entered the cabin, all carpet and walnut and leather and glass and digital displays. An attendant offered a choice of two meals. Feeling like an undeserving interloper I declined both, so she made me a turkey sandwich from the crew's personal supply. She must have thought I was important. On the inbound journey, she stopped Ozzy lighting a cigarette. "I'm paying tens of thousands of dollars for this flight and I can't smoke?" he asked, and she said the owner forbade it. She told him Neil Diamond was a recent customer, and he made the pilot land so he could get off and puff two cigarettes, happy to pay the extra landing fee and fuel cost.

It was one of the most exhilarating nights of my life. I wasn't a multi-millionaire celebrity, high-powered businessman, or elite sport star. Most people go their whole lives without flying in a private jet—not only was I doing it, but I was doing it as a guest of Ozzy.

I was amazed how clear the view was—I was used to being swaddled in low-lying clouds after climbing a few hundred feet, but here, across the barren American Southwest, the visibility was perfect. The sky was pitch-black, but I was enraptured by the rolling canvas of twinkling lights, clusters of yellows and whites and blues and reds, as we raced through the darkness.

When we landed in LA, a trio of limos met us on the tarmac, and I jumped in with Mike and Randy. It was my first time in an American stretch limo with a bar and a phone, and I was going to call my mum, but Randy thought the Osbournes would get charged for it, so I didn't (cutting them a break, right?).

I only had a few hours on the ground, then flew to Las Vegas for two nights, bought a plane ticket to Oakland to see the concert at the Coliseum, and took a bus to the venue—where, again, Bobby said Sharon told him to put me on the plane. I'd considered it a thrilling once-in-a-lifetime experience, flying in a private jet with my idol. Less than seventy-two hours later I was doing it once more.

Ozzy had been on a relentless worldwide slog for a year. He had a precious week's respite at home—yet he and Sharon opened up their home and private family time to me. I spent four nights with them in the Pacific Palisades. My diary reads, "As this trip has gone on it's become more and more incredible, it's like I'm living in a dream world."

The invite was even more remarkable because the next day was Sharon's birthday. A flow of flowers tumbled in nonstop, the most elaborate a four-foot heart-shaped display from Ozzy. Though I hated the thought of his retirement, being alone with him at his home I saw the tour was taking a toll. He was run-down and under the weather and spent most of the day in bed.

The mansion had few personal touches, the rooms sparse and open, the bare minimum of furniture, modern wood doors and windows framing walls painted inoffensive pale shades of white and beige and yellow. It was clear it was a temporary base. The kids Jack and Kelly shared bunks and I slept in with them on another bed, while the eldest child, Aimee, had her own room next door.

Jack was six and loved Legos. When I woke, he was lying on the floor, looking at a couple of boxes his dad had left at the end of his bed when we arrived in the middle of the night. He saw my eyes open and immediately asked me to start building. I joined him on the floor in shorts, putting together a boat and a car. He went to the bathroom, and on his way back, Ozzy wandered out of his bedroom and asked what he was doing. Jack replied, "I'm playing with Stephen."

Ozzy came in and asked, "Did he wake you?" I assured him he didn't, and I was happy to help. Though only twenty-two, I'd good tolerance for kids; there were plenty in our family, and I was used to playing with them.

In Sharon's office I met Michael. He was an assistant then, but within a couple of years he ran it. Good-natured, hardworking, and unassuming, nothing ever bothered him. He said in his interview Sharon asked, "Can you lie?" Then, when he started his job, the first thing she did was send him to buy tampons. We went sightseeing, had dinner on Sunset Strip, then wound up at an exclusive party for the rock magazine *RIP*—a private performance by Bon Jovi for invite-only guests. Tinseltown was so far away from my mundane office back home.

The second morning I walked into the kitchen, and Sharon and Ozzy were sitting talking at the island. Sharon got up. "Good morning, Stephen, let me fix you breakfast," she said.

"I'm fine, don't need a thing, thanks," I said.

"Listen, you naughty boy, don't be silly. Sit down here beside the old man," she said, motioning toward Ozzy. "Coffee? Toast? I insist." She bustled to the counter.

I had interrupted a discussion about the two Costa Mesa dates with Sabbath. She wanted Ozzy to jam with them after his set both nights, while he was determined to save it for the last night as a one-off.

"Boo, listen to me, you gotta do it the first gig as well," she said with her back to us, putting bread into the toaster. "If you don't—"

"Sharon—you're not fucking listening to me! My voice will be fucked! It's hard enough doing the gig with my own band after a year and a fucking whatever-it-is on the road. You want me to do that, then another fucking half an hour with those fuckers, then do it all over again the next night? No fucking way."

She came over and put her hands on the countertop, voice level. "Ozzy, we've sold out both nights, back-to-back. The kids there the first night will feel cheated if they don't get to see you with Sabbath as well." She turned to me. "Stephen—what do you think?"

I froze. How was I supposed to take sides on this one? Support my idol and piss off his wife, or weigh in on her behalf and disagree with Ozzy? Either way, I'd lose. Luckily, Ozzy shot up and walked out, Sharon gave me a rueful smile, and I felt like I'd dodged a bullet. A couple of minutes later he returned, zipping up his fly, Sharon left, and he and I spent the next three hours talking. That happened a few times during my stay and was the highlight of my first taste of California; not the Beverly Hills sightseeing or Hollywood razzamatazz, just Ozzy and me, sometimes joined by Sharon, in the kitchen, chatting.

On my last evening, all five Osbournes took me to dinner at an English pub in Santa Monica. On the way home Sharon drove the SUV, Ozzy in the passenger seat; I was in the next row like the eldest child, the three little ones behind. The kids belted out "Dizzy" by the Wonder Stuff, at the top of their lungs, and Ozzy threw a bottle of water at them, soaking me in the process. At the house, Kelly had a meltdown when told it was bedtime—"She's thrown a wobbler" was their expression when she got upset. She stood at the top of the stairs and screamed at them, while at the bottom Ozzy sang nonsense—"La la la de da"—to her and Sharon danced around him. It was only making Kelly madder, but I couldn't stop laughing, the enduring image of my time with them, just regular parents dealing with a misbehaving child in their own inimitable way.

MY DIARY FOR NOVEMBER 13, 1992: "Absolute mayhem this morning. Tony Iommi was arrested last night for not paying child support for his daughter, and was thrown in jail."

Sharon had to bail Sabbath guitarist Iommi out, literally and figuratively, to save the reunion. When they were still figuring out how to get the $75,000 to him, they at one stage had a private jet standing by to fly me to Sacramento, where he was imprisoned. They were able to wire the finances in the end, but for two hours I envisaged having a cash-stuffed briefcase thrust at me, clutching it to my chest, the handle handcuffed to my wrist, sweating profusely on the jet, unable to relax until I handed it over. It would have been quite the story, but then word came through it was sorted via lawyers.

I had canceled the Barbados vacation (making it up to Fay with a trip to Antigua instead), so after five weeks tending shop at home I headed back to California. Lynn and I flew to LA with a case of clothes from the Osbournes' personal shopper. ("That gear's great, Steve—did you get any of it for yourself?" Ozzy asked. I said no—his designer cashmere sweatsuit equaled two months' wages for me. Besides, all my money went on tracking him around the world.)

Once I was freed from auditioning for a role in a ransom movie, Lynn and I drove south to the Ritz-Carlton in Laguna Niguel. My favorite hotel stay ever. My gargantuan accommodation, paid for by the Osbournes, had an idyllic balcony with a heart-stopping view overlooking the Pacific: the Santa Ana winds turning the sky an unworldly orange-red hue, the beach sweeping in a horseshoe bend, the waves crashing onto the rocks below, the palm trees swaying and rustling as they curved against the breeze, lights twinkling and blinking in the hills.

Ozzy had a room in which to retreat from relatives and friends and spouses and journalists and staff, while the family was in a $2,500-a-night grandiose suite. Lynn and I went up for midnight tea and stayed until 3 a.m., and the next morning, Sharon asked me to look after the kids: Jack left Legos in Ozzy's room, so I went to get it. He opened the door naked as he was heading to the sauna, and we spent ages combing the furniture looking for the tiny figures. I knew he was distracted as we turned over pillows and rooted through luggage—he got nervous before every gig, even more so when it was a special occasion like this, or a show packed with people from the industry like London, New York, or LA—eventually we found them, and I wished him good luck and left.

Dio had quit Sabbath in protest at the support slot, and writer Steffan Chirazi and I went into the pit to watch them perform with Judas Priest singer Rob Halford. We were thrown out, so Steffan found Geezer's wife,

Gloria, who got us back in. Geezer kept throwing his picks at me—I knew it was not motivated by generosity, but he was playing a private game to see how often he could hit me on the head—and their set was excellent. Ozzy's show, meanwhile, was good, not great. I could tell he was holding back for the tour finale the following night, and the sound occasionally swept in and out, as it was a gusty, steep amphitheater. After the encore, I lingered beside his quick-change booth stage left. Geezer and Bill Ward from Sabbath appeared beside me, then Tony walked up. "Are we doing this or not?" he asked Geezer. The answer was no; it didn't surprise me when the houselights came on, and we trooped offstage. We returned to the hotel for the end-of-tour party with the stomach-turning and -churning Jim Rose Circus, and I fell into bed at 4 a.m., thinking about something Ozzy told me:

> "You know, when Sabbath were on, we could take on the world. Sometimes we would do gigs and we'd all be fucked-up, taking acid and doing this and that, but when we got it on we were smoking. I remember once we were supporting Rod Stewart and the Faces at the old Fillmore East hall in New York. We had no money and were staying at this fleapit of a hotel. We couldn't even afford a tour bus and had to pile into a cab to get to the gig. Anyway, in those days you did two shows, a matinee and one later in the evening. We were told we could do a sound check at a certain time, and we went down and sat in the hall to wait for Stewart to finish. But they fucked around and it meant that we didn't get a sound check—and we were pissed, man. We didn't even have to say anything to each other, but we got on that stage and blew that crowd away, man. [Rod Stewart] wouldn't even come out of his dressing room, and tried to get us kicked off the second show."

I'd get to see that band the following night.

THE LAST HURRAH. IT WAS ANARCHY when we arrived, bodies blocking paths and hallways and corridors everywhere, the battle to get to the dressing room like that famous picture of the evacuating Americans fighting off the locals as their helicopter took off from the embassy during the Vietnam War. The energy from a fanatical crowd out front and those of us lucky enough to be backstage pulsed like a living entity.

Ozzy's set was suitably phenomenally raucous, the guys ripping into every song, the rigger in an army costume and wearing an outsized pig mask descending from the lights shooting a giant water gun, Mike's tech dressing as Elvis and waltzing over to Ozzy as he sang, Keith riding his bike onstage.

After the encore, nobody left, and the fans' screaming increased. I've never been to a show that compares with the crackling level of anticipation rippling through the atmosphere that night.

After an endless fifteen-minute lull, it was time for the big event. The Sabbath reunion.

They smoked four songs, Ozzy turning his back on the audience occasionally to make fun of drummer Bill's heart condition. Zakk, Randy, and Mike posted up stage right, as enraptured as anyone, Mike roaring them on, Zakk pulling faces at Geezer, trying to make him laugh.

If Ozzy really was never going to play live again, he was going out on top.

Afterward, there was another party for record company staff. Sharon had commissioned a striking platinum disc display featuring all of Ozzy's solo releases fanned, framed, and mounted in a powerful six-foot collage. When she unveiled it, a record company executive claimed credit for it, telling Ozzy he personally chose the wood and designed it. So Sharon sent him the invoice. When the party ended, a handful of us went to the sumptuous beachfront suite and drank hot chocolate until 4 a.m., just a small gathering with Ozzy and his family, band, and closest friends. It was back in my room that it hit me—after twenty-four years on the road, this had been his last date of his last world tour. It felt like a curtain was coming down. I wrote in my diary, "It's the end of an era. It's sad. . . . I'll really miss the people and the sense of involvement–my memories are very precious."

I delayed my flight home to see Sabbath inducted into the Rockwalk, a hall of fame on Sunset Strip with handprints in concrete, like the stars on Hollywood Boulevard. Rob Halford was to introduce them, and he arrived at the office with muffins and orange juice for everyone, friendly and down-to-earth. But the ceremony didn't go smoothly. Ozzy decided he didn't want to do it, so the other Sabs were told it was off. Then he changed his mind, and it was a scramble to find them and tell them it was back on, and I was ushered into a limo with Ozzy and Rob to the event. They gave Ozzy baby oil for his hands to protect them against the mixture, and had him do a second set of concrete slabs, backup in case an earthquake destroyed those on the sidewalk.

Unfortunately, they couldn't locate Bill, and by the time they found him, he missed it. He was pissed. Sharon suggested Ozzy take the trio for a cup of tea to smooth things over, but it didn't happen. Seeing the dynamic up close was fascinating: four men in their forties who were in a band for a decade and had known each other since childhood, but obviously still had issues, causing friction they found difficult to face.

I received a surprise present to round off the trip—a *No More Tears* double-platinum disc, personalized with my name, more elaborate than my first, cutout photos and logos engraved into the glass.

Lynn hadn't postponed her flight for the ceremony, so the previous day, I drove her to LAX. In the car, I told her I was baffled by the depth of the Osbournes' generosity toward me. Platinum discs, rides in private jets, invites to their home, thousands of dollars on hotels . . . I couldn't work it out. I wasn't a journalist who could give them good press, an industry chief who would enhance their earnings, a TV executive guaranteeing publicity. I offered nothing.

"You're their friend," Lynn said. "Think about it—how many do they really have? They've been burnt so many times down the years, people who get close to them then steal things or try to make money from them. They deal with people every day who want something from them. You don't. You're like their family. They consider you one of their few true friends."

Almost eight years after meeting them in Brazil, I was still struggling to process that. So much of my identity had been wrapped up in being Ozzy's biggest fan, but if he was never touring again, I was happy to be his friend.

PART TWO

ROADIE

#64

SAN DIEGO STATE UNIVERSITY OPEN AIR THEATRE

SAN DIEGO, CALIFORNIA

October 28, 1995

FOR TWO YEARS, I saw the Osbournes often and, perversely, the concert-free years from 1993 to 1995 was my favorite period with them, as I felt part of their special, trusted inner circle. Sharon scaled down her operation and Lynn transitioned to working from home. She asked me to help clear out the office, so I flew to London for a couple of days, and she said I could have anything they were trashing.

In 1993, Ozzy and Sharon sold their home Beel House, a three-hundred-year-old mansion on sixteen acres, after it being on the market for two and a half years. I had stayed there once, the night Lynn got married. It was bought by Matt Aitken, songwriter for Rick Astley and others, but the deal was tetchy and Sharon was mad—she wouldn't leave anything he hadn't paid for, the handyman even destroying a tool bench in the garage. They scheduled an estate sale for the same weekend I was in Bath with my mum, her sister Carol, and my grandmother Jean, as I was treating them to a trip for Christmas. It was a four-hour round drive, but I asked if they would help out, and we spent the day selling stuff to the locals, some of whom were queuing in the rain before the gate opened. My mum bought a curtain she used for years, my aunt a leather jacket. I potted about the estate on a buggy, picking up ornaments Sharon wanted to keep, and Mrs. Aitken turned up to express her displeasure. She seemed like a miserable witch.

In September, I flew over to go with Sharon and Kelly to a Bon Jovi show and met them at the new place they were renting. I asked Ozzy how he was filling his days, and he pointed at a book skyscraper on the coffee table. "You see all them books in this pile? I've read every one," he said, and he insisted I take a memoir about the Balkan War, the retrieval of which resembled a game of Jenga.

Artist Tom Kyffin was commissioned to draw an autobiographical Ozzy comic book and Lynn asked me to help. I went across to London for the night to talk him through important events in Ozzy's life, lending him my scrapbooks, keeping in touch as he worked on it. When it came out at the end of the year, he had copied the photo of Ozzy and me in Rio from *Kerrang!* and painted me into it as a thank-you. Immortalized in a comic book with Ozzy. Wow.

With no tour to sabotage plans, in June 1994 Fay and I lined up a stateside road trip starting in California, and Sharon asked me to take eight-year-old Jack to Ozzy in LA. She brought him, Aimee, and Kelly to Dublin and took us to dinner, then the following morning we crossed the Atlantic via stopovers in both Shannon and Atlanta. Ozzy met us at the gate at LAX and shouted, "Jesus Christ, that was a long trip! He was only a fucking baby when you left." For years after that when Jack was flying, he asked if it was going to be with me, because then he knew he'd have to rough it in coach instead of being in first.

We stayed with Michael and his wife, Denny—after Ozzy, Lynn, and Keith, the Osbourne clan had become my personal accommodation service. Michael and I took Jack to the soccer World Cup semifinal at the Pasadena Rose Bowl, Ozzy giving us his limo to ride there and back in style.

That summer the Osbournes were renovating their new home, Welders House, twenty-five minutes from Heathrow. I have many, many happy memories of days and nights there. Usually Ozzy and I did nothing more than shoot the breeze around the kitchen island. He told Sabbath stories and recounted misdemeanors and adventures; we discussed the news. Or we sat on the sectional in the living area beside it, him with his feet up, resting his elbow on a pillow reading "You can never be too rich or too thin." Underneath the TV was a pint-sized monitor linked to the security system, and we slumped in front of the stream for hours, watching cars go down the lane or deliverymen approach the buzzer. One morning we got downstairs to find a spider spanning a web across the lens and it mesmerized us for days, crawling back and forth across the screen, dilated to a terrifying size like a prop from a 1950s science-fiction B movie. Another time, Ozzy showed me his new rifle and laser sight, then disappeared. Five minutes later he was back, holding a dead rabbit, blood dripping onto the tiled floor. "Quick, Steve, clean this up before the missus comes down the stairs," he said, and I jumped up to grab paper towels.

THAT SAME YEAR, AFTER ELEVEN YEARS working for Sharon, Lynn was let go—with Ozzy retired, their affairs could be handled by Michael in LA. (She was quickly offered another position, though, with Sanctuary, who managed Iron Maiden and others.) As she was winding down, she called me up and told me to come to London, and to bring an empty suitcase. She was putting me in charge of the Ozzy Osbourne Fan Club, so I'd need to carry the filing cabinet contents back to Northern Ireland.

This was the same fan club my mum wrote to almost a decade earlier asking about tickets to Rock in Rio, and, the irony, my mum would now be helping me answer letters.

I sat with her at the kitchen table, an hour into dealing with the fan mail heaped beside us, steam rising from our teacups, arguing about whether to send a signed Ozzy photo to a teenage Irish female letter writer. I'd a stack of seventy in front of me.

"I think she deserves an autograph," said my mum, holding up a page. "Read this! She's a big fan, and look at how much she's written. She's even drawn a wee picture."

I licked an envelope, smoothed it flat with my palm, turned it over, moistened a stamp, pressed it on, and tossed the envelope onto the pile with thirty others. I grabbed a signed promo shot and waved it. "Mum, we can't be sending these out willy-nilly. It has to be something really special. You're so soft—if it was up to you, we'd run out in a week."

I rubbed my eyes, cranky and tired. It had been years since I moved back to Belfast, and I was still living at home. I couldn't afford my own place, paying myself a minimum wage from the business, flying to England monthly to see Fay or meeting her at Heathrow for a trip. Once every two weeks, after a full day in the office, I'd deal with answering fan mail. But I never minded—I loved the responsibility and trust and that it maintained a connection to the Osbournes.

Michael faxed me info from LA—what Ozzy was up to or what new merchandise was coming out—and I used it to draft a newsletter. I faxed it to Sharon, she approved or tweaked it, then I copied it and sent it out to anyone who wrote in, and those already on the mailing list. Sharon was always adamant that if a fan went to the trouble of writing to Ozzy, they must receive a reply.

"I still think she should get one," my mum said. She handed me the next to read and returned to folding photocopies of the newsletter, then stuffing them into white containers. "You were just like her once, remember?"

I was in touch with the office frequently. I knew Ozzy was restless. He'd spent most of his life onstage, not an easy thing to give up.

In early 1995, Michael called with the news I'd been expecting: Ozzy was recording a new album. And was going back on the road.

IN JUNE OZZY BOOKED AN UNPUBLICIZED date at Nottingham's Rock City—scene of the riot after the canceled gig in 1988, keeping his word to make it up—with a new band in tow. Randy returned on drums and Geezer on bass. But Zakk was flirting with Guns N' Roses and wouldn't confirm he was in, so Ozzy lined up Testament's Alex Skolnick. I flew to London, picked up Lynn at Welders, and we drove to the venue chatting excitedly, the unadvertised gig in a small venue a world away in every sense from the "final" show in Costa Mesa.

At least, it was supposed to be. The second the lights went down the fans chanted "Ozzy! Ozzy!" so clearly word had gotten out.

Afterward, Sharon asked Lynn and me about Alex. We both thought he had done well, but I could tell she was lukewarm on him, and a couple of months later she recruited Joe Holmes, thirty-two, who had taken lessons from Randy Rhoads. (I have the only photograph in existence of Alex's sole performance with Ozzy.)

The tour was titled Retirement Sucks. I had dreamed of one day making it to every show on a leg stateside, but it had always been impractical, as they lasted months. However, Retirement Sucks kicked off in October with a four-week run in smaller North American theaters. I flew to the US at the beginning of September to spend a month traveling with friends, then got to Toronto for the first gig. The only other travel I booked was a flight home from New York after the final show. I was hoping to hitch lifts when possible.

This leg was different, though. There was no band bus. Ozzy chartered a small jet, but space was so tight even keyboardist John traveled with the crew instead of the band. The crew had two buses with twelve bunks each, and Bobby invited me to travel on the same bus as Keith. I wouldn't have a bed, but could sleep on the seats.

I booked into the band's hotel and went with Geezer and Randy to rehearsals, catching up with the roadies I knew and meeting the new crew. They always asked, "What do you do?" and I'd stammer, "Nothing. I'm just a fan. I'm a friend of Ozzy and Sharon's." They looked at me, puzzled, and I shrugged, sheepish, and we both went about our business.

Our first long ride was from Montreal to Worcester, Massachusetts. Keith and I drank until 5 a.m., then he headed to his bunk. A minute later he was back. "You know the two rules?" he asked. I did not—it was my first time on a crew bus. "Always sleep with your feet facing the front, so if we stop suddenly and you're flung forward, you don't break your neck. Secondly, don't take a shit on the bus, the toilet is for pissing only." It took me until my fourth tour to learn the cardinal regulations every real worker finds out immediately.

A crew pub crawl was set up for our initial night off, and we woke to discover the guitar tech was in jail for breaking a hotel window. One night off, one roadie arrested.

New York City next. Two days running I chanced upon Joe on a Manhattan sidewalk, and he invited me to hang out with him. I liked him immediately. He was rail-thin, always in combat shorts or pants, softly spoken, and the instant he got back to his room, he strapped on his guitar like it was an extension of his body or he felt naked without it, and he practiced nonstop while chatting.

After the concert Randy took me to the Whiskey Bar, an upscale cocktail joint where the Ozzy-loving manager comped us drinks. Two pretty girls joined us, and after four hours I felt guilty about mooching all night and insisted he let me buy a round. When the check arrived, I realized it was a rookie mistake, and we drank there many times after that, but I never again offered to pay. This wee Belfast lad was way out of his league. Four tours changed some things, but not everything.

The crew left for the next date in DC, but I stayed on to see Geezer's solo band. Joe called that afternoon: a record company executive was treating him and Randy to lunch, and he wanted me to come, even though we had only met five days previously. We got back to a message from Sharon inviting us over, so we spent four hours in their suite, went to Geezer's gig, out to dinner with Sharon, then back to the Whiskey Bar. "Another superb night," I wrote in my diary, for once without hyperbole.

I flew to DC—and landed in the middle of the Million Man March, hundreds of thousands of African Americans mobilized for a demonstration organized by activist Louis Farrakhan. I took the Metro to the venue and never felt more out of place and ill at ease: a pasty-skinned Irishman who, while growing up in one of the whitest parts of the planet, rarely saw a Black person, wandering the streets with my suitcase among the protesters. When I showed up backstage at the Capitol Ballroom, sweating and flustered, the band thought it hilarious.

But no hilarity during his set. I sensed Ozzy was unhappy and struggling, sounding rough in parts, but more tellingly, I saw it in his face, I read his lips as he swore at himself, he was shaking his head and grimacing, his left hand involuntarily flying to his throat and clutching it. He cut the gig short and trashed the dressing room, frustrated and upset.

Backstage, Sharon grabbed me. "Stephen, soon we'll have a bigger plane and then you can come with us," she said. It was another incredibly generous offer, and I seized the moment to tell her I could join as an unpaid worker: helping with luggage, chaperoning, giving Bobby a hand. . . . I didn't need wages and would do it for food, travel, and accommodation. She said to leave it with her, and at 1 a.m. our crew buses departed for Detroit.

We checked into the Omni International, and I turned on the radio—to discover Ozzy had a chest infection and canceled the next two dates, in the Motor City and Chicago. So, with four days until the next show in Houston, we left after one night for the 1,300-mile drive. Our electricity blew, we stopped for hours while both drivers vainly tried to fix it, plowed on without it, detoured to Tennessee to switch drivers, and arrived thirty-two hours later, no one's idea of a fun vacation. At least I'd a bunk, as the burly monitor engineer was too big to fit in one and gave me his, sleeping on the back couch instead.

As a stowaway on a vehicle designed for a dozen the crew nicknamed me "13." Maybe I was unlucky—Ozzy pulled the next three dates. Three and a half concerts in fourteen days. The bigger plane was scrapped. My dream of completing a US leg had turned into a nightmare.

I spent five nights bored and maudlin, trapped in an infuriating Texas suburban purgatory wasteland. I used the downtime to check in on my business, calling and faxing the staff, making sure it was running smoothly. When I bought it, I'd inherited a teenage employee, William King, and four years later, with me on the road five thousand miles away, he was basically in charge.

We got back on track in Kansas City, though Ozzy dropped two songs from the set; next up was St Louis, then we flew to LA. I stayed with Michael and helped him prep the guest list, and we worked on it again on show day. It felt like a full-time job, and when I got to the Hollywood Palladium, I understood why. It was my first experience of Los Angeles: bedlam backstage, hundreds even for the sound check, corridors and dressing rooms and production area thronged with friends and well-wishers and liggers and record company types.

Sharon tossed me her car keys and asked me to deliver the kids to the nanny at their hotel to escape the mania, then I drove to a frenzied "in-store" for the new album, *Ozzmosis*, on the Sunset Strip. It was chaotic, the parking lot crammed, security guards in constant motion like sharks, the queue of fans wrapped around the store like a python circling its prey. Inside, Ozzy and the band along a table like the head guests at a wedding, customers bought the release, then went along the line getting it autographed. I burrowed in beside Ozzy and swept the covers along, trying to make myself useful. After two hours we ducked out, leaving a disappointed mob banging on the windows and yelling as it took another military operation to escape.

THE FOLLOWING AFTERNOON I RODE WITH Michael to the amphitheater at San Diego State University. In the dressing room Geezer gave me a copy of his new album on which he thanked me in the liner notes—what the fuck for I had no idea, all I did was get drunk with him a few times. I was grateful, and nearly a decade after Ozzy first mentioned me on a record, it was humbling to be acknowledged by another rock legend. But that wonderful surprise was overshadowed by the gig.

Ozzy was fired up—joking with the band, messing with the roadies, resurrecting the dropped tracks. He'd just rowed with Sharon, and that often made him unpredictable onstage. He egged the crowd on to get wilder and wilder, they grew increasingly unruly and combustible, and by closer "Crazy Train," with him coaxing them to go nuts, they were a bubbling cauldron. Michael and I were on the soundboard and felt the electricity undulating through the fans, the energy roiling above them like a wave, swelling then escalating. Both of us had seen Ozzy savoring this kind of devilment before, and from our elevated vantage point, we sensed what was coming: the audience stormed the stage.

It was all-hands to the pumps. Michael and I sprinted from the mixer and clambered onstage to help the crew battling the invaders, shoving fans back into the seats, pushing them away from the equipment, and fighting them off the band. Joe, an Ozzy stage-incursion virgin, had a look of "What the fuck is this?" and struggled to keep playing, but Geezer and Randy had seen it all before—Ozzy prowling the stage, basking in the anarchy. We restored order, he encored, then rushed to his plane in case the police showed up. Which they did.

The production manager collared me by the dressing rooms and beckoned me down the hall to a closet. He closed the door behind us.

"Stephen, we've a job for you. Take this and hide it," he whispered, and handed me a video. "It's the master of the gig, and we need to get it outta the building. The cops are asking for it and if they watch it, they might charge him with inciting a riot. We're stalling them in the production office. The runner's waiting at the load-out ramp and he'll take you to the airport. Rent a car and take it to LA. Go."

I shoved the tape down my trousers, walked as quickly as I dared without looking suspicious to meet the runner, got a car, and drove to the band's hotel in LA. They'd booked me a sprawling suite with a gorgeous view over Sunset and I got in at 5 a.m., glancing at the rearview mirror in case of flashing blue lights every few miles. It never occurred to me for a second to refuse to do it.

Sharon woke me at 10:30 a.m., and I drove to their hotel in Marina del Rey

The plan was to edit out any incriminating exhortations before detectives showed up (they never did), and we watched it back, Michael and I popping up out of thin air like bouncer magicians, manhandling fans offstage. A record company executive on the tour made us souvenir laminates reading "I went fucking crazy with Ozzy in San Diego" in commemoration.

I CAUGHT A LIFT TO THE next date, in Phoenix, on Ozzy's plane.

A step up from my last jet adventure, this was even more exclusive transport, a private, private jet, only four of us on board: Ozzy, his assistant, Michael, and me. Although the partying and lack of sleep tugged at my consciousness, I fought the urge to doze: the scenery wondrous, the company exquisite. After the gig I collapsed into my bunk and crashed for eleven hours.

We headed back to Chicago to make up the canceled show and had two nights off, so Geezer treated me to dinner. Like Ozzy, keyboardist John, and tour manager Bobby, fellow middle-aged road warriors who boozed their way around the world and felt they needed to quit alcohol, he, too, had got sober. He replaced that addiction with another, toy collecting. I volunteered to help, so the next day I rented a car, and we spent four hours touring stores. He borrowed my room to talk to a journalist about his solo record, then I accompanied him to a radio station for another interview.

Sharon, who had flown back to England, rang the morning of the Chicago gig about an appearance Ozzy would be making on British TV's *The Big Breakfast*. It involved a fan dance contest, so as I managed the fan club's mailing list, she wanted me to contact four members to fill the spots. It was all a bit vague, but I said I'd handle whatever. After the last US date, I drove to New York, flew to London, took another flight to Belfast, then turned right around to go to Welders to help prepare for the dance. After more than two months away, I stayed home for six hours.

At Welders, I discovered Sharon had listed me as a dance participant.

Not only was I to shake my stuff on live national television, I had eleven hours to locate a partner willing to share my humiliation. I convinced an elementary school teacher friend, who called her principal and asked for permission to be late so she could dance on TV.

I piled into a van with all five Osbournes, amazingly and against all predictions arriving only seven minutes after the 6 a.m. start time. My friend was waiting. There was nothing I was more ill-equipped to do on live TV than dance, so I wore a baseball cap and an XXL Ozzy shirt, and planned to keep my head lowered. But my bid for anonymity was scuppered when a peppy worker in a headset, much too cheerful for the time in the morning, walked up and said, "Stephen! Great, you made it! Let me put this on you," and pinned a jumbo multicolored name tag to my chest.

Ozzy was getting mic'd up, but brushed the tech off to walk over, point at me, and yell, "You're gonna look a right fuckin' cunt, you stupid Irish dimph!" Luckily, the cameras weren't rolling. I'd take smuggling a package past California cops anytime over dancing on live TV.

It was so last-minute my friend didn't have a chance to tell her students why she would be missing from the classroom, and apparently when she was on-screen, some yelled, "Mum! Dad! That's my teacher on TV!" The parents told them to stop imagining things and eat their cereal.

The UK leg of Retirement Sucks, ten concerts in thirteen days, kicked off in Ipswich the following night. I went to them all (two were pulled), traveling around Britain on the hoof, frequently returning to crash at Ozzy's house when I needed to like he was a college roommate.

The last date was in Newcastle, then the tour trundled onto a monthlong trek through continental Europe. But it was time for me to leave. I'd been swept up in an intercontinental fairy tale with my hero, but I knew I was neglecting work. I could call and fax my agency all I wanted every day, but to have a successful business, I needed to be there.

I returned to Belfast, to my life, to my job, to reality.

#76

CONTINENTAL AIRLINES ARENA

EAST RUTHERFORD, NEW JERSEY

January 18, 1996

NUCLEAR EXPLOSIONS ARE NOT usually used as cover for scrapping concerts for birthday parties.

France detonated four nukes in the Pacific between September and November 1995, and in protest, many artists pulled out of shows in the country. Ozzy was due to play Paris at the Zénith, where I had seen him in 1989, on December 3. His birthday. He was also fighting bronchitis.

Whatever the reason—atomic testing, birthday festivities, illness—I knew the cancellation was coming because I had been faxed an invite to his birthday party at Welders.

We ate in the formal dining room, and though I stayed with them frequently, it was the only time we used it: emitting wealth, dark wood and lantern light fixtures, green flowered curtains and expensive framed art, rich red tablecloths, crystal glasses and fine china, ornate elaborate centerpieces of candles and fruit.

It was always the same guests at these intimate get-togethers: the band; Lynn; Bobby; Sharon's niece Gina; a couple of others. "We're a small group, but we all just roll along from place to place, sticking together," Sharon told me about their de facto family (Ozzy was not close to his family; she had well-publicized bust-ups with hers). Though it was Ozzy's party, my birthday was six days earlier, and Sharon gave me an elegant top-shelf black leather bag I still use.

One of my favorite photos was taken that night: Lynn and me seated; standing around us are John and his wife, Jean; Jack on a chair trying to blow out a candle; then Bobby; Randy, one hand on Jack, the other on my chest; Joe; Sharon. An old snapshot may not be framed perfectly or focused correctly, but looking at it stirs a memory, putting you back in the moment and making you smile.

Just like with the *Kerrang!* article and *The Sun* job advert, a third brief innocuous event changed my life. The night before the party, in a London pub, I chatted up an American study-abroad girl, Julie from Gastonia, North Carolina, and as she left in a taxi, she made a split-second decision to hand me a slip of paper with her number.

FOR FOURTEEN MONTHS, OZZY HAD A diary on his record company's website, and I showed up in an entry:

> FRIDAY, 8 DECEMBER 1995
>
> Today we travel to Prague. I've never played here before, but have heard only great things about the city and the crowds. I have lots of friends flying in. . . . My son, Jack; my friend, Stephen Rea from Belfast; my longtime family friend, Lynn

Seager. . . . So you can imagine that everyone here is ready to party in Prague.

I went there because it was the only stop on the European leg with multiple nights, so I got two gigs with one airfare. The Czech Republic had just become accessible and was not yet the tourist mecca it grew into. Economic conditions were harsh—Bobby later told me he and Geezer left behind their toiletries for the hotel workers because they stank.

I took an Irish girl, Belinda, with me, and we flew to London to meet Lynn and Jack. We landed in Eastern Europe, blanketed by ice and snow, and were ushered into a VIP room, where we waited with champagne while our passports were taken to be stamped. Then we were swept off to the Inter-Continental Hotel, where the Osbournes had reserved neighboring suites. They often did that so Sharon could work without disturbing Ozzy, but Sharon decided not to come, and rather than cancel the second suite and get a refund, she gave it to me instead. Rushed through immigration like dignitaries on a royal visit followed by free five-star penthouse accommodation: Belinda didn't know what hit her.

I watched the second night from the pit, and three songs in, Ozzy spotted me. I knew what was coming, but it was too late—he grabbed a bucket of water and dumped it over my head. Mid-December on the Eastern front in a high, huge, freezing hockey arena. I was drenched, dripping wet, shivering like crazy, and quavered to the dressing room to beg Martha, the wardrobe girl, for a dry shirt—but not before receiving a lecture from Bobby: "Now, now, Stephen, you've only yourself to blame, you should know better than to stand in the pit."

Ozzy invited us to his suite for a midnight snack and he was still pissing himself laughing about it. (I asked Belinda twenty-five years later what she remembered about the trip, and she said Ozzy took exception to a decorative flan that came with room service and flung it out the window. I've no recollection of that, maybe because I was used to him pitching food out of hotels.)

AFTER FLYING BACK HOME, I MANAGED just one day in Belfast before receiving a call: Ozzy needed to sign an urgent contract, could I take it to Germany? I hopped onto a plane to London, a waiting car took me to Welders, I picked up the document and rushed back to Heathrow, flew to Munich, and got a taxi to Ozzy's hotel, arriving at midnight. He was on his Lifecycle and said to his assistant, "Sharon's just off the phone telling me to make sure we cover all Steve's expenses. Get a list of everything he spent." Though I'd laid out a fortune in last-minute flights, I wasn't worried—they always took care of me spectacularly. He signed the papers, and I went downstairs to the bar. It happened so fast I hadn't told anyone I was coming, but Joe was wandering about and joined Keith and me for a beer. I was up before dawn, took a taxi to the airport in a savage snowstorm that delayed the flight, flew to Heathrow, was driven to Ozzy's business manager's office, handed over the papers, was taken back to Heathrow, and caught a plane to Belfast. I got home at 10:30 p.m.—on my mum's birthday. Luckily my long-suffering nearest and dearest were used to playing second fiddle to Ozzy.

A few days later the band and crew were sent home for Christmas, but Ozzy had to shoot the video for "See You on the Other Side" on December 23 and Sharon asked me to be his assistant. I stayed at Welders, then spent the day with him on set in London. He was exhausted and napped over lunch. I told the team he was under the weather and left to find a cup of tea, but when I returned, two technicians were about to hammer on his door. "What are you doing? He's knackered and trying to sleep, you don't need him for thirty minutes," I said.

"Oh yes, we know," the makeup artist breezily replied. "But we're worried if he wakes up too soon before going on camera, he'll have bags under his eyes." I shooed them away.

There was a display of peacock feathers lying outside his dressing room, a prop left over from a previous shoot, and Ozzy, always superstitious, told me it was bad luck to have them indoors and wanted them removed. I'd never heard of that, but when I tracked down a worker to do it, they said they also thought it was bad luck and were surprised they hadn't been thrown out earlier.

Ozzy invited me to spend the holidays at Welders. "I mean, if you are doing stuff with your family or whatever that's fine, but the offer's there," he said as Sharon walked in. "He's okay to come to ours for Christmas, right?" he asked her, and she said of course.

I stayed for three nights, eating, drinking, watching TV, riding a quad around their grounds with Jack. The second evening, after Sharon and the kids went to bed, we lit so many candles the fire alarm went off, and because it was wired into the local station, truckloads of firemen turned up. Ozzy lifted £100 from the cash stash and told me to give it to the chief while he dealt with switching it off. I was waiting for the right moment to slip it to him, but Ozzy returned, grabbed it from me, and thrust it at him, saying it was for their benevolent fund.

THE TOUR WAS RESUMING ON NEW Year's Eve with another swing through the US. Even with the postponements and wasted days on my previous North American trip, I couldn't bear the thought of missing out. The first few days of 1996, I wrestled with it. Although being on the road with him was the realization of my childhood dream, it would blow my remaining savings, and devoted as I was to Ozzy, I had to live in the real financial world. Then I thought, *Ah, fuck it*. I was twenty-six, single, lived at home, and had no debts. My outgoings were minimal, and I filtered some travel through my agency as a business expense. I had staff, had paid off the loan I took out to buy it, and it was next door to my dad's shop. When I wasn't swanning around the world with Ozzy I worked hard, usually six days a week, often staying long after we closed.

I cashed in all my airline miles and flew to New York, booking a flight home from LA six weeks later. A last hurrah of scrounging lifts and eating in catering and being my groupie self.

From JFK airport I went to the Essex House, met Sharon, and rode in her limo to the Continental Airlines Arena in East Rutherford. We spent the trip discussing my love life, perpetually convoluted and complicated in my mid-twenties (both she and Lynn always helped with relationship advice). As soon as we arrived, I went hunting for Keith, as my English soccer team had beaten his that day, but the first person I bumped into by Ozzy's dressing room was Martha. As with her predecessors, we'd quickly clicked. I suppose I hit it off with the seamstresses because I hung around the dressing rooms and they were always doing a million things, so there were usually little jobs I could do to help while we talked.

"Hey, hey, welcome back!" she said, and gave me a kiss and a hug. "And congratulations on the new position."

"What position?"

"I hear you're joining the payroll. I was chatting with Bill [the tour accountant] yesterday and he said this leg is all good to go, now we've you on board."

Within hours of landing at JFK, I was gainfully employed: the Osbournes had given me a job. Without even telling me. I think the reasoning was "This fucker turns up everywhere and we can't get rid of him. May as well put him to work."

It was eleven years to the very day since Rock in Rio.

There was never a let's-have-a-meeting-with-Stephen-about-a-job moment. I wasn't offered a position, and we didn't discuss terms and conditions or contracts. For a while I'd helped with luggage and escorting the band places and running errands—and smuggling videos out of gigs—and from that day on I was paid. The change just happened, the transition from a clingy fan and a full-time employee seamless. My life on the road carried on much as it had. It felt so natural, the employment didn't rate a mention in my diary. Not one word, even though teenage Stephen would have sold his soul to Satan to work for Ozzy.

Indeed, backstage everyone knew I was joining the crew. Gossip always rocketed through the grapevine on the road, and the band and roadies all congratulated me. Although obviously delighted, my overwhelming emotion was relief, a belief I'd earned legitimacy, no longer just a freeloader who got in everyone's way as I traveled on Ozzy's plane and slept on the crew's bus or ate the production office's food. My title was assistant tour manager, but really I was Bobby's helper, a gofer for the band.

The crew was paid by direct deposit or check, and on top of that, once a week received a cash "PD," a per diem as a bonus for having to live on the road. I hadn't even thought to ask how much I'd be paid—frankly, I didn't care—and it was twelve days before I found out. I was walking past the production office in Rochester when Bill waved me in.

He was counting out piles of $20 notes and said, "Here, sign this," and handed me a receipt book.

"What's it for?" I asked.

"Your wages for the last two weeks. That's what Sharon told me to pay you. We'll have to give it to you in cash cuz you're not set up in the system."

I was shocked at how much it was, more money per week than the monthly wage I paid myself at the travel agency, my diary reading, "**I can't believe how much fun this is—going everywhere with the band, having all my hotels paid for, and earning really good money!**" Dragging myself out of bed before dawn in winter in Belfast to make 7.5 percent commission on a £29 flight to London never seemed further away and less important.

My handful of responsibilities took an embarrassingly short time. I was in charge of bus luggage: we'd five musicians (including Robert, the offstage backing singer), Bobby, and Bill. At hotels I unloaded it and delivered it to each room, then picked it up when we left, and I handled it at airports as well. We often checked in at an ungodly hour and didn't want a half-asleep porter on the graveyard shift hurling Joe's guitar atop a rickety trolley with a wobbly wheel. I was conscientious about it, but a few times, drowsy, I banged into a corridor or door or elevator and an instrument slid off or toppled over as I wrestled bags out from beneath. It usually went smoothly, me pushing or pulling that contraption with a red-carpeted bottom and tall, thin brass handles you see in hotels, though if there were no carts I got a workout lugging baggage back and forth.

I also dealt with our bus food. More high-level stuff. The venue's in-house caterers cooked meals throughout the day to feed the crew, but the band ate dinner well in advance of curtain-up to digest it before ninety minutes of exertion onstage. An hour after the final bow they were hungry, so I ensured we were stocked with hot food, and we also had a list of snacks and drinks to be provided, as sometimes we had a long ride ahead. In fact, there was a change just after I joined. Sharon came to a couple of concerts at different sites and thought the meals were poor, so she forked out (sorry) for a specialized catering touring company to travel with us. It ate into her bottom line (sorry again), but generously she didn't want roadies subsisting on substandard food.

The security director, spotting I was deliciously underemployed, put me in charge of the guest list, too. It reads like a powerful position, doling out golden tickets in the form of free seats, VIP passes, and laminates, but in reality, it was relaxed. The office faxed me instructions for guests, or the band had friends or family in a particular city, but more often than not the list was short, mostly requests from the crew: "This guy fixed our bikes. . . . A woman didn't charge me for my laundry. . . . I met this cool chick in the bar I'm trying to nail." Occasionally I got a request like "This is my long-lost cousin, but for fuck's sake keep him away from Ozzy and don't let him near the dressing rooms." The initials of the person asking for the pass were written on it, so if the guest ran onstage or broke into Ozzy's room for a turn on his Lifecycle, it could be traced back—and privileges revoked.

Although a laminate was the highest credential and got you everywhere backstage, we often added an extra discreet layer for important events or one-off shows, a tiny gold star sticker, a secret signal you'd permission to enter his inner sanctum.

My last duty was the most important. I operated the teleprompter. Ozzy had a video monitor in front of him and I stood stage left, scrolling through the lyrics like his karaoke helper. Sometimes he dropped tracks, and I had to fire forward; other dates he switched things up and called out titles off the cuff purely to mess with Joe. It wasn't that he had to be reminded of the words to every song in the set, but it was a crutch if he needed it and a quick reference guide—if he romped off to dump water over the front row, or got waylaid trying on bras flung onstage, when he returned to the mic stand he could glance down for the upcoming line. I had to always be on my toes, ready to flash forward or skip back. It was my sole stressful task—the video techs set it up and if it fucked up during a show, there was nothing I could do to fix it, the technicalities of its inner workings beyond me.

Up until then Keith operated it, and that first night, when I finally found him in catering to rip the pish out of him about the soccer result, he was keen to change the subject. "I hear you're gonna be operating the prompter now," he said, then grinned. "You can start tonight."

At showtime I met him at the system, and he galloped me through a two-minute lesson. The remote was connected by a lead and had a couple of basic commands, like jumping back or forward over songs, and a knob you twisted in time to Ozzy's singing.

He handed over the control and stood at my shoulder, ready to jump in if I messed up. I was wrecked with anxiety. I'd got up at midnight Eastern time, flown to London, connected to JFK, and had been awake for twenty-two hours. It was a massive gig, both in terms of being a sold-out show with around eighteen thousand fans, and because it was New York, a vital music industry fulcrum—not an ideal way to ease into my first official day as an Osbourne employee. Though stressed and jet-lagged, the adrenaline kicked in, and by mid-set I relaxed, Keith confident enough to wander off. Afterward, I asked Ozzy how I'd done—he said "Mama, I'm Coming Home" was a bit slow, but otherwise fine. I took that as a win. I guess I was a roadie.

#77–103

RETIREMENT SUCKS TOUR

WINTER LEG

January–February 1996

MY TOUR DIARY SPANS every single day on the road from January until August 1996. It's thirty-five thousand words, and I originally planned to transcribe it—a unique inside account of the last world trek by the greatest heavy rock singer of all time. Then I read it for the first time in decades—and realized it'd bore you. Life on tour was often monotonous.

I was woken around 11 a.m. by Joe or John, sometimes both calling within seconds, and some combination of the three of us went for coffee or breakfast. John was a heavy drinker when we met in '86, but a decade on he was a healthy Buddhist with racquetball equipment, and when we arrived in a city, I hunted for a court to rent for us to play. After the diner / coffee shop / gym I'd have a couple of hours to kill, and I might phone the office in LA, or do some job for Sharon or the band, or call my travel agency. I had confidence in my employees, but I knew it was human nature to slack off when the boss wasn't around and frequently checked we had no major issues. (Though when I talked to William, the first thing he always asked was when was I coming back.) Then around 4 p.m. I grabbed a luggage trolley and called on our riders, collecting their bags and loading them into the storage bays.

We drove to the venue for sound check (only the band; Ozzy arrived a couple of hours later), then we were free for about three hours. Occasionally we left the arena, if we were downtown or if there was an attraction nearby, but usually we hung out. Geezer napped in his bunk while the others were on the bus or in the dressing room, watching videos, chatting, reading, John doing puzzles, Joe glued to his guitar, then we migrated to catering for dinner. Keith bought a soccer ball, and we often had a kick-around while the pair of us religiously walked through every audience in every venue before showtime (to ogle girls). After the gig there was a meet and greet ("grunt and grope," as we affectionately referred to it), with competition winners and guests and industry people, before we boarded the bus and drove to the next town. It could be a short hop of a couple of hours or an overnight journey of seven hundred miles. We might have stayed up drinking and checked into the hotel at 3 a.m., or we may have crawled into our bunks and woke when we arrived.

The 3-a.m.-to-11-a.m. sleep schedule held true for days off, too. They ran the gamut: sometimes we were ensconced in a hoity-toity hotel in Manhattan; sometimes we were marooned in the middle of nowhere outside a dot on the map in the Midwest, grateful to find a suburban mall or an Applebee's. Sometimes we tore up local bars and had wild nights out; sometimes I laid in bed vegetating in front of the TV, my circadian rhythm carved in stone and preventing me from sleeping, despite restlessness and boredom from an all-day wandering exploration of a backwater.

Other times, somewhere like New Haven, Connecticut, could keep you busy. Sharon left a bag in Ozzy's wardrobe case in Manhattan that she needed, so I took a taxi to the venue, picked it up from Martha, then caught a train to New York. I delivered it to the Essex House, and she handed me a present— a regal, weighty picture frame from Tiffany's containing a photo of Kelly and me from

Christmas. A typically generous Osbourne gift. At 3 p.m. I left with Ozzy to a small airfield to fly back to New Haven. By this stage, I was so blasé about flying with him on his personal jet, it merited one sentence in my diary. Jesus Christ.

But although the road was repetitive with little daily deviation, I had the time of my life, thankful every day for the crazy chance I'd been given.

And occasionally, we had a seismic shift.

WE WERE BASED IN NEW YORK from where we were "hubbing"—staying in the same hotel and busing to nearby venues, like New Haven or Philly, then returning afterward each night. When I rejoined the tour I learned Geezer was leaving—he was homesick and didn't want to be on the road anymore. Mike Inez was parachuting in until a permanent replacement was found.

I was thrilled Mike was returning, and Randy was equally delighted—he was getting his hard-partying playmate back.

"I'm in a band with a bunch of L7s, man," he would say, shaking his head, holding up his hands to create a square. They saw plenty of hell-raising in their youth, but John and Geezer were sober, and although Joe had the odd beer, he avoided going out and holed up in his room to practice.

My first full day in Manhattan evidenced the divide: Joe called asking me to accompany him to a coffee shop, then a guitar store, then another Starbucks, while that evening, I got hammered with Randy when an Epic executive took us to a restaurant, a club, and two bars.

Ozzy was sanguine about Geezer's departure. This was one of his oldest mates, whom he'd shared a band with on and off for almost three decades, leaving him in the lurch, but he knew it would all work out. (I tried to follow his lead in the years after, as a business owner, knowing you can always find a replacement.) Mike and Randy were relaxed, too, confident the show would be fine. But Joe was tense, insisting we go to the venue early, making the band sound-check for an hour, then asking Mike to rehearse with him more in the dressing room.

Mike was an immediate accelerant onstage. The energy level exploded through the roof, his arrival revitalizing Ozzy, who soaked every musician with his water gun. Backstage was buzzing, and we stayed up babbling and jabbering on the bus—when we got in, Randy and I drank in Mike's room until 6 a.m.

Occasionally we'd hit a place with a reputation for being boring and it'd be anything but—like Cleveland, the butt of so many jokes for being dull. Martha and I went to catch up with Geezer and watch his solo band in a club, then I fell into bed before midnight. I was woken at 2:30 a.m.: Mike and Randy had brought back a gaggle of dancers from a strip club and wanted me to join them. The following night was another 6 a.m. stint with more strippers. The temperature plummeted: we were on the guest list for Lenny Kravitz, and I showered before we left—the weather was so barbarous, water in my hair turned to ice walking from our van to the gig.

The crazy stripper stalkers who had latched on to us lay in ambush at the hotel, and this time I played host until 4 a.m. As one of our new friends wiggled and wriggled on my lap, I laughed and said, "Boing!" Mike decided it was my new nickname, buying me a mock newspaper he had made at a truck stop with the headline "Boing Springs Forth on Ozzy Tour!" (Revisiting my diary, I discovered he scrawled, "**Boing, boing, boing!!! (666)**" across that page.)

However, answering a 3 a.m. call to accompany the duo in a taxi across the border to Windsor in Canada, where we gambled and drank until dawn, was a brief international exploit that got me a bollocking from Bobby. He woke me at noon and already knew where we'd been—it was impossible to keep anything secret on the road for long.

"Stephen—are you under the impression you have to be with them all the time? Because if you are, I'm telling you now you don't, that's not your job. Leaving the country like that ain't a smart thing to do, you hear me? Lots of things could have gone wrong. Don't let it happen again, okay." A statement, not a question.

Three shows into Mike's return, Sharon woke me at 9:30 a.m. She'd gotten back to England after New York and called to pump me for information on how it was going. I told her the difference between him and Geezer was night and day, he'd reenergized the band, reenergized the show, reenergized Ozzy.

FROM THE NORTHEAST TO THE MIDWEST. Riotous, Ozzy jacked, badgering crowds to climb up and join him, the crew mobilizing into a defensive ring rivaling the Alamo, even a fan in a wheelchair crowd-surfing over the barricade down the front. Moline, Illinois, was so overrun I manhandled someone who turned out to be the opening act's guitarist. (In my defense, it was Munky from Korn; he looked dodgy.) In Madison, Wisconsin, a spiral of madness began when an invader scaled the rig behind the set, then crashed to the ground. Joe jumped into the pit to give a disabled kid a pick, and a frazzled local security guard attacked him for inciting the audience. Mike's bass cut out and he smashed it up, then Joe's tech left his station to chase and trade punches with a fan, so Joe had no guitar for "No More Tears," and they muddled through a bungled unplugged version.

The maelstroms in the Midwest magnified a schism in the band: Mike and Randy embraced the rock 'n' roll hullabaloo, just like Ozzy. Joe, on the other hand, was neurotic about his playing and considered the nightly uproar an obstacle to giving his best. I got on great with all three, and as both a fan and an employee, I empathized with both sides. The pattern from Manhattan often held: I'd have afternoon coffee with Joe, and after shows, when I dropped his guitars to his room, I'd sit and chat for an hour. Then I'd track down Randy and Mike and we'd tear it up with a carousel of locals.

In unlikely Ames, Iowa, the incursion during "Crazy Train" was on a par with San Diego. The audience bum-rushed the stage and kicked over the prompter, while Mike jettisoned his bass and went stage-diving into the crowd. The distraught authorities, fearful the Hilton Coliseum would be torn to pieces, shut down the show. We rushed Ozzy straight from the stage to his plane, convinced he'd be arrested. I swiped his jewelry and gear from the dressing room and was sped to the airfield before he took off. "Well, Steve, what's the word? How many dead tonight?" he asked and laughed, that glint in his eye, when I boarded.

We were mauled daily by blizzards and Randy and Mike fell ill, driving even more of a wedge between them and germophobe Joe. In Fargo, North Dakota, I spent the night with an attractive divorcée. I hurled my guts up the following morning, having picked up Randy and Mike's bug, but the guys riled me nonstop, blaming her. Within minutes of arriving at the gig, Ozzy piled on the abuse as well. Nothing ever got past him.

AS THE AMERICAN LEG NEARED ITS end, we auditioned for a permanent bassist in LA: by invitation in the afternoon, and an evening open cattle call attracting more than one hundred musicians, many of whom were comically bad. Robert Trujillo from Suicidal Tendencies seemed a foregone conclusion, and Joe and Sharon loved him. Ozzy, however, also liked Lizzy Borden's Michael Davis. I thought Ozzy knew Robert was the better option but was posturing a little, perhaps feeling railroaded by the other two. It was his name on the marquee every night, and I got the impression he was making the point that the final decision should be his. At midnight we retired to Jerry's Famous Deli and Sharon and Joe discussed replacing Randy, wanting to replenish the complete rhythm section. I knew then his days were numbered. The next afternoon I went into the office, as I always did on days off in LA, and Sharon told me Robert had the gig.

Mike lived on a sleek boat moored in Marina del Rey beside the Ritz-Carlton, and he ordered room service from the hotel and had them do his laundry. I spent the night on board after the Forum gig, the last date in the States for the time being: we sat on the deck drinking beer as the craft bobbed and weaved, listening to music, smelling the sea, occasionally stretching our legs to lean on the cold metal railings, gazing past the harbor at the twinkling lights of LA playing hide-and-seek between fog gusts drifting through the spring nighttime chill.

"Dude, I'm so happy for you the way it worked out," he told me. "You were the band's best friend, now you're getting paid as well. Paid and laid!" He snorted and clinked my bottle with his.

At 4 a.m. he went belowdecks, and I stayed for a minute, tapping and scratching my near-empty beer along the rough guide rope. I sat in the shadow of a five-star hotel off the Californian coast, reflecting on the previous two months, earning money while partying with rock stars and sleeping with cute American girls. I wanted it to last forever, but there was a six-week break before the next US date in Phoenix, and I needed to get back to Northern Ireland. Retirement sucks. So does a day job.

#108

NIPPON BUDOKAN

TOKYO, JAPAN

March 16, 1996

BUT I DIDN'T GO back to Belfast. Instead, I flew to Tokyo. I never expected in a million years to be on the next leg in Japan. The entourage was slashed to a skeleton crew, the cost of living so atrociously high that wages and per diems were tripled. I assumed I wasn't worth that, and when the production manager asked me for my passport to set it up, I nearly fell off my chair. Belinda, the Belfast girl I'd taken to Prague, had booked a flight to meet me in LA when the leg finished, so I rang to call off her trip—luckily, I had plenty of experience telling women to cancel travel plans because an Ozzy obligation manifested out of thin air.

I knew Japan would be different, but I was surprised by how different. The show day routine was the same, but felt strange. Thousands of fans milled outside the venues, but they chatted quietly, more like conference attendees than hard rock fanatics, no boisterous, music-blaring tailgating like in America. During concerts they were reserved, though the crew veterans told me that for

Japan, the audience was deranged. Ozzy often peeled off his shirt and threw it into the crowd, the front rows tugging and pulling until it was secured. I heard at his previous Budokan stop he pitched them an expensive jacket—and it laid on the ground the whole gig, a roadie retrieving it afterward. I thought back to how I had framed his sweat-soaked, ripped, one-time-use waistcoat plucked from the floor at Rock in Rio.

Every night after escorting the band back to their dressing room, I returned to the stage to pack away the prompter. In Japan, by the time I got back the lightning-quick local stagehands had it in its flight case already, and when doing the bags at hotels, all insisted on sending two bellmen along. I earned three times the money for a third of the work.

In Fukuoka, Bobby suggested that Mike, Randy, and I check out a rock joint called the Cotton Club. But it had been rebranded into a luxuriant karaoke bar with four old geezers—when we swaggered in, all denim and leather and sunglasses and chunky jewelry, one was singing "Danny Boy," so the two rock stars and I were serenaded by an Asian senior murdering a traditional Irish ballad. Later, in the VIP section of a club, I hit on a pretty local with good, but not perfect, English. I invited her back to the hotel, and she was hesitant, but eventually agreed, saying what sounded like "Justa" a few times. On the walk to the elevator, I realized what it was—"Just talk." To my shame, I ditched her, the doors closing on her plaintive face as I hotfooted it to catch up with the others. Every bar and club we hit in every city, we picked up a train of girls like we were long-haired, black-clad Pied Pipers, one night squeezing eight into my room. We went at it so hard that in Tokyo I slept through an earthquake.

But I woke in Nagoya when my dad called with bad news about the travel agency. The seventeenth of each month was the day a large debit hit our account to pay for the airline tickets issued the previous month: if we sold £10,000 worth of tickets in February, our commission was deducted, and on March 17 around £9,000 was taken from our bank. He rang to alert me we were projected to be short, but in the end, we managed to scrape by. I was headed home via New York in a few days, so I said I'd chase up our debtors when I returned.

THE LEXINGTON QUEEN HELD MYTHICAL STATUS among touring artists. Japan was so expensive there were few foreign tourists. Yet it was a society enamored with the Western version of beauty, so young white models made a fortune. Groups came from the States, lodging in packs because of the sky-high rent, and "the Lex" comped their drinks, knowing they'd attract rich, free-spending businessmen. And touring rock bands. It didn't disappoint: I'd never been in a room crammed with so many attractive girls.

Robert Trujillo flew in to learn the live set. Five years older than me, a keen surfer and snowboarder, he looked every inch the California beach bum, chilled as get-out, long black hair, sometimes braided, usually clothed in skateboarding gear. Despite late nights with Mike and Randy, I ate breakfast most days with Joe and Ozzy, and I made a point of banging on Robert's door and inviting him along. We went to amusement arcades together, and the only night in the two-week tour I cried off partying, the two of us still went out to dinner. (I was exhausted after an afternoon buying presents in downtown Tokyo with its barbaric traffic reminding me of *Blade Runner*: monochromic pouring rain; throngs packing the streets, hurrying and scurrying; sidewalks so thick with humanity it was a game of *Frogger* to get to the doors of the towering department stores; blinking neon lights flashing in dazzles off puddles on the pavement.)

Sharon never gave me specific instructions to liaise with new guys, but I felt it made sense. I did everything I could to welcome them to the setup, and although I'd been employed only a couple of months, other than Bobby I knew the Osbournes and their organization better than anyone on the road. Musicians had a tumultuous life, dropping in and out of bands, so making an effort to answer questions and give pointers was the right thing to do.

Japan was a blast. A radical change of scenery and culture after months on the road in Europe and North America, it felt like an intoxicating release, whizzing around the country on bullet trains instead of tour buses, our huge touring juggernaut eviscerated to the bare bones, the few of us left on the same page, filling my time browsing for state-of-the-art electronics, being treated to dinner by famed promoter Mr. Udo, and cavorting with enticing Nipponese girls.

On our last day, Joe, Robert, and I spent hours with Ozzy at breakfast, listening to his tales:

> "We were here one time and I go out and get totally smashed out of my mind on sake. Next thing I know, I'm waking up in some club somewhere and I can hear the Beatles playing.
>
> "I raise my head, and what I see is a Japanese band playing on the stage. I think I'm in the fucking twilight zone or something because it's like everything is not real—it sounds just like the Beatles but it's all these Japanese playing.
>
> "So, I'm beside this bint and I've no idea where I am or where I'm staying, so she takes my key and leads me back to the hotel.
>
> "But what I'd forgotten was that Sharon was out with me. I'm trying to get in the door of my suite and next thing she appears. She takes about a second to size up the situation, then she cracks the tart one, and grabs a picture from the wall and sticks it over my head.
>
> "I wake up the next morning with the frame still around my head."

Our first and last dates in Japan were at the Nippon Budokan, the final gig with the peculiar start time of 5 p.m., no support act. But even though it was an afternoon show it was a banger, Ozzy on form, flashing his bum, doing funny walks, Joe whirring, Mike savoring the last hurrah of his cameo return before returning to Alice in Chains.

Our repeat visits to the Lex meant I put thirty-two Western models on the guest list—surely a record—and with the gig done and dusted, Randy, Mike, and I met them at the club early. We pulled up to find a mob of Japanese fans surrounding the entrance, the bouncers tunneling a gangway for us to run through in a return to the Beatlemania of Rock in Rio. It was a fitting send-off before we dispersed—to LA, to New York, to London; for me, returning, finally, to Belfast.

Safely inside, I scooted back in my seat as the waiter approached. He wiped the table with the back of his hand, the chrome refracting and reflecting the multicolored lights strobing around us, then set down beers that rattled onto the surface despite the paper napkins. He clipped a bow and retreated.

Randy and I toasted while laughing at the antics of a troupe of girls three feet away, edging ever closer toward us, fighting to appear insouciant while ingratiatingly encircling our spot. His smile fled and he became serious.

"Steve, listen brother, I gotta ask you a question. What's up? I've been reading something in your face recently, like you're hiding something. Is everything okay?"

I grimaced, grateful I'd retreated into the shadows, my face hidden in the darkness lurking beyond the sweep of the overpowering disco lights. We were saying farewell to Mike—but I knew Randy was getting replaced, too. We'd been friends for a decade, but I couldn't betray the Osbournes' confidence, and brushed it off.

#120

SOUTHPARK MEADOWS

AUSTIN, TEXAS

May 4, 1996

I WALKED INTO THE cavernous Malibu beach house at 10 p.m. with Aimee. Sharon and Ozzy were intertwined, curled up on the couch, the French doors yawning open to the ocean, a breeze ruffling the fresh flowers on the table.

"They're here," Sharon shouted into the kitchen, alerting Dave, a caterer on the UK leg they loved and had employed as a full-time chef. He appeared, rubbing his hands on his rich cloth apron.

"You guys hungry?" he asked.

I shook my head. We had played Las Vegas the day before, the second date of this leg, then bused overnight to Fresno, where we had a day off. However, I rented a car and drove four hours to LA, as I'd been tasked with taking Aimee to see Oasis at the Universal Ampitheatre. Oasis canceled at 6 p.m.—ironic, as Ozzy then pulled Fresno—so we'd gone for dinner instead.

"Dave, I've an idea," said Sharon. "How about some tea and cake?"

Aimee disappeared to her room, and I settled in beside them, all three of us tired from being back on the road. Kelly and Jack tumbled into the room and, spying us as an exhausted captive audience, with a flourish announced in unison they were performing a magic show. They made us move seats, then took turns introducing tricks, one or the other crawling behind the sofa, not realizing they were still in sight, holding up props and puppets, us feigning amazement at their sleight of hand and conjuring, occasionally setting each other off in fits of laughter.

I was supposed to drive back to Fresno, but Sharon put her foot down about staying. I didn't put up a struggle. Why would I? I was sleeping in my idol's beach house on one of the world's most desirable and expensive stretches of coast. I'd had a few weeks in boring old Belfast, but even those were busy—Belinda and I went to London to attend John's wedding. And I put in long days at the agency, giving William and the staff a chance to take time off, catching up with paperwork, checking in on clients, tallying bank statements, and combing through receipts.

I tried to crash early, but the three kids tortured poor Dave with a baptism of fire, running into his room and messing around, then ducking into my room to hide. The next morning, I found the trio passed out on one bed. (Dave wasn't around long; Ozzy said traveling with a personal chef made him feel like Elvis.)

Dave cooked breakfast for Sharon and me, and we ate at the kitchen table, gazing at the Pacific. I knew how lucky I was to be invited to their home—everyone else on the crew had probably eaten at a Chili's in Fresno—but this family interlude in Malibu, retreat of the Hollywood stars, was the calm before a storm in the unlikely setting of Orem, Utah.

OZZY WAS OUT OF SORTS ONSTAGE at the McKay Events Center until he drenched a guard with his powerful custom-made water gun halfway

in. Then he cheered up immensely. After that, Joe was the problem. Ozzy gestured to him a few times, to speed up or slow down, and Joe got pissed, storming off and refusing to come back for the bow. Ozzy fired after him into the dressing room, yelling at the top of his voice. The band and I hung awkwardly outside until Ozzy came barreling back out, still fuming, Sharon battling to placate him.

"I'm not his fucking father! He needs to grow up!" he shouted, shoving her arm away and almost smashing into a flight case as he slammed open his dressing room door with his fist. I'd seen him lose his temper before, but never with a band member.

His band were employees, and he was the boss. It wasn't a democracy. It wasn't a normal manager/worker office situation like I had in my agency, of course, but still, Ozzy didn't hesitate for a second when he felt he had to act. He was fearless onstage, ready to risk arrest to whip up the audience, but off-stage he also had the balls to make hard calls, no matter how uncomfortable it made the immediate aftermath. Bollocking the guitarist wasn't as much fun as soaking a humorless cop, but occasionally the chief had to lay down the law. (And often, Sharon was *his* boss. Once, I asked Ozzy about the backing vocals on a demo, "See You on the Other Side." They were missing from the final version, but I thought the song better with them. "Yeah? Well, me too," he said. "Go talk to Sharon.")

As luck had it, we'd twenty-one hours on the bus to Cedar Rapids, Iowa. Joe was on tilt, talking it through from every angle, and we sat with him up front, taking turns to chime in and reassure him, like a rock 'n' roll group therapy session. One by one the others hit their bunks until it was just us two, me continuing to calm him until 3:45 a.m.: I liked him and was his friend, and also through a sense of duty to Ozzy, who needed his sidekick in the right headspace.

It was just Joe's personality, indecisive, always needing affirmation, in restaurants asking, "What are you having? What should I order?" and in shops, "Do you like this shirt? How do these pants look?" In Corpus Christi,

Texas, he looked at four different hotel rooms before finding one he was happy with, while in Knoxville, Tennessee, the Hyatt Regency upgraded everyone to suites and Joe, after inspecting his, thought it too big and wanted a smaller room. I trailed him with the luggage cart until we found one he could live with.

His wife told me this story: He tried on a pair of boots in a store on Melrose in LA, but couldn't decide whether to buy them, and walked around, hemming and hawing, looking in every mirror. He asked a shopper for his opinion, and the bloke said they looked good.

"They gotta be right, see, I play guitar, they're to wear onstage," said Joe, and the customer nodded his understanding. He eventually pulled the trigger.

Outside on the sidewalk, his wife said, "Joe—you know who that was?"

He shook his head. "The guy I was talking to? No."

"Bruce Springsteen," she said.

The fight with Joe was an outlier, though, Ozzy over the moon with his new recruits, bassist Robert and Mike Bordin, the drummer from Faith No More, both low-maintenance and low-key. Mike shared my birthday, but was seven years older, and asked me to sit beside him during sound check and sing the new track, "I Just Want You," like an Ozzy stunt double, so he could nail the tempo. My diary reads "**Stayed up until 4 a.m. talking to the two new boys. They are real nice guys and eager to find out about Ozzy and his history.**"

I LOVED SMALLER, OUT-OF-THE-WAY PLACES, THE real America international visitors never visited, like the imaginatively named Normal, Illinois. At these low-pressure gigs, far from the coastal media glare, Ozzy was so relaxed, and took to introducing Joe onstage as "Big Nose."

In Little Rock, Arkansas, I met Keith and some of the crew for a beer at our hotel. We were joined by Connie, the scandalous groupie who claimed to have slept with numerous rock stars and probably did, since she's in Grand Funk Railroad's song "We're an American Band" ("Out on the road for forty days / Last night in Little Rock put me in a haze / Sweet, sweet Connie, doin' her act / She had the whole show and that's a natural fact"). She sat at the bar while we stood around her drinking, listening to stories about the good old days. She got drunker and louder, the tales ever more outlandish, embellishing them by miming the actions. The place was full of conventioneers, horror on their faces, a quiet tipple in their hotel on a Tuesday night in Arkansas wrecked by a notorious groupie. She must have crossed Sharon, though—there was a notice backstage, reading anyone bringing her to the show would be dismissed on the spot.

I kept in touch with Julie, the student I'd met briefly in London, and flew her out a couple of times when we had double days off. She was twenty-three but looked younger, a perception she unwittingly emphasized: when she was asked what she did, she'd reply, "I'm in school." To us Brits, that meant you were in high school, not college, and I'd quickly jump in to clarify.

IN MEMPHIS WE GOT A PRIVATE tour of Graceland, and that night, seconds after coming offstage, Ozzy burst into the dressing room and bubbled, "Fucking hell, I tell you, this is the best band I've ever had, man." They were as giddy as schoolgirls, hyped he was happy, basking in his praise, the vibe on our bus like a sixties love-in.

Then I fucked up.

In Oklahoma City I thought of a prank, at Joe's expense. We spent every afternoon together and played chess on the bus. (I'd swapped entertaining strippers and border skirmishes with Mike and Randy for cerebral games with Joe. Very rock 'n' roll.) Halfway into each show Ozzy introduced the band, their names on the prompter, so to make him smile, I changed "Joe Holmes" to "Mobile Holmes." When Ozzy saw it, he doubled over with laughter and read it out. Joe moaned about it, but seemed okay, and I should have left it there. But in El Paso, I changed it to "Retirement Homes." Again, Ozzy loved it and read it out, but this time Joe went nuts, and after I escorted the band back to the dressing room, he threw a tantrum.

"What the hell you doing?" he yelled. "You're making fun of me in front of thousands of people!"

I set down my Maglite to hold my hands up. "I'm sorry, mate, I didn't realize how much it'd bother you. I only did it to give Ozzy a smile, I didn't mean for it to humiliate you."

He shook his head. "You've gone too far. It's so disrespectful. I'm gonna call Sharon and tell her what you did." He turned away and refused to even look at me, never mind speak to me.

I should have known it'd embarrass him and been more attuned to his feelings. His unwavering dedication to practice earned him a dream gig—and I ridiculed him in front of a packed arena. Shamefaced, I slunk to my bunk early, and it took two days, but his frostiness eventually thawed. Lesson learned.

OZZY WAS A MAN REBORN. IN Biloxi, Mississippi, two cops stood beside me to watch the set, so Ozzy turned the water gun on them. They scarpered, but I couldn't leave the prompter and got drenched—I chalked it up to collateral damage. Four songs into the date in Charlotte, North Carolina, a bra landed at his feet, and he put it on his head and wore it the whole gig. He fired into our dressing room as soon as he left the stage every night, raving, "Even my bad shows are good with this lineup. We've always had one dickhead in the band before."

The Austin date was out of this world. In my top three ever. At Southpark Meadows almost twenty thousand fans jammed in on a baking day and Ozzy poured everything into it, bursting into tears at one point. Normally during the instrumental section of "Suicide Solution" he rested in his quick-change booth, but here he never left the stage and stood beside me, pumping my hand and punching my arm persistently.

Our bus was scheduled to leave the following day for two nights off in Galveston, but he was so blown away by the concert he didn't want us to leave. Instead, he invited us to his suite at the Four Seasons.

"Fucking hell, man, what a show," he said when we walked in, and jumped up from the couch. "I was so fucking wired from that gig I couldn't sleep. I haven't been to bed all night." We crowded him, sitting on the floor or on armrests, as he got up then sat, got up then sat, still hyperactive twenty hours later.

"I tell you what, fuck me, it was a one in a million," he said. "You know the last time I ever got so emotional like that onstage? Donington in 1984."

I was at that show.

As an Ozzy fanatic, I was delighted I saw the two performances in his long career that were so special he cried.

He and Sharon treated us to dinner, him recounting story after story, ordering dessert and coffee, lingering at the table, not wanting the meal to break up. We strolled to the Congress Avenue Bridge, where 1.5 million bats turned the sky black, a humongous colony coiling into the air at dusk, then when night fell, he insisted we go back to his suite, and we stayed another five hours.

#126

THOMPSON-BOLING ARENA

KNOXVILLE, TENNESSEE

May 15, 1996

WE WERE IN THE band's dressing room after sound check at Thompson-Boling Arena when Ozzy came in and sat without saying a word. I was writing, Joe practicing, John doing crossword puzzles. We said hi, but knew something was up—for the first time in weeks he was subdued.

After a beat he spoke, barely more than a whisper. "Sorry, guys, I'm in a down mood. Coming to play here is always really hard for me." He slumped back into the couch and looked at the ceiling.

In March 1982, Knoxville was the last date he played with guitarist Randy Rhoads, who died in a plane crash the following day. He told me:

> "There isn't a single day goes by that I don't think of him. For six months afterwards, Sharon couldn't even look at his picture. When we had to do the video for 'Crazy Train' from the *Tribute* album and I had to open his guitar case, it was

weird, man. Inside were all his little things and chewing gum and stuff.

"But that Kevin DuBrow [singer from Randy's previous band, Quiet Riot]—what an arsehole, man. He went around shooting his fucking mouth off. On the way to the funeral I needed a piss, and we stopped off at a McDonald's. This fucker follows me into the toilet. I didn't know who the fuck he was. He says to me, 'You know Randy was going to come back to me.' I just turned to him and said, 'Well, then we both lost out working with him, didn't we?'"

He said on the way to the funeral, he and Sharon were a mess. They share what he called "a bowel thing" when they are nervous, and she ripped her culottes open in the limo. Ozzy tried to sew them up, but was in such a state he sewed them together instead, and she couldn't even sit down.

"You know, the first gig I did here after his death, the power went out. It feels like purgatory, this place," Ozzy told us. He stayed like that for a few minutes, withdrawn and quiet, and we knew to give him space, the only sounds John clicking his pen against his teeth and Joe running scales. Ozzy scooted forward, bent down, and looked at his hands, slowly revolving a bracelet around and around his wrist. Then he sighed and got up. "Anyway, see you out there, have a good one," he said, and left.

Watching the concert, you'd never have guessed his pre-gig state of mind, as it was as rocking as most on the leg, though he dropped the Sabbath classic "War Pigs," and none of us recalled him doing that before.

He came into the dressing room afterward, much more upbeat, like a weight was lifted. "Thank fuck that one's outta the way, but you know what? This is the first good show I've had here in fourteen years."

#134

EDMONTON COLISEUM

EDMONTON, ALBERTA

June 8, 1996

THE CANADIAN RUN STARTED with something that hadn't happened to Ozzy in twenty-eight years. He walked offstage when his voice gave out.

There was no hint of trouble the previous night. We'd reassembled after our short break and gone to his hotel suite, spending an hour with him, and he was relaxed and rested. Indeed, he arrived early at the venue on show day and was in great form, calling us all into his dressing room to watch the hysterical new intro video he'd filmed that had him superimposed into movie scenes and music videos. Twelve days since the last date, he came into the band's dressing room ten minutes before the gig at General Motors Place. Every night, he warmed up by singing "Paranoid" with Joe accompanying him on guitar—it sounded fine and we walked to the stage.

The opener was on point, but out of nowhere, he faltered during the second track. We looked at each other, unconcerned, assuming it was a blip as he got the cobwebs out of his throat, but by the last chorus his voice had fallen off a cliff. He introduced the third song, "Goodbye to Romance," in a rasp, but only croaked the first verse—then darted offstage and was whisked out of the building before we knew it.

We sleepwalked around, stunned, not knowing what to do. (None of the three advertised acts played: Corrosion of Conformity pulled out after their label made them rerecord their album, and Filter's equipment was impounded at the border.) Unlike both the UK and the US, where riots followed axed shows, the Canucks, resigned, dispersed peacefully, more like the respectful Japanese crowds.

Eventually, we left for the hotel. I thought the Canadian section would be postponed and I'd be straight back home. Within thirty minutes Ozzy rang and told us to come over and I feared the worst, but he was smoking a cigar and in surprisingly good spirits. He felt he let the fans down but was philosophical, saying it was the first time anything like that had happened in his career. He wasn't beating himself up about something he couldn't change, and even when he thought he'd experienced everything after nearly three decades on the road, unexpected challenges lay in ambush.

WE TRAVELED OVERNIGHT TO EDMONTON AS scheduled and had a day off before the date at the Coliseum. We were on tenterhooks, and when Ozzy arrived he was so jittery, it made us worse.

"Wow. I've never seen him like this, he's really edgy," Mike said to me as Ozzy popped in and out of our dressing room, never sitting still for longer than a few seconds, starting to speak, then leaving mid-sentence. It was new to Mike, but I expected it; he always got nervous before important shows, though not to this extent. Adding to the pressure, it was a voluminous near-sold-out arena with thirteen thousand fans, and as we stood at the side of the stage and the lights darkened, they made an unholy row, a deafening variance to how their fellow countrymen filed out of the Vancouver gig.

For the first few songs he kept looking at us and mouthing, "It's crap," while cradling his throat. He was always his own worst critic, but I knew when he relaxed, feeding off the energy of such a huge adoring crowd, he'd battle through it, and by "Perry Mason" he was past the neck-clutching, and we breathed a sigh of relief.

Then it was on to our final show before crossing back to the States, in Toronto. Ozzy came into the dressing room as usual to warm up with Joe. He sounded rough, and hacked and wheezed through "Paranoid." John and I exchanged a look, and as I walked him to the keyboards, he said, "In the past he mighta pulled tonight, you know, thinking he sounded like shit. If he's not on top form, he thinks he's gonna disappoint the kids. But he loves this band more than any other I can remember."

With us expecting a short, ropy set, it was instead stupendous—and Ozzy, keeping everyone on their toes, always able to surprise, announced "War Pigs" as an unprecedented third encore. I'd already escorted the band to the dressing room, and we sprinted back to the stage.

The venue was a picturesque amphitheater on a harbor, and indeed, the Canadian dates provided the most amazing travel backdrop I ever experienced on the road—I even spotted a bear by the highway on our way to Winnipeg. We skirted national and provincial parks, cruising roads that twirled and twisted as we traversed the Rocky Mountains, designated areas of outstanding natural beauty ambushing us around every bend, lakes and trees and spectacular scenery lurking over every incline. Only eight days after fearing the tour would be postponed, we rolled back into New York.

#140

GREAT WOODS CENTER FOR THE PERFORMING ARTS

MANSFIELD, MASSACHUSETTS

June 21, 1996

AFTER CANADA WE'D A week at the Essex House in Manhattan, the start of what would be my final leg touring America. The band performed "I Just Want You" for the *Late Show with David Letterman*, then we went to Mr. Chow's for a typical three-hour Osbourne meal: Ozzy telling funny stories; Sharon chatting with the guys, deftly throwing in business here and there, and picking up the tab. Then we watched the *Letterman* broadcast in their suite.

Sharon summoned me the following morning. Ozzy seemed fine, flopped in front of the TV wearing nothing other than underpants, but she murmured he was grouchy—he stayed awake all night and never came to bed. She gave me $400 and a list of classic rock songs to buy on CD. They wanted them pumped loud between sets to fire up the crowd, so I went to the venue early and used the equipment in his dressing room to make a digital audio tape for Greg, the sound engineer.

The next morning, I was recalled to the penthouse. Sharon had a new job for me. The internet was budding into bloom, and, always at the forefront of fan engagement, she had the idea of a daily diary. It was going to be my job to upload Ozzy's activities to the record company's site. When I walked into their suite, Ozzy, again only underwear-clad, rattled off more songs for the playlist. "At least it sounded like a fucking rock concert for a change last night," he said. He was clearly uninterested in the diary; I was there for two hours and it never came up. Instead, he talked about plans post-tour. He was supposed to write new material in Canada but wanted to stay closer to England. Sharon suggested Ireland, but he spat, "Fuck off, I'm not going to Ireland. It's full of daft cunts," and looked at me and grinned.

I met Joe in the lobby, and he was in a terrible mood: he couldn't find his recording device with ten tapes of ideas stretching back five years. He called me at 3:30 a.m., still having a conniption fit, and I reassured him they were probably in a flight case. We found them at the next venue in Holmdel, New Jersey.

Ozzy's modus operandi, like most acts, was to write and record an album, go on tour to promote it, then repeat the cycle. He didn't have time on the road to write, as even days off were crammed with interviews and media appearances. However, as we were hubbing from New York for a week with multiple non-show days, and Ozzy pulled Hartford after slipping in the shower, extending our stay by three days, Sharon booked the band into Sony Studios.

At lunchtime, we took a limo to the redbrick building in Hell's Kitchen. I got them settled, hung around for an hour and a half to make sure they had everything they needed, then wandered back to the Essex House. When I returned five hours later, I immediately knew something was up. Nerves seemed frayed, though the two songs they worked out sounded promising, both bone-crunching heavy with trippy diversions. Over dinner with John, he shrugged off the atmosphere, telling me it was normal for things to get heated in the studio.

The following day I stayed all seven hours. If creative differences had this effect on guys who liked each other, I dreaded imagining what it was like for musicians who hated each other recording a whole album.

Mike was the grumpiest—strange, as he was usually so laid-back. Joe left the room to keep his temper during the middle of one shouting match, while Robert, equally easygoing, argued with Mike, too. Then Joe accused him of spoiling for a fight. Ozzy arrived at 6:30 p.m. One song he flat-out rejected. He liked the other but wanted the middle section moved to the beginning, and told Joe to lose the effects pedal. It was constructive criticism, but they took it badly: after two days cooped up and mired in a fractious atmosphere, if your boss said half your work was wasted, I guess it would be deflating. Joe stood motionless, silent, his head in his hands, facing the wall.

When Ozzy left, they decided the only way writing would work was with him there.

THE NEXT DATE, IN MANSFIELD, MASSACHUSETTS, was only a hundred miles away, but traffic was insane and it took five hours. It dragged even more because Joe was dissecting Ozzy's comments at the studio, cornering each of us in turn to forensically examine them. Sharon booked them back into Sony for another session, but Joe got it into his head they should postpone writing until after the tour. When we eventually crawled into the venue, Great Woods Center for the Performing Arts, he dived on the phone to her to plead his case—in vain.

Our departure was delayed, as the vehicles were convoying together after the show. Lucky for me—after a week without needing to do it, I realized I hadn't checked if we had bus food. I scrambled to sort it, then everyone retired to their bunks. I sat up front and dozed off.

I was jolted awake by crashing and thumping, and it took me a minute to realize it wasn't a dream. Half asleep, I tugged open the door dividing the middle of the bus where we slept. We had individual TVs in each bunk, and Joe had screamed and punched in his sleep, thrashing so violently he kicked off his new TV and toppled out of his bed. Fortunately, he'd moved from a top bunk to a lower one the previous week (it wasn't only hotel rooms he had trouble settling on), as otherwise he may have broken his arm. He woke on the floor with Mike standing over him. Poor Joe. Two days writing had tortured and shredded his subconscious to pieces.

The two of us went for lunch the following day and I did my best to comfort him, but he was dreading the studio, fixating on how tough he found the first sessions, saying, "I don't know if I can handle it again. If it wasn't for having Elaine [his wife] there to talk to, I would have been driven crazy. When we came back those two nights, I spent hours just walking and walking around the city, trying to get my head straight."

En route to the next date, at Montage Mountain Pavilion, in Scranton, Pennsylvania, a lightning storm slammed us. The strikes edged nearer and nearer, hitting a roadside grass bank so close we heard it fizzle and pop. The clouds pirouetted and raced at an incredible pace, streaking across the darkened sky, then driving rain upgraded into diabolical hail. We were struck dumb, gawping at the weather open-mouthed. It dissipated by the time we pulled into the sixteen-thousand-capacity amphitheater within a ski resort, but lightning had hit the stage multiple times and zapped the power. A side stage tower blew over and ripped through a video screen. Roadies had covered the equipment in haphazardly placed plastic sheets and scrabbled like miners escaping a flooded pit to repair it. They performed so heroically getting the gear back online they fixed it in time for a sound check—unfortunately, convinced they wouldn't meet the deadline, Robert and Mike had left to visit a nearby baseball museum.

Even without the sound check, it was a great show in front of a vast, seething crowd, though Ozzy's voice cracked during "Iron Man." Keith was

Right: The original letter my mum wrote to the Ozzy Osbourne Fan Club in November 1984, leading to a chance to board the Crazy Train. Sharon's secretary Lynn found it in her files years later when she was clearing out the office and returned it to me.

Below: Me at fifteen, about to enter Rock in Rio on January 11, 1985. In Northern Ireland in the 1980s, the shorter the shorts, the better.

OZZY OSBOURNE
% WINTERLAND PRODUCTIONS
SUITE 500
150 REGENT STREET
LONDON
W1R 5FA

023184336. 15 yrs.

Dundonald
Belfast BT16 0EP
Northern Ireland
13/11/84

Dear Sir,

I am writing in the hope that perhaps you can offer some advice on the forthcoming rock concert at which Ozzy Osbourne is appearing in Rio de Janeiro in January 1985.

My son (Stephen Rea) is a fully paid up member of the Ozzy Fan Club. Membership No. is 00090 and he is one of Ozzy's biggest fans. He buys all his LP's and singles and anything that is associated with the man. He writes to pen pals in America and Finland and collects tee-shirts and badges etc. As a special treat and because he never gets to see Ozzy in live concerts – his father is

Above: The first time I met Ozzy—though I was too starstruck to speak to him—in the bar of the Copacabana Palace Hotel, January 1985. I've got an embarrassing teenage moustache; he's wearing teal.

Below: My mum with Ozzy and Sharon, backstage at Avoniel Leisure Centre in Belfast, February 1986. Christian fundamentalists picketed the gig, held during some of the worst violence of the Troubles.

Above: Ozzy, Geezer Butler, and me in July 1988, celebrating the end of the UK club tour in the hotel bar in Glasgow. The next morning, I flew to Amsterdam to meet my girlfriend, the first of many trips I rearranged around Ozzy's touring itinerary.

Left: Ozzy and Geezer helping each other back to Ozzy's room at dawn as the hotel cleaners arrive. They attacked the minibar, I eventually wrangled Geezer to his room, then I skipped sleeping and escorted Zakk to the airport for his morning flight. I was a responsible eighteen-year-old.

Above: Sightseeing on a day off in Paris, April 1989. Left to right: keyboardist John Sinclair, drummer Randy Castillo, me aged nineteen, guitarist Zakk Wylde.

Below: This is the only photo I have with Ozzy and Sharon together, taken in November 1992 at the Ritz-Carlton in Laguna Niguel, celebrating Ozzy's "final" show. I'm dressed up because Lynn told me I had to wear a suit and tie for the party.

Above: Ozzy's birthday party at Welders House, December 1995. Standing left to right: keyboardist John Sinclair, his wife Jean, Jack Osbourne trying to blow out the candles, tour manager Bobby Thomson, drummer Randy Castillo, guitarist Joe Holmes, Sharon. Lynn and I are sitting.

Below: Handing a birthday present to guitarist Joe Holmes in the dressing room post-gig, June 1996. Left to right: keyboardist John Sinclair, offstage singer Robert Mason, bassist Robert Trujillo, me, Joe, drummer Mike Bordin.

Above: Geezer Butler, me, and Tony Iommi in the Black Sabbath dressing room on the Ozzfest reunion tour, 1997. We wore black, all the time. Tour manager Bobby and I often joked about our group, "There is none more black . . ."

Below: Posing onstage in July 1997, before the Ozzfest make-up date in Columbus, Ohio. I'm on the kit of stand-in drummer Shannon Larkin, who played that show after the original date was canceled and the crowd rioted.

Left: With my daughter, Nicola, and bassist Mike Inez in London's Marylebone train station in June 2018. We've been close since I saw his Ozzy debut at the tiny Dublin club McGonagles in January 1991.

Right: My friend Paige Patriarca, me, Ozzy, and my wife, Elicia Ford, outside his dressing room before my last full-length concert. After this show in Houston in September 2018, he only played a further four gigs before retiring from touring.

Right: When Ozzy came to my home in New Orleans in May 2018 to record an episode of the TV show *Ozzy and Jack's World Detour*, we re-created the photo taken in his dressing room at Rock in Rio more than thirty-three years previously. *Photo credit*: Jack Osbourne

Above: Just before Sabbath took the stage at Back to the Beginning, Villa Park, July 2025. Melinda, Lynn, me, and Michael. Combined, the three of them have worked for Sharon for around a century.

Below: Ozzy and me. Our final meeting in his hotel suite, just two weeks before he died, the day after Back to the Beginning. I cried the whole time. More than forty years after our first photo together, our last. *Photo credit*: Melinda Varga

beside me and instantly we both correctly predicted the songs he'd cull from the rest of the set. "How well do we know him?" Keith said, laughing.

After the gig, Joe went into Ozzy's dressing room to make yet another attempt at talking him out of returning to the studio. It was unsuccessful, and the band left on the jet back to New York.

But when we reconvened three days later in Buffalo, Joe told me the studio was productive and stress-free, and as soon as they arrived at the Darien Lake Pavilion, he ushered me into the dressing room to play me the distinctive riff that became "Walk on Water" from the movie soundtrack for *Beavis and Butt-Head Do America.* After all the sleepless nights and bad dreams and anxiety-filled meanderings around Manhattan, it would be the only Ozzy studio track he ever played on.

JOE'S INSECURITIES WERE NEXT LEVEL, AND he also had to deal with Ozzy interrogating him about his diet. Ozzy said when he was growing up, food was so scarce he ate lard sandwiches, and he thought Joe sickly thin. I never saw him eat more than a few bites of anything. Ozzy told me that in an interview, a journalist inquired why he didn't feed his guitar player. Ozzy called him into his dressing room before a gig and asked him if he wanted to see a nutritionist, and onstage introduced him with quips like "If you rubbed him and the wardrobe girl together you could start a campfire. . . . He's straight from the cast of *Schindler's List*. . . . He has only just recovered from being very badly burned." (An equal-opportunity insulter, he also occasionally announced Robert with "Who says I don't employ Indians?")

The moments of comic relief cheered Ozzy when the nonstop touring treadmill was in danger of grinding him down. He'd yell at security for acting like "gorillas," or get flashes of melancholy onstage—in Pittsburgh, for example, referencing the Khobar Towers terrorist attack in Saudi Arabia that killed nineteen people the previous day, lamenting victims who'd never get to have fun again.

After that show, he shuffled into the dressing room and sagged onto the sofa. "I'm fucking exhausted," he said. "Physically, emotionally, and mentally shattered. I need a break." He was spending the day off shooting a cameo for the Howard Stern movie *Private Parts*, but all he wanted to do was lie in bed. When his doctor discovered a broken bone at the top of his back, he was relieved his pain was finally diagnosed, but angry he spent more than $200,000 on MRIs that never picked it up.

By the end of June, when we reached Cleveland, he said the skyrocketing heat meant he felt like he was singing while trapped in an oven and couldn't catch a breath. He railed about the humidity, and the crew poured so much ice on his head the overflow turned the floor into an ice rink. He slipped and tumbled, and when we joked about it with him he said, "Fall? I didn't fall! I just lost my balance."

When we got to the Midwest, away from the zaniness and craziness of high-pressure dates in the Northeast, he relaxed more. After those shows, as soon as he changed, he came into the band's room to chat. He started on a topic and off he went: It could be a concrete train of thought about California, how he was poised to sign the contract for a house in LA when he heard they were installing metal detectors at schools and pulled out. Or more abstract musing, like how he believed life is two doors—when you are young you keep going through one, even though you get repeatedly whacked, until one day you are old enough to know not to. Sometimes it was about a specific something or someone, like when he talked about Michael Beinhorn, the producer of *Ozzmosis*:

> "I hate producers. I want to kill them all. I'd like to line them all up against a wall and shoot the fuckers. I mean, working with Michael Beinhorn was like pulling teeth. Then to make things worse, when I'm doing the album in Paris, Richard Griffiths [the

president of Epic Records]—who is my boss—comes out. He's talking away and I'm gripping the arms of my chair, trying to keep it together. He says, 'That song, "I Just Want You," I don't like the hook. Could you not change it?'

"I could control myself no longer and just said, 'I don't mean any disrespect, Richard, but listen to the words, what am I going to say? I just want Mars?' He answers, 'Well, you're the songwriter.' We leave the room and Sharon says, 'Ozzy . . . ,' and I'm thinking, 'Here we go, I'm going to get a bollocking.' But she says, 'I was so proud of you for standing up for yourself.' So I want to go back in and stab the fucker in the eye."

#150

PINE KNOB MUSIC THEATRE

CLARKSTON, MICHIGAN

July 10, 1996

"YOU'VE GOTTA GO, HE'S not gonna stop until you do!" I yelled in Sharon's ear. She shook her head, digging her heels in, standing her ground.

"Lost and found and turned around by the fire in your eyes," Ozzy sang to sixteen thousand liquored-up fans in Indianapolis on Independence Day. But really, he was singing to Sharon. He was tugging and tugging at her shirt, smiling but insistent, stubbornly determined to drag her from the wings to the spotlight of center stage. It was their wedding anniversary.

When it was clear he wasn't taking no for an answer, she surrendered and let him pull her to his mic stand. He sang with his arms wrapped around her, and she clung to him equally tightly, crying and fighting to free her hands from his embrace to wipe away tears.

My first July 4 in the States was also my most memorable.

The romantic image contrasted sharply to what happened minutes before. We'd only just wrestled back control of the stage. Ozzy had teased the audience into a state of hysteria before "Crazy Train," and dozens scaled our defenses like rampaging Mongols breaching castle walls. One giant stormed across with a topless woman on his shoulders, and she jumped down and tore her pants off, too. Sheds—midsize outdoor venues—tended to have the same layout, a cheaper lawn area farthest from the stage at the back, and those on the grass saw their chance and vaulted the railings separating them from the expensive seats. I was forced to abandon my post at the prompter and hurtled to join the roadies battling the interlopers as it all teeter-tottered on the cusp of pandemonium.

In the tranquility of the dressing room, we gave the couple a set of four towering glass ornaments Bobby and I had picked after two days wandering the local mall (very heavy metal), and Ozzy showed us his present from Sharon, a gold-and-diamond watch. Theirs was a larger-than-life marriage, full of mountains and trenches rather than peaks and troughs, but I gleaned a lot from it. They stuck together—through hundreds of fights about business commitments and drunken incidents and sex with groupies—and were there for one another when it mattered. Each saw their partner as the most important thing in the world.

Another rambunctious stage invasion followed in East Troy, Wisconsin—with more than three thousand tickets sold at the gate it was the biggest walk-up of the tour—Ozzy soaked Mike and Robert and told us, "I love all that bodysurfing shit." After almost a year on the road you would expect him to be jaded, going through the motions, but if anything, the energy intensified, Ozzy spending longer each night bringing the masses to a fever pitch. The back-to-back ruckuses led to our security director quitting, citing a lack of respect. Ozzy thought he was incapable of handling a little rough-and-tumble, saying, "He'll probably go off with Michael Bolton now."

It widened a rift that had creaked open as the band was becoming pissed off by the production team, niggly things that had aggravated. Our juggernaut had been rolling for eleven months. As well as Ozzy, his family and management, and the eight on our bus, the itinerary listed a further fifty eight workers and ten truck and bus drivers. So many bodies in close quarters for that long, it was only natural we got on each other's nerves.

So while production treated it as a disaster and spent the day off attempting to talk the security director into staying, our bus shrugged and carried on. "We never needed a security director before," said Bill, and as tour accountant he was at the vanguard—doing a walk-through after the most uproarious gigs, agreeing on the amount of cash to hand over in compensation for broken chairs and dented barriers.

We nearly had another resignation in Toledo, Ohio, Joe having to talk his new tech out of leaving before the encore. Ozzy was messing with Joe, mouthing one song to him, announcing a different one to the audience, forcing the tech to help Joe make repeated meteoric guitar switches. Then Ozzy pummeled the tech with the water gun, wiping out four different instruments. When the roadie scuttled onstage to change the wah pedal, Ozzy dumped a bucket of water on him and left the bucket on his head. The roadie complained he was humiliated and fumed, "That's it, I'm outta here!" The water hijinks were contagious—Mike sneaked up behind Joe during "Mama" and dribbled a bottle over his head, and Joe went berserk, so if nothing else, musician and roadie were well matched.

If touring was wearing Ozzy down, the mayhem he riled the crowd into producing was replenishing him. It reached a peak at my 150th show, in front of a clamorous crowd of fourteen thousand near Detroit. Ozzy stopped it two songs in because on the lawn they were tearing up sod and tossing it in the air. Our production manager came onstage and pleaded with them to stop, hundreds of monstrous clumps of turf flying above us, a piece cracking Ozzy on the head. They knocked out the cameras, battered the mixing desk, and the promoter was pulling his hair out, as the grass was newly resown.

Before "Crazy Train" Ozzy always said, "The craziest motherfucker gets to come backstage and party with me." (They didn't.) After the missiles halted and the gig resumed, a fan climbed onstage and dropped his pants, jumping up and down and falling over with his bare arse in the air screaming, "I'm the craziest motherfucker! I'm the craziest motherfucker!" Another took off his false leg and pitched it onstage, while someone threw Ozzy a blow-up sex doll—he finished the set with it swaying from a cymbal stand.

It was almost four years since my fiftieth show, when I gave him an engraved tankard to commemorate it in Texas. I was one hundred gigs down the line, but I still faithfully totted up every concert in my journal, still recorded what songs he dropped from the set list, still commented on his voice. I may have been an employee—but I remained as big a fan as ever.

#155

SANDSTONE AMPHITHEATER

BONNER SPRINGS, KANSAS

July 19, 1996

I SAT IN THE dressing room yawning as I wrote in the journal Ozzy bought me. I'd managed only four hours' sleep after the wildest night I ever had on tour, spent with a couple of crazy girls from Nebraska who were in Chicago visiting a third equally insane friend who worked at a strip club. I was fighting the urge to nod off when I was rattled awake by the door flying open and slamming against the wall.

"It's the Irish stud!" Ozzy yelled and barged over to me. He grabbed the journal and riffled through it, grinning. "Why the fuck haven't you filled up this book yet? Concentrate on that and stop spending time pulling chicks in clubs." It was only twelve hours since I got back to my hotel—it never ceased to amaze me how he found out everything so quickly.

The leg was wrapping, but there was time for more drama with Joe at a show outside Kansas City. Ozzy twirled around with his water gun, not realizing Joe had walked toward him. Direct hit. Ozzy never needed an excuse to soak anyone, but this time I saw it was accidental. Joe stopped playing. After a bit, with Ozzy and the band sneaking looks at him, he traded out his guitar, but the new one didn't work. He pounded it into the cabinets, pulled it back, and rammed and jammed it into the speakers, time and time again, then flung it skidding along the stage.

Ozzy loved it, screaming, "Yeah, a tantrum! That's what I like to see!" He orchestrated the crowd to chant, "Oh, c'mon Joe, it's not that bad!" It was priceless, but I was only a few feet away and directly in Joe's line of vision, so I was battling not to laugh. Unsuccessfully. He flung his hair around his head and looked like he wanted to murder someone.

That day we had released our bus: with longer distances between the last shows, John, Bill, and I would go on the crew buses or fly commercial, while the band and Bobby would travel on Ozzy's jet. So, not only was Joe simmering, he was sharing a small plane with Ozzy. He refused to board. I followed him out of the dressing room as he strode to the wardrobe cases stacked down the hall, agitated, wrenching random drawers open then flinging them shut, and fought to placate him.

"I don't care about this anymore," he told me. "Now it's just a job to me."

We finally calmed him down enough to speak to Ozzy privately, and after half an hour, with us walking on eggshells, Ozzy emerged and said, once a month, he'd hold a band meeting to air any grievances (it never happened).

It turned out it wasn't only the ritual drenching eating away at Joe. Every gig, before introducing him, Ozzy said his one wish was that Randy Rhoads could be with him onstage. That upset Joe, though he never mentioned it to any of us. I hadn't thought about it, and I was sure Ozzy hadn't, either, but I took his point—how would you feel if every time your boss said your name, he added that he wished someone else was in your place?

As I'd switched to a crew bus, in Albuquerque, New Mexico, I'd a night on the lash with Keith and lighting tech Ray. I woke fully dressed in a pool of vomit to a voicemail from Bobby. He had flown with the band to the next hub in Denver, and when they arrived, Joe had changed rooms three times—Bobby, less indulgent of our talented, but temperamental, axeman, didn't want to deal with him anymore. I was pulled off the crew bus after one trip to fly with the band from then on.

When we reconvened at the Tingley Coliseum for a rare indoor gig, Ozzy was tired, firing through a short set and cutting two songs and the complete Sabbath medley, and when he introduced Joe to the crowd, that was pared down, too, no mention of Randy. He was in a good mood as he walked into our dressing room afterward—he saw me writing and sat beside me.

"I tell you what, man, I wish I kept a journal on the *Diary of a Madman* tour. Fucking everything happened on that fucking thing: I got divorced and remarried; there were deaths, births, fucking everything." He got up to get a drink, then sat back down, closer to me. He scooched forward, then scooted back, crossed his right leg over his left knee, and leaned into me. I knew he had returned to 1982.

"The crash . . . Man, I know—I KNOW—that if I'd been awake, I'd have been on that plane. I know. You haven't experienced anything until you've smelled burning flesh." He shook his head. "I saw body parts, man. Don Airey had to get therapy afterward."

Then I knew the image fled from his mind, and he was back with us. He turned to Joe, sitting opposite. "Are you happy? No Randy Rhoads tales onstage tonight."

When he left, Joe said, "Are you writing all this stuff in your book? This is friend's stuff, right?"

WE GOT A NEW SUPPORT ACT for a few dates, the three-piece Therapy? from Northern Ireland. They told me Ozzy said I was "fucking my way around America," while he had taken to introducing me as "Errol O'Flynn." In Denver, I intercepted him as soon as he got out of his van.

"Oi, Ozzy—I hear you've been spreading rumors about me to my countrymen," I said.

He posed to punch me and feigned surprise. "How can I be spreading rumors when you're spreading AIDS all around the country?" He put his arm around me as we walked to his dressing room, steering me, turning serious. "Now listen—you need to be good and behave yourself for the last few days on the road, because your missus will be expecting you to have a tank like Jacques Cousteau when you get back. That's an old roadie trick." I nodded sagely—though I didn't have a missus back home, I appreciated the fatherly advice.

Being around Therapy? with their Ulster accents helped me prepare to slip back into my travel agency life. After my dad's call in Nagoya, he rang again in April when I was in Normal, Illinois, with the same warning that our checking account was low, and once more, we only just covered the debit. May and June were fine, but he was on the phone in Columbus, Ohio, with more gloomy news—it looked like another shortfall, and we had twenty-four hours to raise the money. If the charge was denied, we would be blocked from selling tickets, effectively shutting us down. In St. Louis he was in touch for the third successive day: he had persuaded the bank to give us until the end of the week, and the crisis appeared to be over.

Ozzy was almost out of gas with the finishing line in sight, but at the Fiddler's Green date in Colorado, he was still full of mischief, with that gleam in his eye, telling the crowd, "On guitar, Joe Holmes. He used to be a student of Randy Rhoads. . . . Oops, I said it again. . . ." He added, "We're gonna have a tits competition—and a dick contest for the keyboard player," just in case John thought he was immune from piss-taking. Joe gave a wry smile.

BY MOUNTAIN VIEW, CALIFORNIA, OZZY WAS dragging and cut seven songs, making it the shortest set of the tour. He looked shattered before, during, and after. I walked him to his van and he said, "I'm fucking beat, Steve." I replied there was only one gig left, and after that, we'd be going home. He shook his head. "Fuck that. I'm not doing it; I'm trying to get out of it." But he did do the makeup Vancouver date, performed the full set, and it was cracking.

I went into his dressing room afterward to say goodbye as he sat on the floor, going through his bags and bottles of pills, getting everything he wanted out of the flight cases. He looked up and waved, saying, "Have a safe flight. Try to keep your dick in your trousers. See ya at Donington."

Bill handed me $4,000 cash, my wages from that leg, and Robert and I walked back to the hotel, then hit the bar. After ten months of near-unbroken touring, I was ready for two weeks at home.

#160

MONSTERS OF ROCK

DONINGTON PARK RACETRACK
CASTLE DONINGTON, ENGLAND

August 17, 1996

IN THE FORTNIGHT BETWEEN Vancouver and Castle Donington I was crippled by insomnia, and I put it down to jet lag. But it wouldn't be the only time in my life that a bout of prolonged sleeplessness signaled a coming cataclysm. I'm neither religious nor spiritual, but both times my subconscious sensed brewing trouble.

I bought an apartment that February while on the road, in the small town of Holywood a few miles from Belfast (with one *l*—when I told everyone on tour I was buying a place in Holywood, they naturally assumed it was in California, not County Down). On multiple occasions, after tossing and turning all night, I gave up at daybreak and drove to my mum's to pick up my dog and go on marathon walks. I'd drop the dog back, shower, then head into the travel agency for twelve-hour days of catch-up. Too exhausted to go for a beer with friends I hadn't seen in months, the days were a haze, spent in constant brain fog.

I flew to London and walked into the rehearsal studio as Ozzy and the band blasted "Flying High Again." It was loud, so Bobby smiled a hello and we juggled a prompter controller handover mid-verse.

Ozzy was looking at John out of the corner of his eye. The vibe was off. When the song ended John prodded at his keyboard, tentative and playful, even when Ozzy was speaking to them, high-pitched notes punctuating his words.

The guys took a break and I handed John a bottle of water. The smell of cologne emanating from him was overpowering, like he had bathed in it, showered in it, then swam in a pool of it. His eyes were droopy and it looked like he hadn't laid down in weeks.

"Everything okay? You don't look great," I said.

"Yeah, I'm fine, got a cold or something," he answered and shrugged, then returned to his setup.

But Ozzy knew. Addicts can't fool other addicts. Bobby confirmed it later—John had fallen off the wagon hard. Three days before the biggest show of the year and he had relapsed into a raging alcoholic.

On the bus the following day, Bobby asked where John was. I had seen him go to the bathroom, and Bobby strode to the door and wrested the handle with all his strength. It flew open—John was framed in the doorway grasping an upside-down can as he guzzled beer, the liquid cascading down his chin between gulps, the stench of alcohol assaulting me as it fled the room like an escaping prisoner. Bobby lunged at him and clenched his shirt, John thudding off the door and bashing into the mirror as he fought to finish the tin before Bobby grappled it away.

I had spent months on the road with alcoholics and recovering alcoholics, but that moment crystallized the addiction: a man trapped in the disease's clutches, painfully lurching in a battle to consume every drop. We pulled into the next truck stop and Bobby called our hotel to have them remove John's minibar, then rang his wife to ask her to come watch him. He was vital to the performance and his backsliding would be catastrophic, but despite the threat, there was a great atmosphere at our remote hotel. We had it to ourselves and it was like we were kids at sleepaway camp, staying up late and playing tricks on each other.

KISS CO-HEADLINED MONSTERS OF ROCK. IN 1983 they unmasked, but their career stalled, so they reapplied the makeup and recruited the original lineup—this was their first UK appearance since the reunion. They hogged the attention for what was billed as their triumphant return, but it was Ozzy, always best with his back against the wall, who stole the day.

He was a man on a mission, determined to show the English audience he still had fire in his belly nine months since his last British date, conducting the crowd in prolonged soccer-style chanting, cupping his ear as he stalked from one edge of the stage to the other, belting out the classics and the new tracks to tens of thousands of swaying, adoring fans. And John stayed sober.

Kiss guitarist Ace Frehley stood beside me to watch Ozzy's set, though he was in full stage gear, so I couldn't read his expression. We hopped onto golf carts back to the temporary buildings used as dressing rooms. Our compound was separated from Kiss by an eight-foot mesh fence, and as Gene Simmons and Paul Stanley waited to go onstage, Sharon ripped a hole in the cordon to yell at Gene. She peered through the gap, taunting and teasing him, goading him to react, making fun of his costume. She was unrelenting, but he ignored her.

My dad and stepmom came over for the festival, and I took them in to say hello. Ozzy was spent, his voice barely a whisper, drained from the emotion of the show, but he smiled and shook hands.

"Thanks for giving Stephen a job and treating him so well," my dad said. I was twenty-six but still his son, and he was grateful for everything that unfolded since their last meeting at breakfast in Rio.

Donington was special. In 1984, it was my first Ozzy show, and it had traced my growing relationship with the Osbournes. I watched from the crowd at that initial gig. In 1986, I was on the side of the stage. A decade later, I ran the prompter from two feet away.

But the show in 1996 was another milestone, too: technically, that was the last day I ever worked for Ozzy.

DONINGTON FELL ON THE SEVENTEENTH, THE monthly date that hung over us like the Sword of Damocles. Neither my dad nor I could understand how the agency's cash flow was so critical. If the monthly debit was large, it meant bookings were strong, so even allowing for a payment lag from billed corporate clients, why were we unable to cover it? We floated the possibility William was stealing and dismissed it: he had been with us from the start, and we trusted him.

But then, a couple of weeks before the US leg ended, my dad discovered William had forged a letter from our bank to an airline. His scheme unraveled. He'd worked out how to pocket money—when I got back and checked our daily bank deposits, I never cross-referenced his handwritten receipts with customers' records. The reason he'd always asked when I'd be coming home was so he could cover his tracks before I returned. Had he stolen fifty quid a day for six months I would be none the wiser today. Despite being a small operation, we turned over hundreds of thousands of pounds a year, much of it cash. But as I learned after unscrambling the scam and scrutinizing the accounts, what started with a few pounds here and there cannonballed out of control as his greed snowballed.

After the forgery, he resigned before he was fired. I said he could work until I returned at the end of July. (Again, to credit my subconscious, my diary reads "I spoke to William. . . . But then, for some reason, I just couldn't get to sleep. I went to the lobby, watched TV, wrote, but nothing seemed to work. It was 5 a.m. before I drifted off.") That was in the last few weeks before Donington—and he used the opportunity to go for it full tilt, swiping thousands of pounds but not booking anything for vacationers, knowing he was about to leave and I'd have the liability.

Coming home after Monsters of Rock, I battled to save the agency. The deeper I went, the worse it looked. He had swiped hundreds of pounds from families, taking their money but not reserving anything. I didn't just lose what he creamed off the top. I was also on the hook for thousands of pounds' worth of travel that didn't exist. Every day I dreaded going to work, never knowing who was going to walk through the door demanding refunds for flights and accommodations William never booked. Each mail delivery brought more financial horror—court summonses from customers suing me for ghost vacations, invoices demanding payment because faxed copies of checks never turned up. If it was a regular retail store with profit margins of 40 percent, I could have discounted stock to raise capital, but our margins were so razor-thin (7.5 percent commission on a domestic flight, for example), I felt like King Canute battling the ocean.

It was a nightmare lasting months that drove me to exhaustion and close to a nervous breakdown.

I worried I'd lose both my home and my business, and when I was forced to take my car off the road to save on gas and insurance, I knew I had to quit the tour. I had no choice. My office was on life support, and I had angry suppliers to placate, litigious clients to face, a loan to repay—I couldn't swan around America, chasing girls and partying with rock stars. My time with Ozzy taught me that sometimes you had to bite the bullet and face up to tough decisions.

I rang Sharon to apologize for leaving. She was as concerned and understanding as I knew she would be.

"I feel like I'm letting you down," I said, my voice cracking from emotion. "I'm so sorry that—"

"Stephen, listen," she interrupted. "Don't give it a second thought. You gotta do what you gotta do. I'll talk to Ozzy and tell him what happened, don't worry about it. Get everything back to normal and we'll see you soon, okay? We'll miss you."

Before she signed off, I asked to become her preferred travel agency, and she agreed to direct her reservations my way.

I coaxed my agency back to life, and thought about a story Ozzy told me.

> "When Sabbath fired me I holed up in a hotel in Los Angeles for two months. I was living on pizzas, drinking booze, and I had a coke dealer come around every day, with someone sending over chicks, and I'd be fucking them like nobody's business. I closed the curtains and they stayed shut for two months. There was an electric fire in this room that was on a timer and would come on at a certain time. I spent so much time in this dark room that I could tell the exact moment it would come on again. So these chicks would come over, and there'd be empty vodka bottles and dirty pizza boxes and tarts' tights and whatever, and they'd ask, 'What's all this black magic thing about, are you really into it?' And I'd say, 'Nah, of course not,' and then go, 'Boom!' and wave my hand just before the fire lit. They used to fucking freak, man, and go running, screaming from the room."

It was funny, but had a serious point: eventually, you had to stop wallowing and feeling sorry for yourself. Sharon cleaned him up and got him back on track.

My self-pity at the crisis was exacerbated by my depression at missing the last leg that ended in Alaska and Hawaii—the two states I needed to complete the fifty. But I clawed my way out of the pit. I slashed expenses to a minimum, didn't replace an agent when she left, negotiated staggered payments to creditors. And I had my parents, devoted as always. My mum spent days in the office sifting through the financial carnage. My dad gave me an interest-free loan to ride out the peril. More than a decade after Rock in Rio, the wee Belfast lad still needed help from his mummy and daddy.

Ten weeks after flying home from Donington, I was woken by a call at 1:30 a.m. Bobby was ringing from Ozzy's dressing room on the afternoon of the San Bernardino show to say hello. There was a line waiting to speak to me, like Martha and the band. Because I thought I was continuing after Monsters of Rock, I hadn't said any sentimental farewells. And it was bittersweet—crushing to miss it, but uplifting to know I wasn't forgotten.

PART THREE

FRIEND

#161/162

NISSAN PAVILION

BRISTOW, VIRGINIA

May 24, 1997

MY SIXTH DAY ON our private floor of the Ritz-Carlton in McLean, Virginia, outside Washington, DC. Tension ruffled through the deep carpets and expensive furnishings, and to escape the feeling of claustrophobia, I aimlessly wandered the adjoining high-end mall. My name was shouted at earsplitting volume from a quarter of a mile away, and it was Ozzy, shopping with Kelly. They invited me to have tea with them, so we went back to the hotel, then Aimee arrived, then Kelly changed her mind about tea, then Aimee wanted tea, then Ozzy mimed a heart attack, yelling, "You're killing me! Killing me!" and collapsed on the floor, threshing around the lobby, the bemused Ritz staff and guests gaping at Ozzy clutching his chest and moaning and yelping, the girls arguing and crying, me laughing. Never a dull moment.

We knocked the tea on the head and I returned to my room, but I was only there for five minutes when Geezer called. He wanted to go to the mall to buy shoes he saw the previous day at Versace. "I've been to the toilet four times already. I'm cacking myself!" he said. In the food court, where he picked at a baked potato, all he talked about was how nervous he was. We went back to the hotel, he spent an hour fretting in his room, then the two of us met Tony Iommi in the lobby at 6 p.m.

Tony was every bit as anxious. It was a twenty-minute ride to the venue, and he and Geezer spent most of it comparing notes on their stomachs playing up because they were so on edge. As fans, maybe we take professional musicians for granted, thinking they treat live performances as routine and part of the job. I assure you they can get as nervous as you or I might. "I just wish we can get the first one over with and then we'll be fine," Tony said, fidgeting in his seat and fiddling with the seat belt. I swiveled around in the front seat of the town car and tried to distract them, recounting the tricks we played on Ozzy's band while holed up together in our five-star hotel.

Nine months after I'd quit my gig as a roadie to salvage my agency, I was back on the road. In three hours, the original Black Sabbath would play their first proper show in nineteen years.

SHARON HAD SET UP OZZFEST, A hard rock festival, debuting in Arizona and California in 1996 on the leg I missed. The dates were so successful that for 1997 she transformed it into a summer tour, featuring acts like Marilyn Manson and Pantera. Topping the bill, Ozzy pulled double duty. First, he played a shortened solo set, then he returned for a curtailed concert with Sabbath—two greatest-hits shows of nine or ten songs. Every night I worked, I got to see two Ozzy shows. What a job.

Once again, Sharon proved her ingenius management skills. Ozzfest signaled to the Sabbath camp that Ozzy was a star in his own right, and they needed him more than he needed them. It also tested the water to see if the chemistry remained—could they still cut it almost two decades after their last tour? If a fifty-minute sizzling Sabbath sampler was successful, fans would flock back the following year for a full-blown two-hour gig. And it was all under the Ozzfest umbrella, leaving no doubt who deserved the credit.

Meanwhile, I nursed my wheezing business back to stability: I saved money like Ebenezer Scrooge, trashed galivanting around the world on cut-price travel agency deals, and worked long hours for six, often seven days a week. Sharon, true to her word, played a major part in the rescue. She booked her lucrative first-class flights with me, as well as directing staff and assistants and even journalists my way. As everything was handled by Michael in LA, he and I often traded dozens of calls every evening, me doing a full shift in the office, then talking to him after his day started at 6 p.m. my time.

Bobby rang in April, telling me, "Sharon wants you to be a sort of traveling companion for Geezer. You'll look after him, and then during gigs we'll have you back running the prompter for Ozzy and Sabbath. Ozzy's renting a jet, but apparently Tony and Geezer don't wanna fly on it so they're gonna have a bus each." He explained there would be a third bus for Ozzy's band, while Sabbath drummer Bill Ward had opted out of the tour, so Mike, like his employer, would be doing double time, keeping the beat for both sets.

Despite the previous year's financial debacle, I jumped at the chance, delighted to be asked back after leaving them in the lurch, relieved there were no hard feelings. It was different for two reasons: it was only one leg, lasting two months, and once bitten, twice shy: my mum, who took early retirement, went to my agency every day, making sure no one was tempted to be light-fingered.

I got on well with Geezer, but he had quirks and idiosyncrasies, so his list of acceptable companions was likely short. The run was sold in advance to PACE Touring, so officially I worked for them, not the Osbournes, and the wage was generous, more than twice my Ozzy salary.

Bobby let me delay my departure so I could go to London and watch my soccer team, Chelsea, win their first trophy in twenty-six years at Wembley Stadium. We ended up in a Greek restaurant until 4 a.m.—a good rehearsal for returning to life on the road—and the following day I dragged myself on no sleep to Heathrow, still drunk and barely functioning.

I FLEW TO DULLES AND A waiting stretch limo whisked me to my luxury room at the Ritz-Carlton for four days of prep—the crew testing equipment, the musicians rehearsing sets. I slipped seamlessly back into my other life. It was as if I hadn't been away.

I had dinner with Ozzy's band the night I arrived. Because I'd spent day and night with them for months on end the previous tour, I was hyper-tuned to their personalities, and I noticed a subtle shift few would have. Plus, I was in the Ozzy gossip network, so I'd heard what happened while I was away. Joe met the Osbournes to complain about aspects of life in the Ozzysphere: for example, Ozzy using crosses in imagery, something he'd done throughout his long career, and selling "Ozzy Holy Water." Sharon brutally put him in his place—he quit temporarily, and Sharon flirted with bringing Zakk back. When I left, Joe was Ozzy's onstage lieutenant, but I sensed since that put-down, his star had dulled. At dinner, we were talking about everyone having their own bus, and Michael, in from LA, quipped, "And Zakk was going to have his own bus!" I joked that Sabbath guitarist Tony Iommi was like Darth Vader, who'd tempt Joe "to come to the Dark Side"—then wondered if I offended his newfound religious sensibilities.

I needn't have worried. The next day he saw me in the lobby and asked me to go with him to the coffee shop. He wanted to unload, and I was back to being his confidant. He said he called the studio to talk to Bobby one day, and when he heard Zakk in the background, "I totally freaked, man." But he was serene about everything and admitted he was wrong to challenge Sharon's use of Christian imagery on merchandise. He shrugged. "You know, maybe everything happens for a reason and turns out for the best."

After dinner, I went to the Osbournes' suite to say hi. When Ozzy opened the door, he shouted to Sharon that I had arrived, and she came to say hello. I spent three hours with them, eating dessert, drinking coffee, and catching up. They said they were interested in buying a home in Ireland that summer, but Ozzy was uncharacteristically quiet—clearly nervous about the reunion. Sharon got on him about something he was chewing, which he denied until she identified it as a sleeping pill. "You should be a fucking spy, you know," he told her, and spat it out.

AT REHEARSALS THE FOLLOWING DAY, THE scale of everything hit me. There were a million workers, buses layered the parking lot, armies of roadies scudded back and forth, towers of equipment piled around the stage. It was good to see Bill the accountant, while Martha and Greg the sound engineer had become a couple after meeting on the previous tour, but most of the crew had changed. I discovered I no longer had to set up or take down the prompter but just run it during the show—even better, as a delectable double whammy, not only was I relieved of the duty, but the task was assigned to Keith. I knew he'd hate being my prompter bitch.

We had the sixteenth floor of the hotel to ourselves, and it felt like we were renting a stately home or a private cruise ship. I'd get up, wedge my door open with a towel, put on the local rock station, and work on travel arrangements for Sharon. As the morning wore on, I'd hear voices in the hall and poke my head out. Musicians, management, and assistants were coming and going, and they'd ask if I wanted to grab a coffee or take a walk, our own exclusive five-star enclave.

But the Sabs added a different element. I'd known Geezer nine years but never been his employee, and the day he arrived, Sharon called me into her room to give me guidelines about dealing with him, such as his vegan dietary needs and his toy-collecting obsession. For a welcome gift, she had me buy male and female action figures, strip them naked, and leave them on his hotel room pillow, posed as if having sex. He flew in from his home in St. Louis but was jet-lagged, telling me he'd only managed three hours sleep a night since arriving in America the previous week. But he didn't look exhausted—he'd had a facelift in the fourteen months since I'd seen him, knocking years off.

We spent the next afternoon wandering the deluxe mall: Geezer was concerned about his weight and wanted to buy new stage clothes, but he couldn't settle on anything. We retired to a café for a chat, and he confided he was extremely depressed after he left the previous tour—he vacationed in Maui, but aborted it because he felt so miserable. I was in the exact same chair in the exact same coffeehouse at the exact same time as when Joe opened up to me the previous day. I was used to the Osbournes' family atmosphere on the road, but with the Sabs on board as well, I'd be reckoning with a new dynamic and have to straddle both camps.

The evening of the first Sabbath rehearsal, Tony Iommi strode into the lobby: tall, imposing, his trademark aggressive dark mustache, wearing boots and a sweeping leather coat, dressed head to toe in black. The Dark Lord, incarnate. This was my first meeting with him, though our paths had crossed once before, when I interviewed him over the phone while a reporter. Diary from August 15, 1989: "Spoke to Tony Iommi. To be fair, he was really nice. He came across fine, no problem whatsoever, a genuine guy. He even phoned back later to speak to me, asking if I could help get his wife work."

Sure enough, he was friendly and chatty as he rode with Geezer and me to the venue. It was apparent they hadn't seen each other in a while, and as well as catching up on their domestic fronts, they talked about the days leading up to arriving in DC—Tony said his manager refused to let him head stateside until he had the promised up-front money wired into his account.

But I was unsure what to expect. Tony and the Osbournes had a long-running feud in the press, and I'd spent years hearing how terrible he was.

Sharon told me she used to send him turds wrapped in bright blue Tiffany boxes, while I was in the office when Lynn opened nasty letters he sent Sharon. Yet these once-sworn enemies had become friends and bandmates. It was intriguing, and I didn't know how to feel about it.

Never say never, I guess. Not burning bridges was something I'd think about as a business owner in the following years, whether it was returning to a supplier I vowed never to use again or rehiring an employee. But even at the height of the acrimony and animosity, when Ozzy talked about what an arsehole Tony was, he was always in awe of his musical ability, telling me:

> "Randy never liked Sabbath. There were things here and there, but he wasn't really a fan. I don't like Iommi for personal reasons, but that man came up with some incredible riffs. Someone somewhere has a whole stack of tapes with some great sounds that we generated. We used to rent a cottage in Wales or somewhere and just lock ourselves away and jam, man. Then what we used to do was just go in, get out. Come in, do our thing, and then disappear. No interviews or anything. But then MTV came along, and everyone wanted to be a TV star."

Ozzy and Mike were already onstage when we arrived, and Tony and Geezer joined them. I worked the prompter but didn't know the order of the songs, and Ozzy took the piss out of me, waving his arms in the air like a traffic cop, directing me to scroll back, forward, sideways. He seemed unhappy, having it in his head he wasn't ready for the tour, but I was sure it was a psychological, rather than a medical, problem. He was in much better form after they ran the set. Seeing them reunited was special, and a chill raced down my spine when they crunched into the opener. I'd seen Ozzy do Sabbath songs hundreds of times, on many occasions with Geezer on bass, but it sounded different with Tony. In the dressing room the three of them caught up, and Ozzy said, "We should have a cup of tea together," but the others were too tired.

Instead, Bobby, Joe, and I went into Ozzy's suite along with Pete, an Englishman taking my former role as the band's assistant. He, too, had a long history with Ozzy, and the two of them reeled off stories.

Once, they got wasted, fell asleep in the same bed, and slept in, instead of picking up Sharon from the airport. Ozzy woke when he heard her walk into the house and said to Pete, "Fuck! What are we gonna do?"

Pete stood, pulled his jacket on over his pajamas, opened the door to leave, and said, "There's no 'we' about it, old bean."

Another time, Sharon and Ozzy were arguing, and Sharon ordered Pete into the car and fired off, but at the bottom of the drive, the passenger door flew open and Pete tumbled out of the car. He stood, dusted himself down, and said, "This isn't worth two hundred pounds a week," and walked out of the gate.

My journal is also full of stories Geezer told me on that tour about Ozzy when they were in Sabbath:

> "In Germany we sent this guy out to buy us coke. The twat came back with heroin instead, but me and Ozzy decided to snort it anyway. We went back to the hotel, but only made it as far as the steps. We were staying in this really posh place, and there were hundreds of businessmen coming in and out, up and down these fancy steps, just stepping over us. Ozzy was going, 'Oh, I don't like this,' and puking up. Him being sick was making me laugh, then I was puking as well, and I couldn't stop laughing, so I couldn't stop being sick.
>
> "We were in Florida, and Ozzy was mortal. He nicked the hotel manager's motorbike and pissed off on it. The manager called the police and they found him, and threw him in jail. We got this phone call from the cops saying, 'This guy says

> he belongs to you. You need to come down to the station and bail him out.' We just said, 'Nah, it's all right, just keep him there.' He stayed in all night."

Back then the Sabbath guys thought nothing of leaving Ozzy in prison overnight.

The following evening, Geezer and I walked back to the hotel after watching *The Lost World* movie. For the first time he discussed the reunion. He said they all would have loved drummer Bill to do it, but they couldn't rely on him. Bill rang Tony when he heard he was out, but Tony said Bill was cool about it and there was no bitterness. I said everyone was getting on really well and he agreed. He said, "With something like this, you've just gotta put the past behind you. If you look back it'll kill you, you just have to forget about it."

SATURDAY, MAY 24, 1997, WAS THE original Black Sabbath's first headlining gig in almost two decades. Backstage resembled a city preparing for a last-minute hurricane evacuation. Musicians, roadies, liggers, gear coming and going, production staff fluttering about, black boxes rolling in and out like *Space Invaders* on acid, Machine Head blasting onstage, the smell of weed and dry ice and catering food . . . dozens, if not hundreds, of bodies everywhere.

We met Bobby in the parking lot and he marched us through the turmoil into the dressing room: Ozzy materialized immediately, giving off wild energy. He was in and out like an epileptic jackrabbit, shaking more than I'd ever seen. Sharon came in and told Tony to go into Ozzy's room to calm him down. I told her not to send Geezer, because he was even worse. He'd already taken a hundred trips to the bathroom. No one could sit still.

I left the dressing room to run the prompter for Ozzy's set—solid, not spectacular. Obviously, he'd one eye on Sabbath's performance.

We had fifteen minutes. Ozzy barged in flapping a fringed, tasseled shirt like he wore in the seventies, spluttering and shouting like a hyped-up kid. "Look what I found in an old flight case!" he joked. (He hadn't rediscovered a twenty-year-old outfit, it had been tailor-made the previous day in DC.)

Ozzy left again, Tony paced the room, Geezer clenched and unclenched his fists. Then, as the nervousness seemed poised to peak and crest, Mike, who drummed shirtless, stuck his head in. Tony stopped and said, mock serious, "Are you going onstage like that? Where's your black clothes?"

We laughed and the anxiety eased a smidgeon.

I walked them onstage. The houselights went dark. The stage was cleared, so the other acts crowded onto the mixer to watch. The noise from the audience intensified. They couldn't see us because we were behind a Kabuki, the thick black curtain suspended from the lighting rig blocking their view. We turned to watch the intro video playing on the wall of monitors behind us, a compilation of vintage footage from the sixties and seventies. It ended with a crash and explosion. I nodded and smiled at Geezer and flashed him a thumbs-up.

The air-raid siren wailed, Mike thundered into "War Pigs," and it was fabulous. Metal musical magic enveloped us. A historic moment. No rust, no cobwebs, no tentativeness. Nine stone-cold classics (though a couple were curtailed medleys) played by the original members. And I got to experience it from a few feet away.

The song "Black Sabbath" was my surprising highlight because it wasn't one of my favorite tracks. But Tony's solo at the end was sparkling and show-stopping, spastic green lasers zipping and zapping around the cross-strewn stage as he piloted the band into meltdown. ("You should close the show with it," I suggested to him later, never shy about offering an opinion to professional musicians—although he said he was thinking the same thing.)

The crowd's reaction was deafening, and it was also clear the guys enjoyed it. Ozzy clowned around, doing funny walks and making silly faces. A fan in a *Cat in the Hat* hat climbed onstage, and Ozzy pulled it off him and pranced about in it himself. Afterward, Geezer and Tony said his antics relaxed them.

"We're supposed to be all dark and black and satanic, but we were more like a comedy band up there tonight," Tony told me.

At every stop, we had a dressing room for Ozzy, one for his band, and another for Tony and Geezer. Tony's right-hand man, Mick, was also his tech, so he was always working on his rig, meaning I was Tony's de facto assistant as well. Ozzy usually pitched camp in our room, and the pattern for the tour was set that night: we ordered food and he came in to eat. It was the first time I saw them interact for more than a few minutes. What struck me was how relaxed it was, how at home Ozzy was, how they spontaneously fell into old war stories, more like long-lost brothers than the squabbling mercurial artists they had been for years. A torrent of tales, me a transfixed eavesdropper as the most influential heavy rock band in history recalled stealing equipment from tiny English clubs three decades previously. It was well-known Tony made plastic tips for his fingers after a machine accident in a factory—but I didn't realize he kept them in the same little yellow tin box from his mother's shop in the sixties. I asked him about it and Ozzy yelled across the room, "Yeah, Steve, he keeps all sorts of things in there: fingers, ears, bollocks."

Ozzy reveled in the camaraderie, even though, always his own worst critic, he wasn't happy with his voice. At one point he was convinced the set list was wrong (it wasn't), and he kept changing mics, irritated with the sound quality. That, it turned out, was the pattern for the tour, too.

I sat with Geezer on the ride back to the hotel. He said his nerves vanished as soon as the show started, and he was delighted it went well. He told me, "There's just no one like Ozzy, sure there's not? Nobody comes close."

#167/168

ALAMODOME

SAN ANTONIO, TEXAS

May 31, 1997

AFTER A WEEK AT the Ritz-Carlton but only one date, we made our first move. With two bands, crew, management, partners, and family, there was a shit ton of luggage, requiring multiple trips to the lobby to pile up a mountain of cases. Although I was Geezer's assistant, I helped Pete with the baggage. When it was my responsibility, I grabbed a cart and worked solo. Pete's version was more labor-saving. He got cash from Bill the accountant to tip, then commandeered a bellman, watching as he did the heavy lifting and grunt work.

On the way to the airport, Tony told me he went to see *The Exorcist* in Philadelphia, and when he got back to his room, the actor who played the priest was on *The Tonight Show.* The coincidence sent him haywire, and he was so terrified he slept with the light on. The Dark Lord had met me only a couple of days before but was recounting an embarrassing story about being frightened by a movie and a chat show! I knew Ozzy was equally self-deprecating, and I realized the Sabbath guys didn't take themselves, or their image, too seriously. I told Tony he might set off the airport security detector because he was so metal.

I bought lunch at the Burger King departures so vegan Geezer could collect the free *Jurassic Park* watch. While we waited for it, he told me he used to carry a little tape player everywhere, and if anyone did something stupid, he played the James Bond theme. In a hotel elevator in Chicago, Roger Moore—the real James Bond—got on. As he left, his foot caught in the doorway, and Geezer played the music. Apparently, Roger didn't find it amusing.

In Florida, after loading two vans with our skyscraper of bags, Pete and I were chauffeured to our fabulous beachfront Ritz-Carlton in Manalapan. He spent the ride showing me photos of two strippers he was meeting that night and entertaining me with tales from his days with Aerosmith, like when he let two lesbians stay with him in France. Every time he had room service delivered, the half-naked women kissed and groped each other, putting on a display for the staff. The workers fought one another to take food to his suite, and not only did they never charge him, they bombarded him with dishes he hadn't even ordered.

That evening, Gloria Estefan invited us to a private island where she had a house alongside Sylvester Stallone and Madonna. It was elegant and striking, huge lighted candles everywhere in a stunning location—"like a scene from *Scarface*," Sharon said. Afterward we were treated to dinner at her Cuban restaurant in South Beach, then back in my oceanfront room, I opened the balcony French doors and drifted off to the smell of the sea and the sound of the waves. My diary entry ended, "This is the life." No shit, Sherlock.

MY WAKE-UP CALL EVERY MORNING WAS the three little O's tag-teaming me to take them to the pool, the beach, or out on Jet Skis. They badgered me into 360-degree spins and wave jumping, but I was always nervous looking after them when there was physical activity involved, dreading I might be responsible for injuring an Osbourne heir. Over lunch, Tony told me about the time Sabbath played golf in an equally bucolic luxury resort in Fiji. Ozzy spent the whole time clobbering frogs to death with his club, Tony was chasing and stomping on poisonous ants that had attacked him, while Geezer almost killed someone when he whacked a ball against a tree and the ricochet nearly brained them.

Our departure from the idyllic shorefront stay signaled the end of the honeymoon period. It started with grumbles. Geezer was annoyed that in interviews, when Ozzy (never one to miss a windup) was asked why Bill wasn't involved, he answered, "Because Geezer didn't want him." He and Tony thought the deep cut "Behind the Wall of Sleep" was dying on its arse and needed to be switched out. They weren't satisfied with the onstage sound and hauled in the monitor engineer, who got a dressing-down. Mike blasted jazz and funk before concerts and they griped to me about it on opening night. Their complaints became more vehement, so I nabbed Bobby and Sharon: Bobby ordered Mike to turn it down, and Sharon told Martha to stop putting the dressing rooms beside each other.

Their next beef flabbergasted me. Tony and Geezer wanted to play the full versions of "Iron Man" and "Sweet Leaf," instead of bleeding them together as a medley like Ozzy did on solo tours. Geezer, of course, played with Ozzy and knew this—"It's like we're up there every night doing the Ozzy version of Sabbath," he said. *Why was it not dealt with during rehearsals?* I wondered. After all, I knew Ozzy didn't care, it wasn't about ego for him. The lack of communication, the unwillingness to confront the issue before such a monster undertaking, surprised me.

Whatever the reason, in Charlotte, North Carolina, Geezer, Tony, and Mike met to run through the two tracks in their entirety. In my room.

It was the day of a big European soccer game, and I spent ages convincing the unhelpful concierge in our fancy hotel to ring around local sports bars to find one showing it. He finally found a spot and I returned to my room to grab my wallet, but just then Geezer called and asked if they could come over for a rehearsal. I said of course and rang Mike and Tony, and they all appeared ten minutes later.

I couldn't have cared less about the match, aware how lucky I was to witness heavy metal history: Mike drummed on a pillow, the others used tiny practice amps, and it was a freakish diorama: rock superstars, roosted on yellow-and-green comforters in a suburban North Carolina hotel, preparing for a huge show, playing classics they hadn't performed with Ozzy in two decades. While perched on my bed.

That night I reprogrammed the prompter with the extra lyrics, then nipped into Ozzy's room between his sets to confirm he knew about the rejig. He nodded. Then he said, "Steve, my voice is fucked." He was rarely happy with his singing, always judging his performance harsher than anyone else, and when he came into our dressing room later he complained that even when there was no show, he'd media commitments instead of being able to rest his voice.

WE HAD A COUPLE OF NIGHTS in Charlotte, and as Julie lived in nearby Gastonia, I brought her to the gig. John was having trouble with his laptop and asked if she'd look at it, so I took her into the band's dressing room.

Ozzy walked in and came over to see what we were doing.

"Hey, Oz, this is Ju—" I started.

He looked at her, smiled, shook his head, and put his fingers in his ears. "I don't wanna know, I don't wanna know," he said and left, laughing, covering himself for plausible deniability, as he thought I was fooling around with an underage girl. Then on his way to the stage he threw a bottle of water over me.

We flew to San Antonio. Sabbath was replacing "Behind the Wall of Sleep" with "Into the Void," and I went with them to the Alamodome to practice. The crew had set up their gear in a small backstage room, and the volume was earsplitting in an enclosed space—so much power emanating from their amps it ping-ponged around the bare walls in waves, the vibrations shaking material from the ceiling.

We were at the venue early on show day for an MTV interview, and when I asked Geezer how it went, he huffed, then replied, "Okay—when I could get a word in edgeways with Ozzy."

I put the new lyrics into the prompter, but the song was doing the hokey-pokey. Ozzy didn't want to do it; Tony and Geezer did. Bobby asked Ozzy to put it back in for them, and he agreed, reluctantly. Mike was ecstatic. When Tony lit into it, the fifteen thousand fans went nuts, the opening riff sounding out of this world as it screamed to the rafters, the guitars seemingly tuned so low it was as if they were erupting from under our feet, though Ozzy stumbled over the lyrics for the first verse, understandably, as he hadn't sung it since the seventies.

As I stood at the prompter, the sound of the sozzled Saturday night crowd reverberating around the Alamodome, the only enclosed show on the run, the other acts crowding both sides of the stage to watch, I had an epiphany: how unlike a conventional rock tour it was. Jack and I were dancing and laughing, Kelly riding her bike around us, Aimee chatting with their nanny, Bobby shaking his hips in a funny little jig. At that moment, I knew no artist other than Ozzy created an atmosphere like ours, such a relaxed, family feeling, the antithesis of how you'd envisage it to be in the wings watching the original doom merchants, Black Sabbath.

But Ozzy's vocals faltered occasionally, and he also winced and grabbed his back a few times. Post-gig, our dressing room was cheerless and morose.

Ozzy apologized to Geezer, explaining he was struggling with his voice. Geezer was unhappy with his rig's sound, and he and Tony again criticized the monitors. They felt their show was suffering because of Ozzy's solo set and wanted him to chop it down. After waiting nineteen years to re-form they said it should be top-notch—and felt it was being compromised by him singing "Crazy Train" and such beforehand. We left quickly. Gloria, Geezer's wife and manager, had flown in, and she, Geezer, and I were in the hotel elevator when things went further south. I should have seen it coming.

Ozzy was my hero and my recent employer. I'd been friends with him and Sharon for twelve years, and she brought me on board for the tour. I was Geezer's assistant . . . but I ran the prompter for Ozzy during both sets, I babysat the Osbourne kids, I ran errands for Sharon, I helped Pete with luggage for both bands. I had a foot in both the Ozzy and Sabbath organizations—there were individual laminates for each act, and out of hundreds of personnel, I was one of maybe four with access to both dressing rooms. Ozzy and Tony each had a dedicated assistant, while Pete looked after Ozzy's band. I guess Geezer thought he wasn't being treated equally. My job was to take care of him, but I'd other duties as well, sometimes pulling my focus away.

We stood in silence in the elevator. Gloria turned to Geezer. "You want me to ask Stephen why you are the only one who has to walk from the stage back to the dressing room on his own?" He nodded, and she told me they were upset. I apologized, said of course she was right, explained it was an oversight that hadn't occurred to any of us, and promised to fix it.

It was a simple problem. The prompter was stage left, Geezer played bass stage right. After their bow, Bobby escorted Ozzy back to his room, Pete went with Mike, Tony with Mick. But since I was on the opposite side from Geezer, after his tech helped him into his robe, he went back alone. I couldn't get over there to walk with him. If he'd flagged it after the first night we'd have addressed it—after all, it was an easy fix. No one wanted musicians without security or support, open to getting cornered by drunks or nutters.

Gloria looked me in the eye. "If you can't get it dealt with, then we'll bring someone else out to do it."

I was stunned. They were going to fly someone out just for a thirty-second walk? Or was she threatening to fire me?

Chastised, I opened my door to be greeted by a ringing phone. It was Bobby, seething. Pete had told him Geezer was whining about the upcoming midmorning flight to Dallas, and he wanted to call and bollock him. I managed to talk him out of it—I told him what just happened, so it seemed prudent to avoid antagonism. He agreed, sighed, and said, "Stephen, they are just two miserable old cunts anyway."

A COUPLE OF DAYS LATER, I went to lunch with Ozzy's band—just for perfect symmetry—and they complained about him cutting his set due to Sabbath. Poor Ozzy was getting it from both sides. On tour with such a huge, interconnected group, we weaved our own tapestry from weeks of bonding. Ozzy, of course, never got a day off, and it was hardly surprising when he pulled stunts to amuse himself.

I turned on the radio and he was being interviewed. He was asked why Bill wasn't involved, and again said because Geezer didn't want him. Then he added if there were artists listening who wanted to get signed, they should contact Michael in the LA office —and gave the phone number. I was on hold for Michael at the time and thought, *Uh-oh. . . .* I told him when he came on the line and he shouted—only half joking—"He hates me! I'm surprised he didn't give out my home number!" He said Ozzy was in a foul mood because he had to do phoners all day.

Joe still had his hang-ups, literally. I went to dinner with him in a restaurant with a prop car hanging from the ceiling, and he insisted on moving tables in case it crashed down and crushed us. In a coffee shop, he shook hands with a customer, then to his consternation, noticed what looked like track marks on the guy's arms. He was convinced he was a heroin addict who passed him a virus and ran to the restroom to scrub down. Sometimes I didn't know whether I was on the road with a rock guitarist or Howard Hughes.

The morning after Gloria confronted me, Bobby called to say Pete's mother had died and he was leaving temporarily. Twelve hours after getting castigated for my Ozzy duties, I was picking up the slack for more. As it always did on tour, news traveled fast. At the venue in Dallas that night, Ozzy's assistant said to me, "You're looking a bit nervous, son!" and laughed.

With Ozzy insisting his voice was fucked at the previous gig, Geezer was certain he would pull the show at the Starplex, but it was a stormer; once again when Ozzy's back was against the wall, he came out fighting, ripping out lyrics from deep within his soul. For the encore, Tony rifled into "Sabbath Bloody Sabbath," and Ozzy had a fit—I panicked, too, dementedly flicking through the prompter database, searching for the words. It was a windup—the Dark Lord had a sense of humor! Halfway through "Paranoid," Bobby relieved me, and I sprinted around the back of the stage and up the other side, waiting with Geezer's robe to walk him to the dressing room. Problem solved.

Ozzy sauntered into the dressing room, saying he went to the doctor and was diagnosed with a throat infection. "I've been banned from smoking, drinking caffeine, and just about fucking every fucking thing. I had the old microscope down my neck today—did you know a vocal cord looks like a cunt?"

THE FOLLOWING EVENING, SHARON ASKED ME to have dinner with her. She'd heard about Gloria's threat and was sympathetic. She told me the phenomenal amount of money Geezer received for this spurt of short sets and added, "You know, Ozzy has always said Geezer has a bigger ego than Tony."

By the time we got to Cleveland, where we spent hours in toy shops and comic book stores, Geezer was back to complaining a lot, so I assumed things had returned to normal. We were getting tour buses there, and the plan was to ask him if John could ride on his. There were only two of us on it, so it'd be company for him and lessen numbers on the band's bus (four musicians, plus Pete, Bobby, and tour accountant Bill). But with the events of the previous few days, no one wanted to broach it with him—"Because of all his moaning," was how Bobby put it.

One prompter problem solved, one new problem created. With the arrival of his bus, Geezer altered his show day routine. He had turned up as late as possible to keep backstage time to a minimum, but changed it to get to the venue earlier so he could nap in his bunk. (It was eye-popping, the amount he slept.) He wanted me to wake him an hour before the Kabuki drop—right in the heart of Ozzy's set.

I had a confab with Bobby and he said he'd deputize on the prompter while I did it. The first night went like clockwork—once we dodged the attention of a crazy porn star brought onstage by support act Fear Factory to flash her boobs at Ozzy.

The last four dates were spread out—two had journeys of twenty-four hours plus—and we were traveling by road. But after confirming that was what he wanted to do—drive—Geezer changed his mind and decided to fly between them. Bobby told Sharon, and I could tell it wasn't the first wrinkle he'd thrown into planning. She shook her head. "Bobby, from now on, just def him," she said. Meaning, ignore him. With decades of handling artists behind her, she knew when to step in and when to turn a deaf ear. She was doing something right: the management team told me they were selling tickets hand over fist. They'd been offered another six dates, silly money to play Iowa, and extra gigs in Detroit and Boston, as they both sold out in an hour.

#173/174

DEER CREEK MUSIC CENTER

NOBLESVILLE, INDIANA

June 4, 1997

I WOKE IN INDIANAPOLIS, eleven months to the day after celebrating the Fourth of July there. The last thing I wrote in my diary that day reads simply "'Supernaut' tonight." The title of a Sabbath song, a two-word entry, on a routine day with nothing much going on, but it refers to something that happened many times in our dressing room.

I sing to myself constantly, whether I'm pottering around the house, cleaning the bathroom, or dandering to the store. And I did it while messing around the dressing room, organizing photos to be signed, packing up the gear, whatever. As I worked for Sabbath—BLACK SABBATH—I had them in my head, and frequently I'd sing an old song.

Two hours before the gig at Deer Creek, outside Indianapolis, we were in the dressing room while Geezer slept on the bus. Tony stood by the clothes rack, where his practice amp was set up, wearing his guitar, running through exercises, fingers flying up and down the neck. I was pawing through a pile of swag a support band dropped off for us, removing the white T-shirts. ("You take them, I only wear black," Tony told me in the least surprising sentence ever.)

Absentmindedly, bent over with my back to him, I sang, "I wanna reach out, and touch the sky . . ." and BOOM! Tony jumped right into the track, playing alongside my vocals.

My own private karaoke—with the bloke who wrote the fucking riffs.

This happened over and over. I'm a terrible singer, but I'd warble a snatch, he'd play along for twenty seconds, then return to running scales.

Think about that. I started life as a working-class toddler in Northern Ireland, using my grandparents' outside toilet in their tiny terraced house. As a teenager I became a rock fan, listening to bootlegs among the bombs and bullets of Belfast. In adulthood I was friends with Ozzy, and by 1997, I was alone with Tony Iommi in his dressing room, me singing, the master craftsman responsible for some of the most famous tracks in history accompanying me.

THE FOLLOWING EVENING, RETURNING FROM MORE toy shopping, Geezer and I encountered Tony and Mick in the lobby, and they invited me for a beer. We cabbed to the Union Jack Pub on Broad Ripple and plonked at the bar. It was deserted and unassuming with only a couple of other drinkers, fake stained glass, leather chairs, soccer scarves, and all the furnishings and decorations typical of generic English bars across the States. Right away Tony opened up to me, and what started out as a low-key chat over a few pints ended up as one of my most unforgettable evenings ever.

He was the only ever-present Sab for three decades and had a boatful of tales about the many musicians who cycled through; I was the fresh meat who hadn't heard them. He talked about recording the album *Born Again* with singer Ian Gillan: they sank his boat, blew up his tent, and crashed Bill

Ward's car, and said Gillan was a dirty hound who shagged everything, even the woman who cleaned toilets in the local bar. He filled in backstory about Geezer and Gloria as well.

But it wasn't just salacious gossip, and one thing he elaborated on struck home. Throughout my time with Ozzy, and indeed, back to when I was a teenage fan, the narrative was that Tony was the overarching bully in Sabbath. He cracked the whip and coerced the others into doing things his way. Perhaps because he saw me as an "Ozzy guy," Tony wanted to discuss his reputation.

"You know, in the early days, you've no idea how out of it we were all the time," he said. "Drugs, booze, you name it . . . we were a mess. I didn't really have much of a choice, I had to step up and look after things. The rest of them relied on me to be the leader and take charge. And know what? If I hadn't done it, none of the other three were gonna do it. They were outta their minds the whole time. I gotta lotta bad press over the years, calling me domineering, saying I was a dictator, but all I was trying to do was to get us working and making music."

I sipped my way through beer after beer, never interrupting my intimate insight into rock history.

And he revealed that after all the rancor between him and Ozzy, he was nevertheless loving playing with him again, and hoped they'd record together.

We spent hours there. Then, in a bar that was our fourth stop, I met a blonde with a knockout smile whom I told I was Sabbath's offstage keyboardist, a line I used a few times that never worked. She led us to another club, but when we arrived, we realized Mick was missing. Drunk Tony was furious, the fabled temper flaring, ranting and raving that he couldn't believe Mick abandoned him, pledging to fire him in the morning. The blonde offered to drive us to the hotel.

As Tony stepped up to get into her SUV, he lost his balance and fell. He was so wasted he couldn't get back up, floundering on the cement in a bar parking lot at 4 a.m. Even intoxicated I appreciated the scene: the Dark Lord, legendarily formidable in his long black leather jacket, thrashing around, his boots kicking up gravel, fighting to stand, cursing Mick. I was in drunken, hiccuping hysterics, but ducked out of view to avoid a tongue-lashing—if he'd seen me, I would have gotten one, as he was in no mood for humor. Then I composed myself, grabbed him under his armpits to haul him into the back seat, and we headed home.

Five hours later, I woke to discover the blonde beside me, the only time in my life I forgot I'd spent the night with a girl. I walked her to her car (ever the gentleman) and met Pete in the lobby, who provided another shock. Mick had disappeared because he was arrested.

Apparently, he dropped behind us as we walked to the last club, so, drunk and tired, he sat on a porch, where he fell asleep. The homeowner called the police, who whisked him to jail. Hotel security roused Bobby at 3:30 a.m., and he took a cab downtown with $1,000 cash to bail Mick out.

Tony rang me to fill in his blanks, and when I told him, he burst out laughing, saying when he got back, he left a rambling, abusive message for Mick. Geezer also thought it hysterical and said, "Thank you, Lord, for not letting me drink anymore."

Mick was shamefaced and kept apologizing, saying, "I've let everyone down," but the only person annoyed was Bobby, who, to be fair, was whose sleep was shattered. Tony was hell-bent on torturing Mick and wanted me to play along by making him think he was going to lose his job, but every time I looked at him, I couldn't keep my face straight. After delaying our departure for an hour to wait on the jailbird, we left for Pittsburgh.

#175–187

OZZFEST 1997

NORTHEAST LEG

June 7–June 15, 1997

GEEZER CALLED ON OUR afternoon off in Pittsburgh. He found a comic book store in the yellow pages only a ten-minute walk from the hotel, so we headed there after lunch. He was as motivated to hunt down old comics as he was with vintage toys, so I waited while he browsed, flicking through rack after rack. Bored, I wandered the shop and found a stack of music magazines dating back years piled haphazardly on a rickety table in a dusty corner. I accidentally knocked a few to the floor, and as I bent to pick them up, I spotted the *Kerrang!* from twelve years previously featuring Ozzy and me. I snapped it up for $1.

At the venue, everyone thought the photo of him pretending to beat on me in his dressing room bathroom at Rock in Rio was hysterical. I took it to Ozzy, who burst out laughing, then cooed, "Ahhhh, look, it's little Stephen!" I found Sharon in catering to show her, and she wanted to know everything Tony said about Ozzy when he was drunk. Later, Pete, Bobby, and I had a late-night powwow with no musicians around, as Pete was leaving for five days to attend his mother's funeral. He'd just spent $80 on a date, then she told him, "I'll have to introduce you to my friend, she's more your age."

The next stop was Philadelphia, and my old school friend Gordon (the pilot I had visited in Dallas) flew in for a couple of days. Geezer was flying to St. Louis, so Gordon was able to travel with me on the bus. Ozzy's band was going on his plane to New York to meet a producer, so the band's bus would only have John and Bill, while Tony's had him and Mick. Three gas-guzzling vehicles with two passengers each driving six hundred miles to the next stop. (We weren't very environmentally conscious then.) Gordon and I drank until 4 a.m., laughing about how farcical it was that two Belfast youngsters had exclusive overnight use of a Black Sabbath tour bus in the US.

Philly was another humongous gate of around twenty thousand, outselling U2 in town on the same night, and Ozzy stormed into our dressing room like a force of nature in one of his turbocharged effervescent moods, barely pausing for breath as he steamed from story to story, blurting, "Our set blows my own to pieces—it's great playing with you guys again.

"But I wish we could get Bill back," he added, and the other Sabs agreed. He said he'd developed a stock answer when asked about his absence—"I don't know why he's not involved. Ask Sharon."

Despite the headaches he created down the years, it was clear they missed him, and would have preferred him on board.

Geezer got to spend two nights at his house in St. Louis and arrived at the hotel two hours later than the planned departure. Rather than the spell at home rejuvenating him, it made him even more ill-humored, his disposition darkened by a visit to his doctor, who diagnosed an ulcer. He said he was allergic to touring, that he needed a vacation, and he'd never go on the road again, even with his own band. He wanted to move to a cottage in the quiet English county of Cornwall. When I said at least their set was only half as long as a regular headlining slot, he replied, "All tours should be like this one: maximum money for the minimum work."

I collapsed into bed at 5 a.m. and Bobby woke me three hours later with a question. The drivers had to go to the venue at 11 a.m., park the buses, then return to rest at the hotel before our 730-mile journey to Boston post-gig. So the luggage needed to be loaded by 10:45 a.m., he had the band and Tony primed to do it, would Geezer be okay with it? I gave an emphatic no—he never surfaced before lunchtime, and getting up and parting with his stuff by then would put him in a lousy mood.

Instead, when we all left together at 4 p.m., I stuffed his bags into the van around us, and we were glued together for ninety minutes of horrendous traffic. He whined he woke up depressed and reckoned it was a side effect of his ulcer medication—I joked with Sharon he must have been taking it for twenty years.

The sold-out crowd in Detroit, always an Ozzy stronghold, fermented into whirling dervishes for his encore, hurling clumps of lawn onto the stage as we mobilized to limit the traditional invasion. Bobby's muscle memory kicked in and he sprang to his customary crouched position to protect Ozzy—forgetting I went to get Geezer from the bus, and he was operating the prompter. The Fear Factory bassist jumped in to save the day, the flaw in the plan being he didn't know how the prompter worked, so he pushed buttons and twirled knobs, shooting every song on the set list into a speeded-up scroll. Ozzy yelled and Bobby dived back to fix it. We wheeled out Pantera to warn the audience if they didn't stop chucking sod, Sabbath wouldn't perform. Venue staff and promoters watched from the wings, grim-faced. Ozzy laughed and threw a wedge at Joe.

As I walked Sabbath to the stage, Geezer dragged behind, saying he couldn't wait for the gig to be over. I tried to lighten the mood, asking, "Wearing black again tonight, then?" Of course, they'd a blast, helped by a front-row trio of gorgeous topless girls, who rubbed and licked each other. Ozzy kept soaking them with his water gun as he stomped about with a bra draped over his head and a goofy grin, Tony guffawing so hard he almost hyperventilated. It was routine behavior by Ozzy, but Tony hadn't played with him for two decades, and unlike us, hadn't seen him act that way. Afterward, it was a transformed dressing room, Geezer asking if I could get the girls to come every night.

But by Boston he reverted to the mean, and our odyssey around toy stores was conducted to a running commentary of complaints about our hotel. I went for a walk afterward, meeting Ozzy and Kelly outside Banana Republic: inside were Sharon, Aimee, and Jessica, Ozzy's daughter from his first marriage. Ozzy was on the happy pills and grabbed me in a bear hug, saying it was good to see me. He asked me to accompany him to a joke shop and spent $100 on stink bombs—"These are for that Marilyn Manson fucker"—then insisted on trying one at the entrance as soon as we left. We found the girls still shopping in a shoe shop, so Sharon suggested I take Ozzy for coffee.

I bought us drinks and we sat by the window, watching the world go by. As I chatted, he leaned forward and interrupted. "Steve, do you like working for Geezer? Resign and come and work for me."

I was struck dumb. I knew he was still whacked out on something, and I laughed it off. He shook his head. "I'm serious. No one should have to put up with that sort of torture. You're a friend."

I'd never discussed anything with him, so Sharon must have filled him in about the daily toy hunts, Geezer's insatiable appetite for sleep, his uninterrupted moaning. I shrugged and deflected the conversation, then on the walk back to the family he wandered off in a crazy pop-up rainstorm, and Sharon asked me to chase him down. We were both drenched by the time I steered him back.

An informed Ozzy wasn't atypical. Outsiders often underestimated him, mistaking an occasional mumbled word or unsteady gait for a lack of awareness or intelligence. But he was razor-sharp in many areas and a keen observer—a great way to approach both personal and business matters: say nothing, watch and listen, let them underestimate you. People always reveal themselves—"give them enough rope," as Sharon used to put it.

The singer for Geezer's solo band lived in Boston and came to the gig, and Geezer told me to bring him onto the bus, but usher him out after ten minutes. I was incessantly wrong-footed by Geezer's shyness, and realized in the nine years I'd known him, he'd never formally introduced me to anyone. The singer was a bouncer in his day (or night) job, and Geezer wound him up the whole time, convincing him their drummer quit to represent the US at the Nintendo World Championship. He had no idea what was happening and seemed relieved when I made up an excuse to kick him out.

We spent the drive to Manhattan talking about Geezer's solo project. He said, "It's going to be a bit crap going on tour with my own band after this tour." Just a few days previously he said he was allergic to being on the road and would never do it again, but since then his mood had swung to discussing his upcoming dates. Just before bed, he told me Sabbath felt like his band once more with him an integral part, rather than when he was only a hired hand playing with Ozzy.

I'D LOOKED FORWARD TO SEEING THE famous Giants Stadium in East Rutherford, New Jersey, and as I walked onto the field my first impression was awe-inspiring, the stands rising straight up like cliffs, the backstage lot a sea of glinting metallic chrome. The corridors around the dressing rooms resembled Times Square at midnight on New Year's Eve, and Geezer had enough after five minutes. I walked him to his bunk for a lie-down, and on the way back Bobby got me to put my watch forward ten minutes so we could herd the musicians early, the pair of us synchronized like a military operation, the only time we ever did it.

Ozzy was on at 7 p.m. and Geezer wanted to be woken at 7:20 p.m., but Bobby forgot to relieve me from the prompter. He remembered ten minutes late and I spurted to the bus. Geezer was already awake, sarcastically slow-clapping when I boarded. I apologized and explained. He said, "So, it's bollocks to Geezer, then. The teleprompter is more important than me."

But their concert was awesome, the audience's roar in recognition at the intro to "War Pigs" deafening. Geezer stage right, head bobbing, frenetic, Tony only a few feet from me, composed, confident, occasionally flashing the devil horns as he strode around the stage, Ozzy leaping, prancing, emptying his lungs. For the outro of the song "Black Sabbath," I watched transfixed as lasers bounced out above the cauldron of humanity, the music flying over the heads of tens of thousands of fans massed like Mongol hordes poised for invasion. . . . The memory of standing onstage for Sabbath in Giants Stadium still gives me goose bumps.

Sabbath wasn't happy, though. A whipping wind played havoc with their audio, and they were worried something would be thrown at them (Ozzy later told me Tony once got cracked in New York, and every time he returned, he couldn't stop thinking about it). Meanwhile, Ozzy groused, "My set is fucking abysmal, man," and didn't want anyone near him.

Jack insisted on riding with us back to the city—even an eleven-year-old was doling out stick about some exaggerated story he heard about me and a stripper in Dallas—and after I delivered him to Ozzy and Sharon, we revisited our old haunt the Whiskey Bar. I fell into bed at 4 a.m., the next day there was more toy shopping, then nine hours to Columbus, Ohio, most of which Geezer slept through. After a couple of hours chatting to Joe in his room I turned in at 1:30 a.m. My last quiet night of the tour.

#188, 202/203

POLARIS AMPHITHEATER

COLUMBUS, OHIO

June 17 & July 1, 1997

I BREEZED INTO THE Polaris Amphitheater in Columbus, Ohio, at 5 p.m. as Geezer, of course, slept on the bus. I tracked down a phone he could use for an interview, then sat in the dressing room listening to the Dark Lord's stories.

I went to catering and realized there was no Ozzy. I asked Martha when he was due and she replied, "Half an hour ago." I ate with Keith against a backdrop of furtive whispering into walkie-talkies. I saw Bobby and asked what was up.

"Ozzy's late. He shoulda been here an hour ago," he said.

"We still on for tonight?"

He arched an eyebrow. "Your guess is as good as mine." I knew right then the gig would be pulled and went to tell Geezer. I tracked down Mick and whispered that he should check in with Tony, but he didn't get what I was hinting at. Eventually I spelled it out for him—I forgot most of the roadies were not Ozzy veterans, unable to sniff a cancellation in the air.

Our leaders retreated to the parking lot to hatch a plan. An Ozzfest jam was suggested, a set featuring the other acts playing Ozzy and Sabbath songs. Bobby told them it was an awful idea. However, the guy with the most Ozzy experience was overruled.

I got Geezer, and told him and Tony the show was off.

"Should we fire him?" joked Tony, deadpan, and we cracked up.

"Good to see he hasn't changed," said Geezer.

They were angry and disappointed and didn't want anything to do with the jam. "It's a dilution of the show," said Tony.

The all-star session ignited a rumpus backstage. Musicians charged into the band's dressing room to rehearse, revving an insane amount of noise, whooping and hollering and high-fiving . . . as Geezer started his interview on the phone next door. He couldn't hear, so I went to ask them to quiet down, making me popular with every other Ozzfest artist.

Joe washed his hands of it, saying, "After ten minutes they're all gonna start chanting 'Ozzy!'" But he changed his mind, yelling at the others, "C'mon! Let's do it!"

Mike hit the whiskey, a rarity to see him let rip, and phoned his wife, shouting how great everything was.

Pete Steele from Type O Negative asked me to put the lyrics to "N.I.B." into the prompter, so that track was added to whatever set list was being compiled by somebody somewhere. It was already a mess before a lick was played, but we caravaned to the stage, Mike, swigging from a bottle, flashing me his dick.

What snookered any chance of it working was the introduction by Phil Anselmo from Pantera. Instead of a clear statement like "Everyone, Ozzy is sick and can't play, you'll get refunded, but we're gonna jam a couple of songs for you," his rambling, muddled announcement was unintelligible. We couldn't make out what he said standing two yards away, so the bewildered fans out front had no chance.

It got worse. Two musicians I didn't recognize dived onto Ozzy's water guns and never gave them up, spraying water all over the stage, causing Robert to slip and fall during "Suicide Solution." We'd Machine Head singer Robb Flynn, Phil from Pantera, and Burt from Fear Factory, but the whole episode was ill-advised and shambolic, reeking with a the-idiots-have-taken-over-the-asylum vibe. Marilyn Manson appeared for "Crazy Train" but had no clue how it went, so he smashed a bottle of wine on the drum riser and threw beer into the crowd. Pete Steele came on to do "N.I.B.," but it turned out the band didn't know it, so he walked off again.

Phil reappeared to say goodbye, had two bottles thrown at him, and fled. We followed his lead and retreated to the safety of backstage. The crowd tore down the perimeter fence, overturned a car, and smashed up the box office. Police choppers arrived, sweeping with searchlights. We watched live reports on local TV in catering. The Ozzy old-timers had seen it all before; the newbies were acting like we heralded the Four Horsemen of the Apocalypse.

Again, counterintuitively, the cancellation resuscitated Geezer. On the six-hour trip to Chicago we sat up until 4 a.m. and he reeled off story after story about Sabbath and his drinking days. It was just like how Ozzy went on long monologues from topic to topic, and as soon as he called it a night, I transcribed his tales in my journal:

> How Ozzy blew off a gig in Philadelphia on the first tour, and their manager Patrick Meehan sent a security guard with a gun to drag him onstage. . . .
>
> In Germany, they bought air rifles and took potshots at a police station opposite their hotel from Bill's balcony. When they were spotted, they bolted to their rooms—Bill, who wasn't even involved, was passed out on his bed, and took the rap.
>
> Another time in Germany, Tony didn't realize they had been arrested, and thought the police were giving them a lift back to the hotel. . . .
>
> In Finland, Geezer wanted to blow up the hotel by driving a car into it. He flew to Barcelona to avoid being charged, but

> was picked up when they landed—still drunk, at the station he invited the attractive cop back to his hotel. . . .
>
> Once, he thought it would be a good idea to dig up his father's coffin, then he fell asleep upside down in a tree, convinced it would stop him getting a hangover.

Sharon rang at ten the next morning for details on the ill-fated jam. I saw her later and she relayed what happened on the plane to the show—Ozzy's doctor told him he needed three days' rest, but he didn't tell her until they were airborne, too late to get word to the venue. It led to an epic screaming match. He threw an almighty wobbler on the plane and hammered on the door to get out midair. When they landed he ran around the runway like a man possessed, and she sent Robert, who was with them on the jet, to try to calm him down. I'd never seen her so tired and stressed—she looked like the weight of the world was on her shoulders. She told me the canceled date would be tacked on at the end of the tour.

Geezer had an interview with a music magazine journalist to talk about his solo band's album and tour, and not wanting a journalist in his private space, asked to use my room. I sat reading in the hall until Sharon called me into theirs: the magazine photographer wanted to shoot Sabbath that evening, but she told me to refuse—it was in Geezer's contract he wouldn't do solo press while on the road with Sabbath, and though they'd let it slide thus far, this latest request was a bridge too far.

Geezer was unhappy about that, and when I woke him at 9 p.m. for the gig and told him Ozzy was already encoring, he complained about the quick run time upsetting his schedule. Then he had a stop over tour programs he wanted signed by every act but the Pantera road manager hadn't returned to me. The good-natured Geezer who regaled me for hours with brilliant old shenanigans only hours previously was gone.

We were hubbing from Chicago, and for days on end I'd toy shop with him in the Windy City. I went to a nearby mall to leave film to be developed, then returned later with him, so stopped off to pick up the prints. He got angry we'd to wait behind another customer. So after thirty minutes in a store with his moaning particularly virulent, I cracked. I said I needed to pick up contacts from the optometrist before it closed at 6 p.m. and ducked out. I just needed a break.

At the next show, Sharon called me into Ozzy's room and said she heard what happened. I told her about Geezer's constant complaints about anything and everything, and how I was dragged around toy stores for hours. She laughed, but she also brought back up his illicit string of interviews promoting his own band. She was juggling so much. She'd moved the band's room because Mike's loud music was still bothering Sabbath—but they'd put it beside Ozzy, and it was driving him nuts, too. "Go in and cut his hands off," she told Bobby.

I FLOORED THE ACCELERATOR IN THE juddering cart as we meandered along a barely discernible rutted muddy trail between the hodgepodge of buses and trucks backstage on a glorious Saturday evening. Four days after the chaos of Columbus we were at the Alpine Valley Music Theatre in East Troy, Wisconsin, and it was hiving with thirty-four thousand fans, three times what we attracted just one year earlier in 1996, stretching as far as the eye could see up the hill, the stage surrounded by a golf course like a moat circling a keep, picturesque chalets dotting the environs. I was driving Kelly and her friends on a tour of the grounds, but they wanted back to catch Marilyn Manson's set. I was in no hurry—the shock-rockers had not endeared themselves to us. ("Marilyn Manson" was the name of the front man, and the band.)

They threw their weight around from the get-go. At their first date, I checked the prompter during their show and their security guard pulled my pass and interrogated me why I was onstage. When I ducked into the pit, one of the crew tried to grab my camera, demanded the film, and threatened to eject me.

Marilyn Manson, real name Brian Warner, was at the height of his devil-worshipping notoriety, but we considered it amateur hour compared to Sabbath, a pale, gimmicky imitation of the originals (and the best) who cultivated that image three decades previously. Once, I was chatting with Tony on his bus when we spotted Manson standing beside us in the parking lot—he always dressed in black and wore two weird, differently colored contact lenses, but he'd a pager clipped to his belt. Knowing he couldn't tell who we were behind our tinted glass, I opened a small window and shouted, "Brian! Brian! What's the pager for? Is it in case Satan needs to get in touch with you?" and Tony laughed so hard he spat out his tea. Brian ignored me.

In Milwaukee, projectiles rained onto the stage, and Brian taunted, "You pussies at the back have terrible aim," which obviously invited a further cascade of bottles, cups, and cans. The audience chanted, "Ozzy! Ozzy!" throughout, and he cut out twenty minutes early and sloped off. In contrast, Ozzy was inspired, running over three songs into Sabbath's set and yelling in my ear, "Get me my tasseled shirt!" He ripped off his regular stage wear with that manic expression he got, put on the top, and shouted, "Now it feels like Black Sabbath!" Tony's fingers flying along the frets on his outros.

But even after replacing the monitors, the band was still furious with the sound onstage. "I want to kill that guy," said Tony about the new monitor engineer, and Ozzy raved at the top of his voice that the system was "a bunch of crap and the cheapest bunch of crap around." He said he couldn't help laughing when he walked across to Tony and had no idea where they were in the song, while when Tony played a snatch of "Sabbath Bloody Sabbath," he couldn't make out what track it was. "Then I come offstage and get a bollocking from Sharon for not getting into the gig," Ozzy said, "but I can't hear a fucking thing."

WE FLEW TO DENVER. PETE STAYED at the airport for the luggage, and when he brought Geezer's case to his room, it was ripped. Pete spotted the tear at the carousel and filled out the damage form on his behalf to claim compensation, but it put Geezer in a grumpy mood. He wanted to go to a toy store, but Sharon had asked me to book flights for her, so I told him I needed ten minutes to call my office; already pissed, he said he couldn't wait and stormed off.

Mike was committed to going back to his band Faith No More, meaning he couldn't do the makeup date in Columbus, so Shannon Larkin, the Ugly Kid Joe drummer, came to watch the show. Tony wanted a former Sab, Bobby Rondinelli, who was touring with Blue Öyster Cult, to do it. Rondinelli agreed and organized Blue Öyster Cult's old drummer as his cover for one concert—but then rejected the offer when told it only paid $1,000.

Robert had played with Shannon and advocated for him. When he was out of earshot, he grabbed my shoulders and said, "Dude! He's great! He says he can kick Rondinelli's ass! He just wants one shot at it, he says let him play two songs with them and he'll prove he can do it."

I took Shannon into the dressing room and introduced him to Tony, but when he left Tony told me, "I've seen that drummer play. He's crap." I got Geezer, who had been napping, and the Columbus gig was all the two of them talked about. Tony said he'd made multiple calls to Rondinelli to persuade him to do it, but Tony didn't blame him for turning it down for a grand. He said, "I think it's just gonna be a case of us having to grin and bear it."

It was funny, how much time and effort they were putting into a fifty-five-minute date in Columbus. Everything was shrouded in history and politics. Tony and Geezer even discussed asking Bill Ward. Geezer thought it might be insulting. Tony thought it wouldn't be if they asked the right way. They wondered if there were business concerns precluding it.

Then there was Ozzy. I was talking to Shannon in the hall outside our dressing room when he appeared. "Think you can handle it?" he asked Shannon.

"I won't let you down," Shannon replied.

Ozzy nodded. "Good enough for me," he said, and walked off.

A five-second interaction. Sabbath was vexed by the drummer situation, endlessly discussing it, convinced it wasn't going to work, troubled by a temporary substitute for a quick-fire set. Ozzy, though, had faith his manager secured a suitable surrogate. He wasn't second-guessing Sharon's decision, even though he was the one who would carry the show onstage in front of thousands.

In Phoenix, we booked a studio for Joe and Robert to rehearse with Shannon for Ozzy's gig. I rode with them there, but when we arrived, word had leaked that Ozzy's band was arriving. I took the bloke in charge aside and told him it wasn't cool for everyone to stand around and watch, so we kicked them all out. The guys spent a couple of minutes tuning up, but if Shannon was nervous, it didn't show. They launched into "I Don't Know"—and from the opening bars, he sounded astounding. "Let's go home now!" I yelled after the closing chords. They ran the set, and for a first practice we all thought it jaw-dropping.

I sang two tracks to help Shannon with the timing. The band wanted me to do the whole concert, but I was too shy, finally reluctantly agreeing to belt out a couple, even though I sounded terrible, so I'd a story to tell my grandchildren. ("Hey, kids, ever heard about the time your granddad stood in for Ozzy Osbourne with his band?") Sharon had returned to England to pick up the kids and wanted to know how it went, so when we got back to the hotel, I called to say Shannon had been a star. Then Robert, Joe, and I took Shannon for a few beers, as the Sabbath run-through was the next morning, and he was nervous.

Twelve hours later, Sabbath walked onstage for sound check at the Desert Sky Pavilion. Ozzy wasn't there, and without a singer, Tony refused to play. It was indicative of how seriously he took the reunion, wanting even a sound check to be perfect. "It was embarrassing playing in front of people when we were sorting stuff out, even if it wasn't a public performance," he told me.

Bobby handed me the mic, but I was terrified: it was one thing to sing with them in their dressing room, another to do it with Ozzy's band in a studio—this was fronting Black Sabbath with hundreds of workers watching. So Bobby tracked down the singer from Fear Factory instead, but although I ran the prompter he didn't know the songs, so he came in off-time and sang in the wrong places—in particular the track "Black Sabbath" was a mangled disaster. But Geezer and Tony heard enough to think Shannon could handle it—Geezer said to him, "Well done," after "War Pigs."

I STAYED UP LATE TALKING TO Joe and Robert, and got one hour of sleep before my phone rang. It was my mum, in a tizzy, and I knew it was serious if she was calling at 4 a.m.

She gabbled in one take, "I've just had Sharon on the phone from a taxi because her and the kids are booked on the nonstop from Gatwick to Phoenix, but they're stuck in traffic on the M25 and she doesn't think they're gonna make the flight and it's the only one today and she wants to know can we help. Can we? Is there anything I can do?"

I turned on the light, sat up, and rubbed my eyes, fighting to wake up and think.

She launched in again. "I've checked all the other airlines and British Airways are the only ones with a flight, so I don't—"

"Mum, it's okay, don't panic, do this: Call the special number for BA first-class reservations. Give them the locator and her Executive Club number because she's gold level. Tell them she's running late and request special assistance to rush them through the airport. She's such a good customer they'll maybe do it for them."

They were met at check-in, hurtled through security, sped through immigration—only for the gate staff to spot that Aimee's passport was four months out of date. They wouldn't let her board.

We needed a plan B, so they jumped into a car to Heathrow, me hoping the officers at the busier airport wouldn't spot the expired document, and I'd my mum boogie to book them tickets to LA instead. It worked, and after three hours of transatlantic calls, my poor mother growing ever more feverish each time, they made the gig after jumping onto a private plane from California, dragging along Michael, who said, "I was kidnapped!"

Although it wasn't the final date, we were losing some acts after Phoenix, so we had the end-of-tour party. It was like the last day of school, throngs of musicians, management, crew, and entourages lining the corridors at the venue. Ozzy was in a playful mood, jumping me in the hall to mock-punch me on the ear, then grabbing a handful of stink bombs and disappearing. He returned laughing and gagging. "They were all standing there, all these tattooed fuckers, rock stars, chicks—they all fucked off once they smelled them, though." Even Geezer radiated a sunnier disposition. A journalist asked him how he learned to play the bass: Geezer, straight-faced, said Frank Sinatra taught him.

THE FOLLOWING DAY, WE WENT TOY shopping, then out to dinner, and Geezer told me he'd enjoyed the tour. I nearly choked on my pizza. I silently gave thanks I was his assistant on a fun trek, and imagined how miserable he'd have been on the road if this had been a tour he hadn't enjoyed.

After eating, the two of us hopped onto Tony's bus to a rehearsal space an hour away from our hotel in Scottsdale. When we arrived I burst out laughing—it was a blazing Friday night in late June, and we'd rented a garage in an industrial complex in the middle of nowhere. The doors to most units were open, and teenagers milled outside, drinking and smoking, oblivious that arguably the greatest hard rock band ever had turned up to blast heavy metal classics. It was tiny and pokey and dark and we walked into a row: Ozzy's band was there with Shannon, and Bobby told them their time was up, but Joe wanted longer, yelling they'd only had twenty minutes. Bobby won. Sabbath ran the set, and although Shannon got pointers after every song, Tony and Geezer were delighted with him.

Sometimes, my mind drifts back to the incongruity of that scene. The hot, dusty landscape, the taste of the desert in my throat, the perpetual buzzing lights of the gray, bland commercial buildings reminding me of Brobdingnagian flycatchers, the smell of the slimy carpet, the chatter and murmur of the part-time musicians clustering outside, the bang of the metallic doors, the cramped, ill-lit studio, literal "garage bands" tuning up and bashing various mutilations of standard rock covers. And in the middle of it—Black Sabbath. We didn't speak to anyone, no one recognized them, there were no gaggles hanging outside our door. Did some guitarist wander out from the sweatbox on a cigarette break, hear Tony Iommi ripping through "Sweet Leaf," and mutter to himself, "Hmmm, those guys next door sound decent"?

SAN BERNARDINO WAS THE LAST SCHEDULED stop. Ozzy was unsure his voice would hold up and flip-flopped with a cancellation, but his solo set was great, and when I reported back to Sharon, holding a meeting in the production office, she rolled her eyes in an I-knew-he'd-be-fine kind of way. Tony painted his goatee pink for a laugh: his daughter was there, and Geezer said it was odd hearing him called "Dad" for the first time. (Geezer colored his mustache pink, too, but wiped it off before showtime.) Tony's daughter wanted Marilyn Manson's autograph, but Tony wouldn't let her go into his dressing room and sent a roadie to get it.

Sabbath was smoking, and the lads thought it was one of the best of the tour. Ozzy was on fire, mucking about, pulling faces and doing funny walks. It was Mike's last date before he returned to Faith No More, but Ozzy forgot to introduce him during his solo gig. So, during Sabbath's set, he gave him a huge buildup, saying he was a fantastic guy, a fantastic drummer, going on and on—then shouted, "Now, fuck off!"

Afterward, no abatement in the LA scene, barely room to move as doors flung open and slammed closed with management types and record company employees, while apart from the few of us heading to the makeup Columbus stop, it was the end of the road, so we were inundated with crew and support bands wanting cymbals and drumheads signed for souvenirs. Sepultura, who had supported Ozzy the past summer, asked about my business, and I was touched they remembered why I left in 1996.

But amid the Tinseltown wackiness, more clouds of doom. Geezer sarcastically told Gloria they should run a competition for the first employee of his label to spot his record in a store. She replied, "Are you psychic? How can you moan about something that hasn't even happened?" He was upset we were flying to Columbus via Chicago and told me to switch his ticket to a stop-off in St. Louis. I worked on that until he changed his mind and said not to bother. Then he was annoyed we'd a limo to the airport because he wanted a town car. We flew to Ohio and spent our last afternoon together toy shopping. For old times' sake.

TWO WEEKS AFTER THE SHAMBLES OF the jam in Columbus, we were back. Backstage felt eerie, like we'd crash-landed on a desert island, the contrast especially marked after LA. Neurosis was the support, but all the other buses and trucks and crew and musicians had gone—no video guys or laser techs, a stripped-down stage without backdrops, props, or effects. The sound check was scrapped as, en route to Columbus, the air-conditioning on Ozzy's jet malfunctioned. The heat spiked, smoke billowed from the unit, and they turned around and changed planes. When I told Geezer, he puffed out his cheeks and said, "Thank God I wasn't on it, I would have been freaking out."

In the last minutes before the show, Shannon felt brittle and Ozzy delighted in winding him up further at every opportunity. Ozzy came in between sets, saying, "My voice is fucked, so just go up there and have a laugh. The audience will." Right to the end, underestimating himself. Before the Sabs went on, Shannon presented the three of them with bookmarks to thank them for letting him play, an unlikely gift for the masters of metal, but a tangible token of appreciation for what it meant to him.

Then, for the last time, I walked them onstage.

Black Sabbath signed off with a belter. The 19,000 fans—1,500 more than the original show—were instantaneously into it, jumping en masse, their herd mentality transplanting excitement to the band. Ozzy soaked Geezer with the water gun, then turned it on Tony—Bobby and I stared at each other, braced for the backlash—but Tony laughed it off and pulled down Ozzy's trousers in retaliation (later, he said it was hard to get him back for anything because he does everything to himself). Ozzy whipped out his dick and waved it around, introduced Shannon as Cheetah, and said Bill wasn't there because Geezer hated him. Even Geezer smiled at that.

Afterward Ozzy came into the dressing room, and while the three of them ate and I packed up around them, they conducted a lengthy postmortem, both on the tour and the drumming situation. Ozzy did nearly all the talking.

He said, "This has been fucking great, but I don't know about you guys, it just feels to me like there's been something missing. I mean, Bill . . ." He trailed off, sat back, and crossed his legs. "I tell ya, when I was in LA, somebody gave me a local paper that had an interview with him in it. And you know what he said? 'I'd play with Sabbath for free.' What a load of bollocks. It was his fucking manager who put the mockers on the whole fucking thing last time."

He said four years previously Sharon predicted to him that if there was ever a reunion, Bill wouldn't be part of it. But Geezer and Tony agreed they would have preferred to have him onstage with them, and all three said they wanted him back in the band if he got in condition to play.

"Say what you want about the mad old bastard, but he was fucking light-years ahead of his time," said Ozzy.

"He invented techno with his drumming," said Geezer.

"What the fuck's techno?" asked Ozzy, and as often happened, that thought led him down a rabbit hole and a rant about the music Louis, his son from his first marriage, listened to, saying it sounded like there was something wrong with the heating unit.

He was interrupted by Shannon sticking his head in the door to say goodbye. They told him he did well, so he left happy, departing to Geezer's nonsensical farewell: "I'll see you in Belgium."

Later Shannon asked me, "Is the Ozzfest going to Europe?" and I explained it meant absolutely nothing and was just his sense of humor.

MY LAST DAY WITH GEEZER STAYED true to form.

Five minutes before our limo to the airport was due, I rang Mick to make sure he was ready. We had been celebrating with Shannon until 5 a.m. and I woke him—he slept through his wakeup call. Geezer threw a fit in the lobby. He was determined to leave him behind, and it was all I could do to talk him out of it, reassuring him we'd plenty of time. He didn't speak on the ride, and in departures he was still mad at Mick, so there was no drawn-out farewell. I gave him a present, a framed photo I took of him in the sea in Florida, and he thanked me, then flew to St. Louis, while Mick and I headed to LA.

With Geezer airborne, as Mick and I had a farewell beer in the terminal,

I reflected on the tour. What was going on with him? Why was he so angry when inconvenienced by a few minutes the odd time? I can't overemphasize how unhappy he was, moaning nonstop about everything around the clock. It didn't make sense. After years of touring with an underperforming Sabbath, or being a hired hand with Ozzy, he was back with his own band, garnering rave reviews, earning a fortune. He was transformed from the guy I went drinking with in Darlington in 1988, in Paris in 1989, or even the teetotaler I hung with in Chicago in 1995. An occasional late-night delve into sepia-tinged rollicking stories was a flash of the old Geezer, his shoulders shaking as he chuckled uncontrollably, but those were few and far between. He said he suffered from depression after leaving Ozzy's band, fifteen months previously. Despite his career getting spectacularly back on track, perhaps he was still waging a private war against debilitating mental health issues.

Maybe he felt I was foisted upon him by Sharon. Tony always picked up the tab at dinner with Mick, and the Osbournes never let anyone pay for anything. However he and I split checks, though he always chose the restaurant and earned more than fifty times my wage. I was paid royally and never expected a free ride, but perhaps his not offering to treat me once was symptomatic of some festering resentment.

However, part of it was my fault. I'm laid-back, but I found the job a struggle. Six weeks straight, with a couple of days off, I spent traipsing around toy stores, holding his bags for hours while he flicked through comics and pored over *Star Wars* figures, him complaining nonstop. It took it out of me. But it was my job, and I should have been better at it. I realized I wasn't cut out to be a personal assistant. Friendship and employment were different.

At LAX I rented a car to drive to Sharon's new office. She turned up with Cube, a band of English teenagers in town to meet with record companies, then Aimee and Kelly arrived, and I was told I was taking them all to the Magic Mountain theme park. I loved how they considered me part of the family, and I was used to rolling with whatever. I chaperoned a bunch of sixteen-year-olds and the girls on rides for four hours.

IT WAS 1:30 A.M. WHEN I finally climbed aboard Mike Inez's boat, him greeting me with "Did Black Sabbath's keyboard player get laid or what?" and guffawing, so I knew Keith spilled the beans to him about my trusty pickup line. I crawled into bed at 3 a.m., but he woke me the following morning by calling, "Hey, Stephen—your part in 'Johnny Blade' is next up!" so I knew it was going to run and run. He was dating the singer Poe, and she joined in with the piss-taking, calling me "Thirteen," my old crew nickname. It was merciless.

My second Fourth of July in the States was spent at a party hosted by Guns N' Roses drummer Matt Sorum, high in the Hollywood Hills, a primo pad with an awe-inspiring view. From his patio we watched the fireworks popping all around as multiple municipalities alternated through displays, a landscape of shimmering lights, the panorama breathtaking as the chromatic bursts splashed into life below, not above.

Sharon invited me over on July 6. No one was home, but the Osbournes appeared twenty minutes later and Ozzy hopped out of the car, ran over, and said, "Can you do me a favor—go to Toys 'R' Us for me," and bent double, laughing. Tony was there, too, and I left him and the Osbournes chatting in the kitchen while I played laser tag with Jack and Kelly. After that we jumped into the pool for a couple of hours, then I went with all five Osbournes to see *Men in Black*, but it was sold out. We went to dinner instead. Afterward I took Jack and Aimee to the 10 p.m. showing, and dropped them home after midnight.

Ozzy and Sharon were watching TV, and before I left, I thanked her for giving me the chance to go back on the road. I didn't want her to think I was ungrateful, difficult though it was at times with Geezer. Ozzy told me he was knackered, saying it was the hardest thing he had ever done, and he was glad it was over.

"Oh, give him a couple of months at home and he'll be fine," said Sharon, pinching his cheek and smiling.

I left the next day. My diary reads "I usually look forward to getting home after a tour, but I am not at all this time. I was on the deck of Mike's boat thinking, *Why am I going from Sunset Boulevard to Belfast?*"

#205

NEC

BIRMINGHAM, ENGLAND

December 5, 1997

THEY REELED IN BILL Ward. All four original Black Sabbath members would play together for the first time in two decades.

Or maybe they wouldn't. Just forty-eight hours before the big event, Bill confronted Sharon. He threatened to walk away from the two hometown shows in Birmingham unless he received more money. He thought he had her over a barrel and she'd crumble.

He hadn't reckoned with Mrs. O.

She flew into the chilly production office we'd set up in the depths of an English winter and mobilized her team, all of us snapping to attention, scrambling on every available line. Michael jumped on the phone to Vinny Appice in LA, the Sabbath drummer from the Ronnie James Dio era, and persuaded him to fly over. I reserved a flight and hotel room, giving him forty-five minutes to throw his stuff together. Bobby sent a car to his home, the production manager tracked down a kit, someone arranged a tape of songs, all in a few minutes. While we worked, Sharon danced around the room, swaying her hips and waving her skirt, singing, "La di la di la" at the top of her voice. I don't know whether it was her way of dealing with the stress, or if she was showing us there was no need for consternation.

Two hours later, she told Bill if he didn't do it, they had Vinny ready and waiting. His participation was always in doubt, so she had a concert advertising poster that didn't feature him—and she unfurled it with a flourish. "Look—your face isn't even on this. We don't need you. Why do you think you deserve the same amount of money as my husband?" (Ironically, she planned to present him with a whack of cash anyway, as both shows were near sellouts.)

Bill backed down from his late-stage brinkmanship. He seemed a reasonable bloke but surrounded by nutcases—his assistant was a kooky fella in a beret and blue John Lennon glasses who looked permanently angry.

FOUR DAYS BEFORE THE FIRST GIG, I flew to Birmingham and hired a minivan; I was the driver and runner as well as handling travel. The next morning, I drove to Heathrow to pick up Sharon's management crew arriving from LA, then we went back to the Midlands and checked into the same hotel we stayed at for Donington in 1996. We had two days of run-through for sound and production at the NEC.

Five months after the US tour I got on great with Geezer and Tony—it was those around them who were the problem. The difference between an event run by Sharon and one put on by Sabbath was stunning. Ozzy fostered an easygoing family atmosphere—here the vibe was bitter. When they went out under the Ozzfest umbrella it was obvious Ozzy was the star, but back home on their old stomping ground, Sabbath viewed the reunion as a more collective undertaking. Gloria wanted to put flyers on seats advertising a

Geezer solo show, and that caused an argument. She hit back, countering that the merchandise stalls sold Ozzy shirts. Tony's manager reveled in posturing, while the whackos with Bill were an hourly headache. I drove Sharon to the hotel, and she told me how aggravating it was—if she wanted to do anything, she was forced to consult three others, none of whom had achieved anything like as much success in the business.

The day before the first date was Ozzy's birthday, and I went with Sharon and the kids into his room to wake him up. He was solemn, saying he hadn't slept well and was worried about the show—still riddled with insecurity despite a career every singer would have sold their soul for. I bought him a pair of stone devil bookends—"You stupid fucker, what didya do that for?" was his typically Ozzy response.

At the venue, anxiety dripped from the rafters, a cauldron of negative emotions. I picked up Geezer from his house and he was a bundle of nerves, and you could smell the rancor wafting from Bill's camp—not helped by Vinny's presence, like Banquo's ghost at Macbeth's banquet—while the cherry on top of this crucible of passive aggressiveness was Geoff Nicholls, the band's real offstage keyboard player. (John fulfilled that role in the States.) I'd impersonated him to pull chicks; it turned out he was a royal pain in the arse.

Bobby and I were in the hall when Geoff asked us to find him a dressing room, even though he wasn't changing for the concert. Bobby didn't reply and shot me a look.

"It's a psychological thing, walking out of somewhere and onto the stage," Geoff said.

Bobby blindly reached behind him and opened the nearest door. "Here—use that room," he said, and I turned away so he wouldn't see me laughing. We took to calling Geoff "the Lion King" because of his eighties hurricane of a blond wig and caricatured rock star getup—and sang, "In the jungle, the mighty jungle," whenever he entered a room.

We Osbourne employees were friends for years and knew each other's foibles and moods. Dissolving into the Sabbath machine—on their home turf—was a mentally exhausting experience. Yet once they hit the stage, the bickering and pettiness evaporated. Sabbath was supersonic, the audience in raptures, howling along to anthems they hadn't heard played by the original members in nineteen years, Ozzy's vocals on "Spiral Architect" in particular searing into my heart.

There were heavy hitters there, like Queen guitarist Brian May, while Henry Rollins came in specially from the US. I asked him to write me an excuse note: Julie had flown over from North Carolina and was waiting for me in Northern Ireland. After both dates we sat with Sharon in the lobby drinking coffee and eating cookies. She and Ozzy had to stay in England, but Aimee and Kelly needed to get back to school in California, so Michael volunteered me to take them—"Led like a lamb to the slaughter," he joked later. Julie was a Rollins fan, so he chivalrously scribbled me a get-out-of-jail note, as she'd be in Belfast on her own for a week.

I skipped going to bed, drove to Heathrow for the 7 a.m. flight back to Belfast, had three hours at home, then went right back to the airport and flew to Welders. Sharon woke me at lunchtime and we were driven to the airport, Ozzy checking through my head for gray hairs before I left. In LA, we had a suite at the Beverly Hills Hotel and I shuttled the kids between tutors, interspersed with shopping trips to the Beverly Center.

After three days Sharon arrived and I went into the office every day, helping with anything from writing press releases to addressing Christmas cards. Sharon was both manager and mom—and occasionally manager to her kids and mom to musicians. Aimee, fourteen, could be a handful: Sharon bought three extortionately priced tickets for the *Titanic* movie premiere for her, Aimee, and Kelly, but Aimee wanted to go with her friend, not her sister. "You've ruined everything," she screamed at her, and I felt for Sharon—first Sabbath, then the difficult teenage years.

I took on my last assignment for the Osbournes. Ozzy was doing three weeks in Oceania, and with Mike indisposed with Faith No More, Sharon asked Randy Castillo back. Then she worried Joe wasn't cutting it in the studio, so called Zakk. With those two on board, she thought she might as well go the whole hog and get Mike Inez as well, re-creating the *No More Tears* lineup. That was a tough call—Sharon said she felt terrible about ditching Robert, and the kids begged her not to.

She took us all out to dinner—the old (new) band and Robert, who must have wondered why they were there. I had arranged to go out on Sunset the following night with Joe and Robert, but I just couldn't face them, knowing they were about to get canned for the tour. I said I had to look after the girls for Sharon and cried off, and went to the movies instead.

The next morning, I was packing up when Michael called. Joe, unexpectedly, was in reception, with a demo tape for Sharon. She was on her way back from a business meeting, so he asked me to run interference. I sprinted to the lobby, found Joe, and told him Sharon was going to be out for hours and he could leave it with me. He was in no rush to depart, shooting the breeze, but I was bullshitting on the hoof, ushering him out without seeming like I was ushering him out.

It was painful. I was fond of both Joe and Robert, but my first loyalty was to the Osbournes. It always had been—even as a roadie on epic tours, my friendship with Ozzy and Sharon was more important than anything.

I flew out of Los Angeles and touched down in Belfast on December 14, my mum's birthday. I brought outrageously expensive silk pajamas from the Beverly Hills Hotel for her. Handing them over was a physical symbol of me parting with my glamorous, five-star Hollywood life. My time working for Ozzy was over. The next day I went to the office, just a bloke with a run-of-the-mill job in an Ulster travel agency.

PART FOUR
LIGGER

#208

GREAT WOODS CENTER FOR THE PERFORMING ARTS

MANSFIELD, MASSACHUSETTS

July 9, 1998

THE SUMMER OF 1998, after the NEC gigs in December, the four original Sabs re-formed. Sort of.

As expected, Bill's health was the problem. After all the bluster and disputes, they finally inked a deal—then he suffered a heart attack during rehearsals. Vinny, the bloke parachuted into Birmingham after Bill's brinkmanship, returned as the drummer, not a standby.

But Keith and I were out.

I would have loved to have been on the short European run, so I was disappointed, but when I hadn't received a call a couple of months out, I knew I hadn't made the cut. Later, Keith and I heard we were victims of politics; the Ozzfest was Sharon's creation, she controlled every aspect—and Sabbath wanted a bigger role. We weren't owed a thing: we enjoyed the ride, and neither of us harbored an ounce of acrimony.

But I wanted to see the gig, even if it was at my own expense, so my friend Patrick and I booked a weekend in Budapest for the opening date in June. I met him at Heathrow, and as we turned the corner to the gate, we were assaulted by a flying mane of yellow hair—keyboard player Geoff Nicholls. I looked past him and a row of seats hummed with black leather, as the band was on our flight. I wondered why I didn't see Geezer, then spotted him at the desk, him and his assistant arguing with the gate agent about hand luggage, and I'd a wee chuckle that I didn't have that headache anymore.

When we landed, we jumped onto their bus downtown, just like old times (or six months previously). Not content with that freeloading, we also mooched a ride with them to the stadium on show day. We went to their hotel to meet, and in the lobby saw Ozzy, lounging on a couch, bored, and eager to chat. "Sharon is out buying half of fucking Yugoslavia," he said, then launched into what happened with Bill, saying, "We had to get Carmine Appice back," and I took the piss out of him for mixing up Vinny with his brother, who was also a drummer.

I was back to being young Stephen. Patrick and I stood on the stage for Sabbath, and it was superlative. We rode back in Ozzy's van, and he was amped, a nonstop blitz of tales that had us in stitches.

> "In the Sabbath days, we all fucked this chick and we all got a dose—I mean all of us—the band, the crew, everyone. So we all file down to this clinic and they're all saying, 'Go on, Ozzy, you go first, tell the bint what's wrong with you.'
>
> "So I go up to this chick and my bottle goes. I point to my neck and say, 'I've hurt my neck' when she asks what the problem is. She says, 'Take a seat over there, then, sir.'
>
> "Next thing, the rest of them go up one by one and they all say, 'I've got the same as him.' The poor girl didn't know what was going on."

A couple of weeks later the Ozzfest debuted in England with a bumper gate of fifty thousand at Milton Keynes Bowl (I stood beside actress Minnie Driver onstage as she rocked out to the Foo Fighters), then Ozzy had a month stateside with his solo band. I got a bus from Belfast to Dublin, flew to Boston, rented a car, and drove to Mansfield, Massachusetts.

I caught up with everyone, then watched the concert, one of Ozzy's best in years, the first time I ever heard "Believer," a rarely played track from the seminal *Diary of a Madman* album, his voice spine-tingling after giving up smoking a few months before. The production manager's teenage nephew operated the prompter, which made me laugh. Instead of denting my ego to see it was a job so simple a schoolboy could do it, it made me grateful the Osbournes had fashioned a job on tour for me. It was my third gig in a month, across half the world: Hungary, England, and the US.

I was a fan again, blowing my savings globe-trotting to watch my hero.

After the show, I sat in the band's dressing room talking to them until they had to board the bus. Sharon, who also had a bus for her and the kids, made a point of coming in to say goodbye, and said she'd see me at the next stop in Pittsburgh. She assumed I was riding on the band's bus, but it was a one-shot deal for me. Joe had been hammering at me to go with them since he came offstage to catch up, wanting me to leave my car at the gig, ride the bus to their hotel in Pittsburgh, take a taxi to the airport the next day, jump onto a flight back to Boston, then take another taxi forty miles to pick up the car.

I mean, I was tempted. Just for old times' sake. But nine hours on the bus with the lads overnight was going to cost me hundreds of dollars. I was still a huge fan, but I was also a twenty-eight-year-old (halfway) responsible adult and couldn't justify that. Teenage Stephen would have been so disappointed. Instead, I said my farewells and crashed at a cheap airport motel after being on the go for twenty-six hours, writing in my diary, "**It felt different today, not the same excitement. There is no doubt I am growing up—I don't think it's a good thing!**"

A FEW MONTHS LATER, A FEDEX messenger walked into my office and handed me an envelope—I think it was the first package I ever received from an international courier. I ripped open the cardboard to reveal a ridiculously splendid invitation to Ozzy's fiftieth-birthday party at the Beverly Hills Hotel. I had a plus-one, but greedy as always, I put in a cheeky request and asked to bring two guests, my mum and Julie.

The Osbournes were as accommodating as always, and I flew to LA with my mum and Lynn, flying in Julie from North Carolina.

We walked down a sweeping staircase into the Crystal Ballroom at the Beverly Hills Hotel, and although only minutes after the 8 p.m. start, the party was heaving, many of the four hundred guests arriving early.

A string ensemble welcomed us, playing what I thought was background music, as we stopped for a rest halfway down. My mum's knee was troubling her so she was using a cane, and an attendant asked if she wanted to jump into the elevator instead. "Oh no, I'm fine, I don't want to miss a thing," she replied, examining the hollow banister, overflowing with jelly beans and marshmallows. At the bottom, four giant glass crosses cradled mammoth candles, and as we glided across the white fur–lined floor, my mum said to me, "That's an Ozzy song those musicians are playing, right? I recognize it." I stopped walking and listened—it was, indeed, a classical version of "No More Tears." The Ozzy fanatic schooled by his mother at his hero's party.

It was like nothing I had ever experienced, even after years of hobnobbing with multimillionaire rock stars. Mike Inez called it "Ozzyland," and I knew what he meant, it seemed like every musician he ever employed was there, as well as stars like the Red Hot Chili Peppers' singer Anthony Kiedis.

The second we walked into the main room, Ozzy spotted us and came over, smiling. He remembered my mum right away, though he hadn't seen her in thirteen years. We caught up for a minute, then I said we didn't want to hog his time, but he told me he didn't know half the guests. I introduced him to Julie, and he shook her hand with that devilish look in his eye, saying, "Ohhhhhh, I can tell you a few stories about this guy. . . ."

"Ozzy—someone wants you over there," I said, butting in, and we laughed. But I was glad we had a special moment together among the hurly-burly—after all, I would never have met her if I hadn't been in London for his birthday party in 1995.

We moved on across the room to where Ross Halfin, the *Kerrang!* photographer who took our photo at Rock in Rio, had set up a studio. He took a picture, and it was set into an Ozzy wallet, though Ross was kind enough to send me a high-definition print when we got home as well.

We delved farther into the interconnecting venue, past huge balloons tethered to the furnishings with images of Ozzy's face morphing through different ages projected onto them. There were waterfalls and ice sculptures, and as we were funneled outside, dozens of trees with hundreds of white flowers individually hand-tied on lined the passageway. A host of ethnic food stations were set up in the courtyard, like the Indian tent, where they threw petals as you entered before you sat cross-legged on a bed listening to sitar music.

Through another door, roulette and poker tables, the croupiers handing you envelopes of cash to play with, the bills featuring Ozzy's face. We explored every nook and cranny: an artist carved animals out of candle wax; a fortune teller twirled tarot cards; a Chinese psychic read your palm; gorgeous models in revealing outfits were draped in snakes. Hovering around us as we coasted through the attractions, cigarette girls circulated, handing out sweets, matches, chocolate bats, and napkins, all inscribed with "Ozzy's 50th." And as you'd expect at his party, music everywhere—myriad entertainment spanning drag queens to a swing band to fifties-style dancers.

At 11 p.m. Ozzy cut his crucifix-shaped cake, but I knew he was uncomfortable with the fuss, as offstage he was always embarrassed to be the center of attention. When a fifty-strong gospel choir sang "Happy Birthday," I kept my eyes on him, and sure enough, he used the distraction to duck out. The party ended a couple of hours later, though I, my mum, and Julie sat with Sharon until 2:30 a.m. I told Ozzy's son Louis I was knocked out by the extravagance. "Yeah, Dad told me they spent forty thousand dollars on it," he said. I knew that was rubbish, and probably what Sharon told Ozzy. The following day I found out that forty grand didn't even cover the flower bill.

Three days after the party, Lynn and I went to their new house, only a few doors down from the Beverly Hills Hotel. I had Ozzy's birthday present, but he was out, so Sharon told me to wait for him. We sat chatting in the kitchen for a couple of hours before he came home. He was much more at ease away from the hullabaloo, and when I handed him my present he joked, "Is it ticking?" Almost fourteen years later, I was still the kid from the Troubles in Northern Ireland. After tearing off the paper he held up the thick, squat box I wrapped it in and said, "A house brick! Just what I always wanted!" Really it was a World War II book.

We had always been bonded by our shared fascination with the conflict. The gift sparked him telling me about his recent trip to Auschwitz, a place he had wanted to see for decades, and as often happened, it led us into an epic discussion about wartime destinations we'd visited.

The following day I drove my mum to Las Vegas for two nights, and while we were away, Lynn stayed with Sharon for emotional support—Ozzy went into the Cedars-Sinai clinic the same day we left for a new detox treatment that flushed his system, then hours later, their dog, Tank, drowned in their pool. We returned for three more days in LA, and the afternoon we left Sharon insisted we visit for tea. She laid on a magnificent spread that tells you so much about her generous character. Her husband detoxing, the beloved family pet dead in tragic circumstances, a hectic work schedule—and yet she put everything aside to entertain Lynn, my mum, and me.

Friends who worked for British Airways got us into the executive lounge and upgraded for the twelve-hour flight back to London, so my mum went home in style. As we sipped champagne in business class, she kept repeating, “Can you believe Sharon Osbourne actually served me tea in her dining room?” It was fourteen years since my mum wrote that letter to the fan club, and I sensed the story she had set in motion was winding down.

#212

NEC

BIRMINGHAM, ENGLAND

December 22, 1999

MY MUM HAD SUCH a ball in LA that for her Christmas present, I booked us back to the States eight weeks later. Five nights in Manhattan—of course, the trip wasn't completely altruistic on my part, as it coincided with Sabbath playing the Continental Airlines Arena (now called the Meadowlands Arena) in New Jersey. I flew in Julie to meet us, and I waited at the box office with her laminate. Dave Grohl appeared but wasn't on the guest list, so I introduced myself and gave him Julie's. I knew Michael would replace it.

Two fans who looked like Beavis and Butt-Head personified queued beside me, and one nudged the other. "Dude, that's the guy who split up Nirvana," he said. The other shrugged. "Well, somebody needed to split them up."

It was a fabulous show we watched from the mixer with Lars Ulrich and ex–tennis player John McEnroe, and I heard my favorite Sabbath song, "After Forever," live for the first time. I hung by the dressing rooms to say hello, but for the first time in years I didn't pop in, as it was the usual helter-skelter Big

Apple mess in the hallway, and I didn't want to add to the volume of liggers begging for an audience. Michael told me later Ozzy was saving his voice and only nodding or shaking his head anyway. That made me feel better—three years earlier, almost to the day, the same venue was my first official date as part of the road crew.

I flew to England twice to see Sabbath in December 1999, a gig in London and two in Birmingham. When the original band reunited for the first time in two decades for their triumphant homecoming appearances in December 1997, it was a jaw-dropping spectacle and the expectation insane. It was only natural the excitement level dropped after that, two years of touring dulling the sheen of the re-formation.

Indeed, the second Birmingham concert signaled an ending to me. Afterward, I was reluctant to poke my head into either Ozzy's or Sabbath's dressing room and balanced on a flight case at the end of the hall as well-wishers, friends, and family fluxed around. Once I'd have ambled down the corridor, knocked on the door, and said hello, but as I sat in the drafty backstage, detached, idly kicking the hard, cold metal container, I distinctly remember feeling like an outsider, like I no longer belonged.

Ozzy was being walked to his car and stopped when he saw me.

"Hey, Steve, how's it going? Ready for Christmas?" he asked.

"Doing great, Oz, how are you?" I replied, but then he had to leave, and that was the extent of our interaction.

AS THE MILLENNIUM TICKED OVER, MY relationship with the Osbournes, and with those around them, changed. Connections were forged on the road, where we spent twenty-four hours living on top of each other, working together cheek by jowl, every day for months. We lived in a social bubble decades before the term was coined. Instead, it turned into a regular friendship like perhaps you had with schoolmates whom you once knew well, but only saw now and then. Of course, some of those guys shape you or help guide your life path.

I feel humbled and privileged I was part of their inner circle between 1985 and 1999. I began as a wide-eyed fifteen-year-old fanatic, became a trusted staffer, and by the time I was thirty, I had matured into a loyal confidant. I bet during Ozzy's five-decade career in such a brutal occupation, few were so close for so long. Even regular friendships peter out, never mind those forged in a celebrity crucible and amplified through the lens of fame with its inherent pressures.

Ozzy's life changed, too. He never again did a world tour on the same scale after Retirement Sucks, and in the following twenty-four years he only released three studio albums. Sabbath played shows, but while I revered Sabbath's spot atop the pantheon of rock, I remained first and foremost a fan of Ozzy's solo output. Rather than spend weeks crisscrossing the States to see a handful of gigs, I vacationed in places like Cambodia and Antarctica. The more time elapsed, the fewer tour personnel I knew, and the orbit of employees, friends, and band members circuiting the Osbournes revised.

With the twentieth century drawing to a close, it was time for Ozzy to ease up his road work, and for me to—reluctantly—grow up as we entered our next act.

#213

MILTON KEYNES BOWL

MILTON KEYNES, ENGLAND

May 26, 2001

IN 2000 I MARRIED Julie and I owed it to Ozzy—we met because I was in London for his birthday party in 1995. We honeymooned at a Maui hotel he recommended and stopped in LA for three days on the way home—it coincided with his birthday, so we called to see him. He dramatically propelled open the front door, yelling, "Mister and missus!" He looked great, enthusing over where we were in Hawaii and reliving a disastrous vacation in Tahiti, and showing off Sharon's present, a statue of Satan.

My agency rallied, much of the turnaround down to Sharon giving me her business. I worked it out—combining my wages for touring with Geezer with the Osbourne commission on flights, I recouped the money stolen by my office thief, and cleared my dad's loan. I wrote to her to express my gratitude.

When Sabbath headlined the Ozzfest at Milton Keynes in May 2001, I got the chance to tell her in person. I went backstage and tracked her down in the production office. She hugged me and said, "Thank you for your letter, it was so sweet," but it was me who needed to thank her.

I got calls for Ozzy World matters regularly. The nanny at Welders would ring; there were overnight faxes from Michael in LA and flights for their business manager, Colin, in London. Louis and Ozzy's daughter from his first marriage, Jessica, often got in touch, asking if I knew Ozzy's travel plans, or because Sharon was flying them to California to visit. My little high street Belfast travel agency was a nerve center for all things Osbourne.

OCCASIONALLY I WAS UNDER ORDERS TO feign ignorance to certain callers. Maybe Sharon was at a clandestine artist meeting, perhaps a journalist was booked on a cheaper flight with a layover than a musician on a nonstop, or Ozzy was in London but wanted to avoid an annoying relation.

But I was an old hand at it, as on the road, I told countless wee white lies. I apologized I didn't know where Sharon was when a pain in the arse from her past turned up backstage, called Ozzy away to fictitious appointments to cut short meet and greets, and apologetically interrupted interviews when an urgent call came into the production office for one of the band.

I was almost rumbled when I'd a drink on our day off with a pretty girl from the management office of a support act. She inquired what I'd been doing, and I said Ozzy pulled a radio appearance at the last minute, so I dashed over with the band instead. She wondered how we explained his no-show, and I said we told them his grandmother died.

"That's our standard cop-out for getting him out of things he doesn't want to do, we say she's just passed away," I explained.

"But she really did die last week, right?" she asked.

It hit me—we used the excuse to get him out of a photo shoot with her band five days previously.

"Oh yes, she passed last week, that's where we got the idea," I said, and changed the subject. You could tell the same lie over and over again and get away with it before the internet.

When I was staying at Welders during the Retirement Sucks UK dates, I faked being Ozzy on a phoner, disguising my voice, banging the receiver and crunching paper, attempting to convince the interviewer there was interference so he'd end it quickly. "You know you're going to hell with the rest of us, don't you, Stephen?" Sharon would say when she roped me into doing something nefarious, and cackle.

She expanded her artist stable to include the Smashing Pumpkins, and to celebrate the new millennium, MTV ran an elaborate contest called Blind Date, in which winners were flown to Dublin for a private show at a tiny theater, unaware who would perform. She invited Julie and me along and we got to experience a mega act rocking a box-sized venue.

Twenty days later, Michael woke me in the middle of the night. Sharon was fed up with singer Billy Corgan, notoriously difficult to work with, and quit on the spot. She needed first-class tickets for her, her assistant, Aimee, and the tour manager to get home to LAX. I grabbed the pen and pad I kept by my bed and booked them on the next flight out of Munich.

"Put everything on this card," her assistant said, giving me an American Express number. "Put anything else you like on it. You want to buy a house with it?" he asked as Sharon and the tour manager laughed in the background. Billy's office rang a few days later, asking what the charge was for and where I got the number, but they never disputed it.

I reconnected with Ross Halfin, the photographer from Rio, when Sharon had him call to reserve a flight to the States for a photo shoot with Ozzy. From then on, he gave me his bookings, and thanks to him I'd one of my most unforgettable travel agency moments. He rang from Led Zeppelin guitarist Jimmy Page's place, as one of Jimmy's domestic staff wanted a flight to Brazil. When I phoned back an hour later, Jimmy answered, saying he was alone. Envisage the dialogue if Jimmy Page spoke to a bloke with an Irish accent about a South American trip he knew nothing about because it was his housekeeper's. After a couple of minutes of muddled miscommunication, I suggested I ring back later, and he agreed. I was ecstatic—our conversation went EXACTLY how I imagined it would if I ever caught a befuddled seventies guitar god off guard at home.

IN 2002, ***BLIZZARD OF OZZ*** **AND** *Diary of a Madman* were reissued with bonus material, and Michael, knowing I had been a devoted collector, asked me to courier him the different versions of the early singles. I was happy to help, glad to reprise my role from the eighties, when Lynn called me "our consultant." He gave me their account number so I could charge the cost to them, but the Belfast branch of FedEx couldn't process it. Instead, he said to pay the fee and send an invoice to the business manager, Colin, who would reimburse me.

I blame no one but myself. I should have paid extra to insure the package. The vinyl took years to collect, and I packed it all into a box and handed it to the messenger. Among those records was my most precious piece of memorabilia, a bona fide rock artifact, a "Crazy Train" 7-inch single signed by the original band: Ozzy, Bob Daisley, Lee Kerslake, and Randy Rhoads. But niggling away at me was that Colin's office was perpetually busy, and it would take a while for them to get around to paying me. I was so dumb. The parcel cost about £40 to send, and enhanced insurance wouldn't have added much more.

Two weeks after it was picked up, Michael asked when I'd be sending it. Realizing it hadn't arrived, I called the company. They lost track of it in Memphis. Michael was incredulous I sent a sleeve with Randy's autograph—he hadn't realized it was a signed copy. He emailed, "Are you crazy!!??"

I called FedEx daily for updates, while Michael had a colleague monitor eBay in case it popped up. After a month, I accepted it was gone and filled in a claim form. Michael sent me a supporting letter from Sharon, explaining how precious the item was, and it was so rare, even the Osbournes didn't own Randy's autograph. I didn't know that and it shocked me.

My pilot friend Gordon had a pal who flew for FedEx, and he checked with him—they had a warehouse for undelivered packages without labels, and the guy inquired if he was allowed to rummage through them to look for it. But it was a no-go.

FedEx paid me $100. It was the maximum under their terms.

More than two decades down the line, I still catch myself imagining what happened to that shipment. Did it bounce around in a delivery truck and get wedged under a seat, tumble out of a bag at an airport and get thrown into the trash, or perhaps an employee spotted it was going to Sharon Osbourne's office and stole it? Did the contents end up on an auction site? Were they fenced to a memorabilia store? Tossed into a landfill in Tennessee? Who knows.

I received a "special thanks" on both album reissues, and Colin generously sent replacements for some of the records. But even now, I search the web the odd time at nights, hoping to buy a replacement.

IN 2002, FROM OUT OF NOWHERE, Ozzy became even more famous. In March, the family (minus Aimee) flared into international stars when their MTV series, *The Osbournes*, was an overnight record-smashing phenomenon. I couldn't understand what the fuss was about. I assumed everyone knew that's how they were: they shouted and screamed, but they loved one another and were, underneath it all, just a family trundling along as they earned a living and navigated life like everyone else.

A couple of years into *The Osbournes*, Ozzy told me that the previous day he was talking to a woman and mentioned his music, and she didn't know he was a singer. She only knew him as a TV star, not a rock star.

I felt protective and defensive when viewers poked fun at Ozzy, and I knew footage was edited and massaged. In one scene he struggled with working the TV remote, but to me it didn't prove he was a bumbling buffoon, it was because he owned an elaborate, space-age system. I knew, because the same remote baffled me, and I was twenty years younger.

When the show debuted in the UK, I flew to London to watch Ozzy record a chat show at the BBC Television Centre. He was appearing at Party at the Palace, a concert to be broadcast live celebrating the Golden Jubilee of Queen Elizabeth II, at Buckingham Palace the following month. I sat with Sharon and Lynn in the canteen as they talked with the producer: there I was, in BBC headquarters, sipping tea, as they fine-tuned plans for a show honoring the Queen at Buckingham Palace. Could you shoehorn in any more motifs of the British establishment?

SHARON ALWAYS LOVED TO THROW A party, and after *The Osbournes* catapulted their fame to a new level, she ended 2002 with the greatest blowout I've been lucky enough to attend. The Osbournes arranged to renew their vows, twenty years after their wedding, on December 31, again at the Beverly Hills Hotel.

Unfortunately, one of my oldest friends from Ozzyland wouldn't be there—Randy losing a sudden, shocking fight with cancer that March. Nearly two decades later, Michael told me I was in the opening scene of a documentary about him, *The Life, Blood and Rhythm of Randy Castillo*, walking past Ozzy's dressing room at the Budokan in Tokyo. It had photos of him battling illness—I was glad I never saw him like that. I remember him healthy.

The invitation was even more decadently scandalous than that to Ozzy's fiftieth, delivered in a royal purple satin envelope, my name handwritten in gold ink calligraphy, an imitation jewel used as the clasp for the fine thread tying it together. Against all the odds, in the world's most rough-and-tumble industry, where their union mixed business and pleasure, their bond remained unbreakable.

Julie and I touched down in LAX three days early amid Osbourne-mania. Kelly had launched a singing career and sold out two nights at the Roxy on Sunset—Michael couldn't even put me on the guest list, as she added fifty names just before showtime, though he got us in the next night, along with my friend Gordon and his wife. Indeed, in a nod to cheeky younger Stephen, Keith happened to be in town on vacation and I convinced the doorman to let him in as well, though the VIP area was such a mob scene we were squished against a wall.

Ozzy arrived, but left halfway through (I found out the next day he'd been self-medicating and, half-tranquilized, thought he was attending a Rolling Stones gig). For the closer, "Papa Don't Preach," she urged the audience to rush the stage and join her, just like her dad did with "Crazy Train." Lynn led me into the dressing room so I could congratulate her, and I chatted with Sharon, then we hit the after-party.

Jack saw us come up the stairs and walked over to hug me, clutching a beer, though he was only seventeen. I squeezed his arm and said I was so happy for him the TV program was such a sensation. He gave a rueful smile. "Thanks, dude, but I tell you, I think the drawbacks of all this fame are beginning to outweigh the benefits." Before he could elaborate, another guest tapped his shoulder to get his attention and launched into a story.

ON NEW YEAR'S EVE WE HAD our names checked off, gave up our cameras, got our hands stamped, were ushered into a reception area, waited until the doors opened, then tumbled into a room flooded with a sea of white roses and crystal decorations. The rabbi said they had only a few friends watching in 1982, but this time it'd be a few million, as the ceremony was being filmed for later broadcasting on *The Osbournes*.

As we recessed down a staircase we were handed a Sharon Osbourne credit card with her photo. It served two purposes: it entitled you to $1,000 worth of gambling at the casino, and when you showed it at a row of mini designer stores set up in the courtyard, each gave you a gift. Mike's drum tech, whose wife was the professional planner organizing the party, told me they planned for five hundred guests, but were expecting seven hundred, so warned me to hoover up the merchandise first (Justin Timberlake called the previous day asking for eight invites). It was a hardcore scrum around the Rodeo Drive–style pop-up shops, wives and girlfriends of millionaire musicians and actors and Hollywood personalities pushing and shoving and elbowing to snag the luxury limited-edition cargo of candles, watches, jewelry, and makeup.

Marilyn Manson's girlfriend, Dita Von Teese, stripped while in a whopping wineglass, a crooner belted out lounge versions of Ozzy songs, we'd a special souvenir edition of the *National Enquirer* (the *National Ozzquirer*), while the attendees were a barometer of their new elevated Tinseltown status: actor Jon Lovitz, comedian Chris Rock, singer Robbie Williams.

Michael introduced me to Rudy Sarzo, the bassist of the beloved Randy Rhoads–era lineup. It was the highlight of my night. He enthralled us with stories from Ozzy and Sharon's original wedding in Hawaii, and from the bachelor party visit the night before to the Korean brothel that was part of rock folklore.

The Village People hit the stage to ring in the new year. That's how I welcomed 2003—dancing to "YMCA" in Beverly Hills with rock stars and celebrities. Just like when I was that teenager in Rio, I took a moment to wonder what I'd done to deserve it. When it wrapped, Julie retired to the hotel and I went with Robert and Whit from Ugly Kid Joe to a penthouse overlooking Sunset, staggering out at 5:30 a.m. The UK celebrity magazine *NOW* ran a six-page spread detailing the extravaganza—the invites cost £6,000, Sharon's jewelry was valued at $1 million—but it being the Osbournes, there was more drama to come.

On New Year's Day we went back to the hotel, spending the afternoon by the pool with Lynn, her partner Paul, and some of Ozzy's family. At the table beside us were Tobey Maguire and Leonardo DiCaprio, Matthew Perry sat a few feet away, and we shared the elevator with Warren Beatty. It was another world. Ozzy had gone home, no doubt overwhelmed by the hoopla—he had a complicated relationship with his relatives, and they said they hadn't seen him since they arrived. His brother referred to him as "John"—the one and only time I ever heard Ozzy called that (as a kid his mates shortened his surname to Ozzy and the nickname stuck).

Sharon treated a handful of us to dinner—"It's so ridiculous—so ridiculous—that you are here! That you traveled all this way," she kept saying to me. During the meal she repeatedly stepped out to use her phone. When she invited us back to her bungalow at midnight, we found out why.

Each party guest received a raffle ticket, the prize an outrageous necklace worth $43,000. The winner turned out to be a gate-crasher. Sharon's assistants were trying to track her down. As we stood in the bungalow, we discussed it with her staff, security guard, and nurses, some of whom were convinced the draw was rigged: Kelly was supposed to do it, but she was replaced at the last minute, and no one knew why. Sharon was furious—she had been hoping the winner would be an employee or friend, not an interloper. She wondered if she could sue her for the cost of the event, which was $2,000 a head. And then . . . the police showed up. Six cops—six!—rapped on the door. The girl had reported Sharon for threatening her.

She was the picture of innocence. "Me? Look at me. How could I threaten anyone and act like a gangster? The only gangster I know is Don Corleone." We told them what happened, they said it seemed like a civil, not a criminal, matter, and left.

She waited a beat after the door closed, then said, "Do I deserve a fucking

Oscar or what!" and we all collapsed in laughter. She always said her dad was a gangster, so I guess she got it honest.

It cleared out, but Lynn, Julie, and I stayed until 1:30 a.m. to help choose wedding photos to be released the following morning to the media. Sharon asked if we were available to get together the next day, but it was clear she'd stupefying demands on her time, and everyone wanted a piece of her. Referring to their new superstardom, she shook her head and said, "Stephen, this year has been crazy." An understatement for sure. The only tinge of disappointment was I hadn't spoken to Ozzy, so I asked her to say hi from me. It was the last blowout I was invited to, and I sensed that at the time, writing in my diary, "The party was a great way to go out and leave my Osbourne adventure."

#214

VOODOO FEST

CITY PARK
NEW ORLEANS, LOUISIANA

October 30, 2010

IN JUNE 2004, WE immigrated to the States. Julie missed home, and after twelve years as a travel agent, I was ready for a new challenge in the New World. I painfully pared down my Ozzy collection and mentioned to Michael I'd dozens of posters and T-shirts that didn't make the cut: he told Sharon, who said to send them to LA, and she would buy them. That less-valuable FedEx box arrived safely.

Before we left, I saw Kelly and Jack in Ireland in the space of a few weeks. Kelly played in Dublin, but I was delayed driving down and only made the last two songs. The promoter's representative, a garrulous bloke, escorted me to the VIP area, then took me to the dressing room to say hello afterward.

But that two-hundred-mile round trip for a ten-minute show paid off two weeks later. The Red Hot Chili Peppers headlined Slane Castle, an outdoor festival in County Meath, and Lynn, whose generosity toward me still knew no bounds after all these years, arranged passes. The guest section was bleachers on a hill, and we wandered down to get closer, but were stopped at the first barrier. Who appeared but the friendly fella from Kelly's gig.

"You're the lad who's friends with the Osbournes, right?" he said. "Come with me." He marched off, us on his heels, past every checkpoint and bouncer, into a near-empty enclosed area at the front. We watched the Foo Fighters and Chili Peppers from a few feet away. To this day I don't know his name or what his job was, but it was one of the best gigs I've seen.

The following week, Jack flew to Belfast for a TV show, the first time any Osbourne was in Northern Ireland other than for a concert I believe, and I spent the day with him and Lynn at the studio. Jack and I were in his dressing room with the host discussing funny websites when we were interrupted by my cell ringing, and to my embarrassment, the ringtone blared the Sabbath classic "Paranoid." But Jack loved it and asked where I got it so he could download it, too.

Sadly, the summer before we moved, Ozzyland suffered another body blow when Bobby died. He was an integral, trusted part of the Osbournes' life for two decades, handling multiple jobs on tour, working with other acts for Sharon when her management branched out, organizing logistics while rehearsing and recording. He succumbed to throat cancer at only fifty, while, of course, on the road with Ozzy. A great guy who took me under his wing, to whom I owe a lot.

With the loss of Bobby and Randy soon together, it felt like my time with Ozzy was slipping into the mists of history. Immersed in writing this book, with all things Ozzy ruminating and rattling inside my brain, a fact whacked me around the head at 11 p.m. in bed—I've seen four solo dates this millennium. In the nineties I went to more in a week. I had over a decade between gigs. I'd no idea the gaps were so long, the shows so few. The fan who flew to Brazil, who didn't want to miss a performance anywhere on earth, was averaging one concert every five years this century. I saw Sabbath live only once after Milton Keynes in 2001 before they retired from touring in 2017.

Extenuating circumstances are myriad. Ozzy's tours shortened: for instance, the trek I worked on, Retirement Sucks, lasted fifteen months, but the one to support his 2010 album, *Scream*, was only thirty-odd North American dates, while the Ozzfest never came within three hundred miles of our new home in New Orleans. I still jumped on every itinerary as soon as it was released and scoured it for potential trips, but in my stateside life, money has always been an issue.

In my travel agency days, I was self-employed with unlimited £20 round trip tickets on fifty-minute flights to England to catch gigs. Living in Louisiana, both the distance to shows and the cost of airfare and accommodation were prohibitive. I've never held a full-time job since settling here, scratching a living from a mishmash of teaching and freelance writing, working at my daughter's private school in return for cheap tuition. Julie was the main breadwinner; what little spare cash we had for trips went on visits to family.

On July 21, 2007, my two lifelong passions collided when both Chelsea, my soccer club, and the Ozzfest were in the LA area. I dreamed about watching Chelsea in the afternoon, then driving to San Bernardino to see Ozzy. I researched flights and messaged Michael, asking if I could stay with him. The problem was, Julie was pregnant with a due date of early August.

We went to her checkup in June, and when her ob-gyn asked if we had any questions, I cleared my throat, clasped my hands, and leaned forward. "So, Doctor . . . whaddya think the chances are that the baby could come early?"

Julie narrowed her eyes at me and shook her head, a warning look I'd seen Sharon give Ozzy.

"It's hard to say," the doctor replied. "I mean, there are so many—"

"Yes, I'm sure," I cut her off, "but if you had to bet today. I mean, is it possible it could arrive two weeks premature or—"

Julie raised her hand. "Stephen, no. Stop it. You aren't going," she said, and explained to the doctor what was going on.

I became friends with the doctor, Becky, as our daughters went to the same school, and years later she told me that when I asked the question, she thought I was joking, and it was only when she read my book *Finn McCool's Football Club*, about my love of soccer and our pub team's story during Hurricane Katrina, that she realized I was serious.

Nicola was born on July 31, and money got even tighter as I became a stay-at-home dad for the next four years. I was a father at thirty-seven—the same age Ozzy was when Jack was born. A decade on from touring the world with him, I was looking after my baby daughter full-time, changing diapers and going to story time at the library. When I met Ozzy, I was a kid and he was an icon, but we both ended up as regular guys with a wife and family.

OZZY HAS PLAYED NEW ORLEANS TWICE since I moved here, headlining Halloween's three-day Voodoo Fest. The 2010 edition was the first solo date I'd caught in more than a decade—indeed, I hadn't spoken to any of the Osbournes in years since starting my new life in the States. I caught up with the entourage first, as Michael and his wife, Denny, came in for the weekend and I'd breakfast with Martha and Greg.

Keith happened to be visiting from England, and twenty minutes before showtime, we stood outside Ozzy's dressing room, in a high school sports stadium, while his assistant told him we were there. I knew he was always nervous before a gig and afterward when he was relaxed was a better time to chat, but he was "doing a runner"—not returning to his dressing room when the set ended, but sprinting offstage and into a van to be whisked to the airport, beating the post-festival traffic.

He came out, smiling, looking fit and healthy. "Steve, how you doin', old bean?" and shook my hand. "Were you here through all that hurricane stuff?"

We discussed Katrina briefly, Keith took a photo of us together, but I could tell Ozzy was thinking about the concert, and we didn't hang around. Jack was with him, and he, too, came out to say hi and also ask about Katrina.

We went to the mixer and stood behind Greg. The songs had hardly changed since the eighties, with only one track from his latest album, *Scream.* But surprisingly, he resurrected "Killer of Giants" from *The Ultimate Sin.* In 1986 as a teenager, I stood on the soundboard to watch him do it in a drafty leisure center in terrorist-ravaged Belfast—twenty-four years later I had the same vantage point to listen to the same song as a father in my new home on the other side of the world.

#216

VOODOO FEST

CITY PARK
NEW ORLEANS, LOUISIANA

October 31, 2015

IN 2013, I DROVE six hours to see Sabbath kick off their tour in Houston. It was tremendous, four songs from *13*, Ozzy's first full-length record with them in thirty-five years. Afterward, my friend Paul and I went into the dressing room to talk to Ozzy and Sharon. As we caught up, an unmistakable thick Brummie accent rang out, "I thought I heard a Protestant in here."

Geezer, laughing, shoulders shaking, was standing at the open dressing room door, and he came in to talk about soccer. They all packed up and left, then when I was speaking with Martha in the corridor, Tony came past on his way out. I said hello and got a photo with him, but I don't think he remembered me—sixteen years later, I suppose he'd forgotten me helping him off the ground in an Indianapolis parking lot. Gloria kindly took me to breakfast the next morning at her hotel, no sign of Geezer, so I guessed his long lie-ins were still a thing.

Two years later, Ozzy returned to Voodoo Fest with a hybrid solo-Sabbath show. The appearance was billed as "Ozzy and friends" and featured Geezer, along with guest guitarists Tom Morello from Rage Against the Machine and Slash from Guns N' Roses.

It poured all day, and backstage was a quagmire, every step sucking your shoes off. Beforehand, I got to spend time with Sharon, Gloria, and Kelly as we huddled in the catering tent to escape the elements, but I never saw Ozzy or Geezer. The guest hangout enclosure by the dressing rooms was a saturated mud bath, so no one hung out. I didn't want to disturb Ozzy pre-show, and although Gloria told me to bang on the dressing room door and say hi to Geezer, I didn't feel comfortable barging in, as he shared a room with Tom and Slash. I knew Slash wouldn't remember me from our all-night rager at his in 1995.

As I closed in on fifty, I spent less time with middle-aged Ozzy and Geezer at gigs than I had as a pimply teenager. But I was still bonded to his musicians and roadies, even if the ties loosened over the years.

I was at Voodoo Fest with Ray, the lighting tech from Retirement Sucks, who also moved to New Orleans after marrying a local. I hadn't seen him in eight years but spotted him on the sidewalk from my car weeks after immigrating. His daughter went to Nicola's school, so the small, private all-girls joint in the exclusive Garden District had two students with Ozzy roadies for fathers.

We had passes for the guest stage, and we climbed the stairs to an elevated metal platform erected stage left. Kelly appeared for two minutes to check out the view, but otherwise, we had it to ourselves the whole set, no one else allowed so close, the organization still treating me spectacularly. We could see over the backline, the amps the guitarists use for onstage sound, as the three special guests joked out of the audience's sight line.

I loved it as much as ever, Ozzy showing no sign of slowing, still doing his frog leaps and dumping buckets of water, the improvement in live audio technology helping his voice sound crystal clear. Ray worked on two tours, but it was his first Ozzy concert as a fan, not an employee, and he, too, was impressed. Half of the sixteen songs were Sabbath's with half of Sabbath onstage, and Ozzy lobbed in a throwback, "Shot in the Dark," his big hit from *The Ultimate Sin*, a track he hadn't performed in years. Geezer saw me in the gantry—Chelsea lost, 3–1, that day, and throughout the night he flashed three fingers at me and laughed. Almost three decades after meeting him, some things hadn't changed.

WHILE OZZY APPEARANCES IN LOUISIANA WERE rare, the extended "family" passed through more often. He's had almost forty band members—one for every year of his solo career—but it's two bassists I've remained closest to.

Straight after No More Tours ended in 1992, Mike Inez joined Alice in Chains, and I flew to London to see his debut with them two months later (he always insisted the first time I saw him, in Dublin, was a live rehearsal, not a proper gig, but he can't argue about this one!). We've been friends for more than three decades, but the incident we revisit most is his visit to Belfast on that tour in March 1993. We were hanging in their second-floor dressing room while drummer Sean Kinney dropped unopened beer cans out the window to fans at the stage door. Then he shouted, "Are you okay?" A tin smacked a teenage girl in the face. The tour manager rushed down and brought her up, her nose busted open and her clothes blood-splattered. The band fussed over her, signing CDs and posters. "Dude, you think she'll sue us?" Mike whispered. I said no, this was Northern Ireland, not New York, and when her boyfriend talked his way in, he said a cursory hello to her, then concentrated on autograph collecting.

Only six weeks after we set up home in New Orleans, in August 2004, Mike sold out the House of Blues with Heart, whom he joined for an album and tour, and we had a couple of late nights reliving old times and partying in the French Quarter.

Twelve months on, there was no partying in the Big Easy. As Hurricane Katrina drew a bead on the city, we ignorant transplants underestimated the danger posed by a historic Category 5 storm. We fled our newly purchased house at the last minute with no more than an overnight bag as the monster crashed ashore. With no evacuation plan we haphazardly crisscrossed the South on the hoof, east to Mississippi, back west through northern Louisiana, and into Texas, battling to stay ahead of the devastating winds.

My pilot friend Gordon told me to get to Dallas and he'd arrange a flight out, and finally, after two days of desperate, anguished-filled driving, we made it to DFW. Most cell towers in the region were destroyed in the flood, and the few working overloaded as distressed evacuees fought to contact friends and family. Sitting in the airport food court, exhausted, silent, beat from the ordeal, my phone rang for the first time since the disaster. It was Mike—making sure we were okay, asking what he could do to help. He said he'd had us on redial for hours.

Alice in Chains re-formed, and he returned to a still-recovering New Orleans with them in October 2007. I took him to visit the devastated Lower Ninth Ward, then swung by mine so he could see three-month-old Nicola, who cried her eyes out the whole time. I took him to his hotel, we planned a quick drink at the rooftop bar, one led to another, and it turned into another marathon Quarter adventure.

I went to his wedding at his manager's home in the mountains of California with a host of rock stars. He's so popular in the business because he never changed and remains warm, funny, and genuine, still calling me often just to shoot the breeze. Although he sold his boat, he always invites me to stay. In 2018, I caught Alice in Chains three times in five months. They played in London while I was there with Nicola—the following day, we went to Mike's hotel for coffee, and this time she didn't cry. When they came back to the Crescent City we strolled along Bourbon Street again, but Mike had been sober a while, so he stuck to nonalcoholic beer. Maybe some things do change.

MEANWHILE, ROBERT TRUJILLO JOINED METALLICA AFTER Ozzy's band, and is also one of the friendliest, most unpretentious blokes you could ever meet. Metallica came to town a few months after I immigrated in 2004 on his first tour, and we met up to catch some live music and have a beer. Four years later they hubbed from here, and one of their managers owned a French Quarter condo. I passed a lazy afternoon with Robert and singer James Hetfield on the balcony, eating expensive hors d'oeuvres and sipping champagne, watching tourists drift by beneath.

At their hotel I heard an English accent in the lobby—it was *Kerrang!* photographer Ross Halfin, who'd flown in to shoot the band—funny how thousands of miles from the UK, and more than two decades later, I was still bumping into the Rock in Rio crew. In fact, both Metallica and Alice in Chains played Rock in Rio in 2013. I'd been messaging with Mike about a painful personal issue, so he hunted down Robert backstage to tell him, and when he returned to the States, Robert called to give me a pep talk.

Metallica headlined Voodoo Fest in 2012 and he rang a couple of weeks out for a favor: his wife, Chloe, had never been to New Orleans; could I show her around for a few hours? The band arrived on their private plane, and I drove to the executive terminal, where I was escorted to the runway when they landed—I'd never driven up to a runway before. I picked up Chloe for an afternoon of sightseeing, then she called their tour manager to open the back gate for us. I kept getting waved through until I was twenty feet from their dressing room—"rock star parking" in every sense.

I watched from the same raised stage-left platform, then Chloe appeared to say they were doing a runner but Robert wanted to say goodbye. She led me down to his side of the stage so we could snatch a minute between the end of the set and the encore. He dragged me onstage and his tech snapped a photo of us. Me onstage with Metallica. My cell lit up with texts from friends in the audience who saw me.

In 2018, Robert and Chloe were back for a few days, as a documentary he produced was in the New Orleans Film Festival. While Chloe shopped, Robert and I lost track of time over lunch, and I realized I'd to pick up Nicola from school. We went to get her, and it still makes me laugh—my eleven-year-old daughter at an upper-crust school collected by the Metallica bassist.

The following year, I returned to Ireland to see Metallica's gigantic outdoor gig at Slane Castle, and a couple of days before leaving, I took Nicola to stay in a retrofitted school bus in the country. Robert texted from the runway in LAX, about to depart for Dublin, asking if I'd an Irish friend who could lend him a guitar and practice amp for a couple of days. I messaged a bunch of mates, marveling at the bizarreness: I was staying in a school bus in the North Carolina mountains, trying to borrow equipment for a musician before their prestigious show on the other side of the planet. Just helping out a pal—who happened to be in one of the world's biggest acts—and I owed it all to Ozzy.

#217

MOONSTOCK FESTIVAL

WALKER'S BLUFF WINERY
CARTERVILLE, ILLINOIS

August 21, 2017

EIGHTEEN YEARS AFTER *THE Big Breakfast*, I was back dancing at a TV show for the Osbournes.

Sharon used *The Osbournes* as a launchpad to forge a stellar career on the small screen. She was a host on the daytime TV discussion program *The Talk* when it came to New Orleans in 2013. I was one of five men in an audience of hundreds, and the warm-up comedian had us come onstage and dance in turn, thankfully only for the spectators, not a nationwide broadcast. Afterward we visited her in her dressing room. Guests received products from all the sponsors, and before I left, she made sure I was stocked with vouchers to claim everything online, from blenders to heated bag chairs to Spanx.

Four years later, it was Ozzy and Jack in town filming their TV series—at my house. A couple of months beforehand, Michael called to say they were headed here for an episode of *Ozzy and Jack's World Detour*, in which they traveled the country exploring offbeat and unusual historical sites, and I volunteered to help with local advice or logistics. They wanted to shoot in the LaLaurie Mansion, an infamous house in the Quarter with a grisly reputation, reputed to be the most haunted home in America. I knew the owner, another Michael, and offered to put a word in for Jack: no one had filmed inside it before, but he was a rock fan, and if he was to let anyone break the duck it would be Ozzy. When I spoke to him, though, Jack's office had already been in touch, and it was sorted. I assumed they didn't need me after all, but planned to swing by the mansion and say hi while they were shooting.

A few days out, the production company rang and asked to meet. They had this idea for Ozzy and Jack to call on me to catch up on old times, as they'd never had a segment featuring anyone from Ozzy's past. Three guys came over, I guess to check that I wasn't a whack job who lived in a dump. They gave me a performance contract and a nondisclosure agreement, warning I could be liable for $50,000 if I talked about it in advance. They had an RV and equipment vehicles and SUVs and vans for bodyguards and cameramen and sound recordists and directors and assistants—it seemed more roadies and gear for Ozzy visiting my three-bedroom house than we had when he headlined stadiums. They needed lots of parking, so I banged on my neighbors' doors and pleaded, "I've a favor to ask. I can't tell you why, but could you please park your car on another block tomorrow?"

The crew arrived, set up, mic'd me up, and gave me instructions. The director said, "Don't open the door as soon as they arrive. We don't want it to look like you're standing at the door waiting for them." (Which I was.) "Instead," he said, "hold off for a while, and I'll give you the signal to let them in."

When I didn't answer immediately, Jack pushed open the door and came in.

We joked our way through a couple of hours, shooting the shit in my living room. Jack asked how I met his dad, and Ozzy and I reminisced, all the time ignoring the sound techs and cameramen crowded around us, the director leaving us alone to chat. I brought up the morning in 1988 when Sharon sent her sleeper chair to Lynn's for me to use.

"It was such a kind thing to do for me, but you won't remember that, Ozzy," I said.

"I bloody do! It was my fucking chair!" he roared. "I wondered where it had disappeared to when I went to use it!"

I made tea and we moved to the dining room. I'd dug out a pile of photos and we flicked through them, triggering memories for Ozzy, and we recalled past bandmates and tours. When we wrapped, and I thought they'd stopped filming, I told Ozzy I wanted to be serious for a minute.

"Ozzy, I just wanted to say, I feel so privileged to have spent time with you. I was paid to travel the world with the man I consider the greatest heavy rock singer ever. I'm just happy for the time I got to spend with you."

Ozzy jumped up. "Stroke me. I can go home now. You've topped me off for the next five years."

Just like that afternoon in a Manhattan hotel suite twenty-one years previously when I thanked him for buying me the journal I used to write this book. His fame grew more than either of us could have imagined, thanks to TV, but he was the same old Ozzy: still reluctant to accept praise, still squirming when you paid him compliments.

Of course they used that clip in the show.

THAT EVENING THEY FILMED IN THE LaLaurie Mansion, and though it was Nicola's exam week, I thought meeting Ozzy justified a late night. I took her into the kitchen to introduce her to him as the crew set up.

I said, "Ozzy, this is my daughter, Nicola. You're the reason she's alive. If I hadn't been in London for your birthday party in 1995, I'd never have met and married her mum. So it's all your fault."

Michael had given me a gift for her: a one-off Sabbath hoodie from their Hollywood Bowl date made specially for family and friends (I never got one). Nicola wore it, so I've a photo of her, in Black Sabbath gear, with Ozzy, the Prince of Darkness, in the LaLaurie Mansion, the nation's most haunted home. So metal.

The episode I was featured in aired in December. I watched the premiere at the LaLaurie Mansion with the owner, Michael, his housekeeper, and her daughter, all of whom appeared in it, and texted Jack a photo of us. I featured briefly and my name was on-screen fleetingly, but even so, there was an immediate reaction. Within minutes I received a tsunami of Facebook friend requests—a woman in New York writing, "You are very handsome and I love your voice"—then letters turned up begging for backstage passes and autographs.

Spending the day with Ozzy provoked me to react, too. I still saw him as a singer, not a TV star, and I resolved to catch him live. After making only two gigs in fifteen years, I saw two in thirteen months.

THE FIRST WAS MOONSTOCK, THE MOST otherworldly show Ozzy ever played in his zany career. Michael mentioned it four months out when we were in contact about the TV shoot. An Illinois vineyard owner offered Ozzy a fortune to perform at 1:30 p.m. on the Monday the path of near totality of a solar eclipse was passing over Carterville, Illinois. His winery was in nearby Walker's Bluff, and the contract stipulated Ozzy was to go onstage and sing "Bark at the Moon" exactly when the eclipse started. Who knew wine came from Illinois? I emailed Michael it sounded so batshit crazy I was tempted to go if I could scare up some friends. He urged me on, replying: "You should go to Moonstock. What could be better than seeing Ozzy during a total solar eclipse at 1:30 in the afternoon? It's like seeing the Prince of Darkness in total darkness."

I roped in two mates confusingly called Jonathon and Jonathan, and Jonathan's girlfriend, Sarah, came, too. We used his roomy BMW for the 1,300-mile round trip rather than my thirteen-year-old Honda with no AC. Although the concert was booked only a few months earlier, tourists had reserved accommodation years in advance to witness the extraordinary event and were descending on the eclipse's track slashing a diagonal swath across the country. The available rooms could have been cited for price gouging, but I came across a couple renting their house for the first time and snagged a deal only forty miles from the venue.

We arrived in Missouri and were greeted by the host, an older lady who lived next door. She showed Sarah the three bedrooms and said she'd organize a camp bed.

"No, it's okay, I'm dating one of them," Sarah said.

"Oh God. Really? Which one?" she answered with a horrified look, managing to insult all four of us simultaneously in an admirable feat of succinctness.

Everything about the concert was strange. "Moonstock" was a play on "Woodstock," but unlike that famous festival, in Carterville Ozzy was the only act. We saw a solitary sign advertising it on the way.

It was suffocatingly hot, even after thirteen years of acclimatization to New Orleans summers. The site was in a valley where the heat settled. It was the first time in years I couldn't get a cell signal due to topography—even to text I'd to leave the complex and walk up the hill for service.

Which was a problem when we were on the guest list, but there was no guest list.

The young worker on the gate said she'd try to find someone to help, and in the meantime, I turned around to tramp back up the slope to text Michael. When I returned, a middle-aged woman had appeared at the entrance. I gave my name and she said, "Yeahhhhh . . . that sounds familiar. I maybe saw it in an email somewhere."

So the nonexistent guest list would have totaled "Stephen Rea + 3." The staff didn't know what to do with us. It seemed their first time organizing any event, never mind a concert by a rock icon, but they smiled, thrust us VIP passes, and pointed us toward a cool bar. I trudged to higher ground to tell Michael we were in, and thankfully, just at that moment, Ozzy's security guy called. There was a meet and greet we could jump into—but it was happening right then.

I sprinted back down, lassoed the others, ran to a tent, got directed to another tent, blundered up a different hill, found a building atop a bluff. We were wheezing and sweating but hadn't missed it, dozens of fans queuing. A steward came out and asked if I was Ozzy's friend. I guess she was told to look for anyone out of breath and late. We waited, I saw Martha and Greg—who had married—then they announced Ozzy's plane was delayed, and the grunt-and-grope postponed until afterward. I knew he'd already landed, and assumed that being his usual anxious self, he wanted to get through the gig first.

We walked back to the field and the eclipse inched to life. Workers handed out souvenir glasses to watch the trajectory as a sliver of the moon nudged in front of the sun. A galaxy of seats at the front of the stage was cordoned off for the premium payers, but it was so scorching they were empty, as the attendees sheltered in concession tents. In my favorite Ozzy audience photo ever, the two Johnnies and I are sitting in the front row, wearing eclipse glasses and peering at the sun, no one else even in the frame.

I've been to hundreds of shows on all six inhabited continents. I can count on the fingers of one hand when the hairs stood up on my arms because I was experiencing something so special. When Ozzy ran onstage as the sky blackened, launching into "Bark at the Moon," it was like I was whisked to another universe in a different dimension. We were close, and I saw on his face how knocked out by it he was, too. He did fourteen songs, didn't phone it in, the best set I'd seen in eons.

After the meet and greet, I went into the dressing room, which wasn't a dressing room but a converted space in a winery flecked with flight cases, oak barrels, leather seats, stone walls, and mounted mosaics. The band had their own area, so it was only Ozzy, Sharon, and Martha, who was flitting about packing up: no line of record company executives or straggling liggers or competition winners to glad-hand and schmooze.

Years fell away as Sharon and I gossiped about ex–band members and mutual friends, just as we did after Sabbath shows two decades previously, and she asked after my family. It felt criminally laid-back, and they were equally amazed at the surrealness of it all, and by the amount of money Ozzy was paid.

Meanwhile, Ozzy and I slipped seamlessly back into our favorite discussion topic, World War II. The producer of *Ozzy and Jack's World Detour* told me Hitler's horse was buried on a former plantation in Louisiana, and they planned to take Ozzy to the grave. A month after the filming, I tracked it down. It was a saga, the site a private home with no public access, the summer afternoon heat meaning the area was deserted, no one around to ask for permission, the sketchy directions years out of date, me conscious of the high gun ownership in rural parishes as I blattered about trying to find the grave of a horse.

"Isn't it mental it ended up there?" Ozzy said when I told him about it, and we laughed at the absurdity of it being buried in a New Orleans suburb.

"Ever see that documentary about Hitler's grave? You know the mad fucker ended up under a car park?" he asked. After more than thirty years of friendship, we remained bonded by our fascination with the war, and Hitler. And his horse.

The vineyard owner arrived, and Sharon introduced us, and he said, "So you're the guy on the guest list. I wondered who that was." My friends came in to get a photo with Ozzy, then left to buy me the collector's edition Moonstock wine as a gift (I've never opened it).

"The guy on the guest list." I was back to being a ligger. No job, no responsibility, just posing about backstage and getting in the way of the real employees. Still, thirty-two years after Rock in Rio, I had decades of special friendships to treasure as I faded into the sunset.

The Osbournes left for their plane. I stayed for an hour in the dressing room with Martha as she tied up and packed, chatting away like the old days. A last moment in the sun. Or the moon.

#218

CYNTHIA WOODS MITCHELL PAVILION

HOUSTON, TEXAS

September 28, 2018

IF MOONSTOCK HAD BEEN my final Ozzy concert, it would have been a fittingly batty gig to cap off my Ozzy fanaticism. But in 2018 he announced No More Tours 2—with knowing irony—and I knew I had to catch his last tour to say goodbye to the rock 'n' roll rebel who was so important to me for so long. And I needed to complete the circle. When I first met him, six thousand miles away and thirty-three years earlier, I was a lad, and he was a father on his second marriage. By the time of the tour, I was closing in on fifty, with my own child and ex-wife.

Julie and I divorced and I was dating Elicia, a lawyer, originally from Mississippi, whom I met when she took my writing class. She wasn't a heavy metal fan and had more refined musical tastes—she loved the symphony, and weeks after this show, she dragged me to my first opera, *Eugene Onegin*, in Russian of all things. She wasn't even born when I saw Ozzy at Rock in Rio.

But I wanted her to meet him, so she agreed to come along, and with our friends Paige and Paul, we drove to Houston's Cynthia Woods Mitchell Pavilion. Martha found us in catering and escorted us to hang outside his dressing room. She had a helper. No one on the road with Ozzy ever deserved one more. It was our only chance to say hi, as Ozzy was doing a runner afterward. I knew how jittery he always was pre-gig and how tough it was to get an audience, and told Elicia we might not see him. We waited in the corridor for maybe ten minutes.

Then the door opened, and he barreled out, hand outstretched. "Steve, how ya doing? I can't stay long, I've gotta get ready for this gig and—"

I raised my hands. He didn't have to explain, I knew exactly how he felt, I'd seen it so many times, and was touched and humbled he'd interrupted his preconcert routine for us. I didn't want to intrude further.

"I know, Ozzy, just wanted to say hello and wish you all the best for the gig. And I wanted to introduce my girlfriend. This is Elicia."

"Girlfriend! I can't keep up with you!" he shouted.

She put out her hand, and as he took it to shake, he flashed me a look, that glint in his eye, and made a joke about where her hand had been. He said it quick and low and no one else understood it, but he and I laughed. A wee private moment between us.

Paige took a selfie, then he retreated to his sanctuary, and we went out front.

AT MY LAST FULL-LENGTH OZZY CONCERT, true to form, my friends and I were treated like royalty with laminates and fantastic seats. It was terrific, the sound crystalline. The set list barely changed since the original No More Tours trek twenty-six years previously, but why would it? Fans still wanted to hear some of the stone-cold greatest rock songs ever. He still packed arenas and sheds after fifty years.

It felt special, though, middle-aged dad that I was, because the set list was a journey through my history, too. Three Sabbath classics. Four tracks from his debut solo album, the one I listened to repeatedly before I even hit my teens. "Shot in the Dark" from *The Ultimate Sin*, the tour I'd first jumped the bus on in 1986. Three hits from No More Tears, where I stood on the side of the stage in California, thinking it was the end of the road. Zakk's solo spot hitting "Perry Mason" from the *Ozzmosis* release when I became an employee, and, of course, closer "Crazy Train," Ozzy, after all these years, still imploring the crowd to "Go fuckin' craaaaaaazy!"

My soundtrack, spanning four decades.

What happened to me will never happen again. What are the odds a teen admirer will write to Ed Sheeran or Taylor Swift and become friends? The music business changed. When I was in charge of the guest list, the crew scrawled names on a receipt or napkin. Those days are long gone. Every seat is precious and must be accounted for, even for the biggest acts. Hopping on a band bus or an invitation to share a private jet? Never happening again. Some of our roadies still tour, though I hear things are different now, confidentiality agreements and tickets for blood relatives only.

I was the right kid with the right lack of self-awareness in the right place at the right time with the right parents. And I worshipped the right rock star—one managed by his wife, who made business a family affair. They changed my life.

AS THE ENCORE PEAKED TO A crescendo, with Ozzy singing the last line of "Paranoid," I thought back to my adolescence during the Troubles in

Belfast, examining my past dispassionately and with fresh appreciation. And I knew everything came down to my parents.

My mum wrote the letter. Let me skip school to ride a tour bus with Ozzy Osbourne.

My dad paid for me to go to Brazil. Supported and encouraged my love of music.

The band took their bow, and Ozzy lifted the mic to his mouth. I knew what he would say. He ended every performance the same way, and although he looked out over the audience, he was talking to everyone onstage and on the crew as well.

"Thank you," he said. "I love you all."

#219

BACK TO THE BEGINNING

VILLA PARK
BIRMINGHAM, ENGLAND

July 5, 2025

IN FEBRUARY 2025, LYNN texted asking me to call her. I replied I'd do it in the morning, conscious of the six-hour time difference, but she answered: "Best today if you can."

The following afternoon, the Back to the Beginning show was announced for July 5. One final gig for both Ozzy and Sabbath at Aston Villa's soccer stadium in Birmingham, a stone's throw from where they formed a lifetime before. Joining them were a who's who of rock acts, playing for free, paying homage to the original masters of metal, the likes of Metallica, Guns N' Roses, and Alice in Chains. Lynn, who still worked for Sharon part-time, gave me the heads-up so I could book one of the last rooms at a hotel they were using, a seven-minute walk from the venue. Which I did.

For a minute, I wondered if I should make the nine-thousand-mile round trip. Ozzy looked and sounded fantastic in Houston in 2018—after more than two hundred gigs, was that the way I wanted to remember him live? But it was a fleeting thought. I knew I had to see his last stage performance.

Tickets went on sale at 4 a.m. New Orleans time, so I woke to screenshots from British friends who tried to buy them, the Ticketmaster site reading for one, "You are now in the queue. 120,597 people ahead of you." I was trusting somebody, somewhere, would get me in.

A few weeks later I flew to Belfast. My mum was selling her house and needed help clearing it out, and as I rooted through the attic, I found Ozzy photos, paintings, posters. . . . In the depths of her roof space, it was a timely reminder of how much he featured in my life for so long.

As it happened, Adam Wakeman, the keyboardist for both Ozzy and Sabbath, was playing in Northern Ireland with his side project, Jazz Sabbath. He put me on the guest list, and we had a drink afterward.

I said, "I bet you're getting hammered for tickets for the show, right?"

He chuckled. "I'm gonna do an Instagram post with all the crazy requests, blokes I haven't heard from in years asking for seven."

I told him I didn't have a ticket, but was hoping to attend. He put down his pint and said, "I'm playing all day. I'm in the band. I'm onstage with both the all-star jams, with Ozzy, with Sabbath—and I've just spent a thousand pounds on tickets for my family."

I froze, processing what he said. I blew out my cheeks. "Well, fuck-a-doodle-doo then," I said. "I guess I'll be listening to it from outside." I grimaced, then gulped the rest of my beer.

That was Friday. All weekend I fretted, weighing up my options, calculating how much I'd pay to scalp. On Monday, I flew to London to stay with Lynn—I hadn't seen her in three years, and the visit was planned before the announcement. She met me in the arrivals hall, we drove to her house, then I sat with her and her partner, Paul, in the kitchen. We'd been catching up for hours before we even mentioned the show . . . then she said I didn't need a ticket because she'd listed me as being on the crew. They would find jobs for me to do. Waves of relief washed over me like I'd been drenched by Ozzy's water gun.

Lynn, forty years after Rock in Rio, was still my fairy godmother.

I LANDED IN BIRMINGHAM ON JUNE 29, rented a car, and picked up Lynn at her downtown hotel. She had been in the city a few days but was moving to the upmarket golf resort in the countryside where Ozzy and Sharon were staying, half an hour away.

She had more luggage than I'd seen some support acts travel with on a two-month US tour. The new place was chockablock, packed with middle-aged guests in chinos and button-ups, but I parked a few feet from the front door, blocking the entrance to unload.

"Okay if I abandon it here for a minute, mate? I'm just nipping in for a cup of tea," I asked the bellhop. He said it'd be fine for twenty minutes. I left eight hours later.

Lynn and I caught up over afternoon tea on the sun-dappled terrace overlooking the first tee. The entourage filtered back from rehearsals, and I stayed for dinner with Lynn, Michael, and his wife, Denny, both of whom I hadn't seen in nine bloody years! We were joined by Melinda, who has worked closely with Sharon since 2001. She didn't think we'd met, but she had my number in her phone, and I was sure we had bumped into each other before.

Sharon and Kelly came down to say hello—I hadn't seen Sharon since Moonstock in 2017, Kelly even longer, Voodoo Fest in 2015. We had a drink after dinner, then I drove to where I was staying, the home of a married couple I knew from my journalism days in the city. It was a trek, on the opposite side of the UK's second-largest city, but it was free. I spent the next day touring the special exhibitions in the city that tied in with Back to the Beginning, and it felt like something of a homecoming for me as well, as I visited my old haunts from when I worked there, thirty-five years earlier.

The next day, Melinda decided I needed to stay at their hotel. I was a "runner"—picking up family and staff, buying supplies, carting stuff back and forth to Villa Park. Just like that, I was welcomed back into the fold, a trusted member of the Osbourne family. It was like I'd never been away. As Mike Inez often said, "Once you're in, you're in."

We ate breakfast together, worked all day, went to eat, and had a drink or two afterward. Long hours, little sleep, early starts. There was so much to organize, so many moving parts, a never-ending wave of logistical challenges for the unprecedented hard rock event.

The Ozzy and Sabbath sound checks were Thursday, forty-eight hours before the gig. It was the first time I'd seen Ozzy in the flesh in seven years, since our last meeting at that show in Texas. He'd suffered a string of health issues since then and was fighting Parkinson's.

He was pushed in a wheelchair to a hydraulic ramp underneath the stage, transferred to a Gothic throne, then lifted up. We walked out front to hear him run through "Mama, I'm Coming Home" with Zakk on guitar and Mike Inez on bass. It was a charged song anyway, but watching Ozzy, listening to his vocals, his hand shaking as he gripped the mic, made my eyes well. When Sabbath took the stage, Mike walked out to join me.

"Dude, what were you thinking when you said you might not come?" he asked. "You couldn't have missed this for the world."

He was right. For the next two days, backstage was like the craziest high school reunion ever. Guitarist Jake E. Lee and I re-created a photo of us together, him grimacing and pulling my hair, taken thirty-nine years earlier.

Band members I hadn't seen in decades, roadies I once shared a bus with, music journalists I'd gotten drunk with . . . Everyone and anyone who passed through the Land of Ozz descended upon Villa Park in Aston, the neighborhood where he grew up, to pay homage. No egos, no drama. The night before the show, I drove Lynn, Michael, Melinda, and her husband,

Steve, the half mile to Lodge Road, Ozzy's childhood home. There were a few fans also making the pilgrimage, but they good-naturedly let us bustle in ahead of them to take a group photo crowded outside the small, terraced house. We look so happy in it.

I WAS GIVEN A JOB ON show day: Sharon had a poster she wanted autographed by every musician performing in the show. I grabbed it and left her dressing room—Guns N' Roses had just finished sound-checking, and guitarist Slash was heading back to the hotel.

I held the poster out along with a Sharpie and told him what it was for. He took the pen, laid the poster on a flight case, then paused, his hand hovering over it.

"Is this really for Sharon?" he asked, looking me in the eye.

"I assure you, it really is," I replied. He nodded and signed it, the first to do so.

I spent the day running up and down stairs and back and forth across the stage and along corridors tracking down bands, and the members of both supergroups. The dressing rooms were spread over a vast area, with so many acts and solo stars and crew and production, every bathroom and nook and cranny and cupboard under the stairs had a famous rocker lurking inside.

I went into Sabbath's dressing room to get their signatures, and to help Michael with another forty-four posters. These were to be signed only by the four Sabs and divided among them. I chatted with Geezer and Tony as we did it, Geezer making fun of my accent and my soccer team, inviting me to come visit him in the States, Tony saying he remembered me from the nineties, Bill shirtless, warming up, all casual and relaxed, as the clock ticked down to showtime.

Finally, in to see Ozzy, Michael unfurling the posters for him to sign as I slid them along, me marveling at how lucky I was, back in the fold only days previously, but trusted to be one of only a handful allowed to visit the inner sanctum of rock royalty as they prepared for the pinnacle of their professional lives.

I locked Sharon's poster in the car for safe keeping. It had maybe eighty signatures, out of around ninety artists who would be performing. The only one in the world, a unique piece of heavy metal memorabilia. What a special role, to be the bloke who got those autographs. And maybe on some astral level, whatever I did wrong that led to me losing my Randy Rhoads autograph, this balanced the cosmic ledger.

I saw little of the other bands' sets. But there was no way I was missing Ozzy—five solo songs, four with Sabbath. Team Osbourne, those who had worked for him for decades, watched from the VIP platform out front. He sounded superb, visibly moved by the outpouring of love from tens of thousands of fans who flew from all around the world to be part of history.

To our amazement, Ozzy came to the afterparty—we thought for sure he'd be physically and emotionally spent. From his perch in an oversized leather chair, he saw me and pointed, so I walked over.

I shook his hand. "Ozzy, that was fantastic tonight. You sounded brilliant," I said.

He gave a half smile and shrugged. "Yeah, it wasn't bad, was it?" he said.

For Ozzy, the most self-critical person I ever met, never happy with how he sounded, it was as self-congratulatory as I ever heard. We chatted a moment, but I didn't want to monopolize his time and moved off.

Then from ten feet away, I realized that with me gone, he was exposed to dozens of liggers he didn't know. I said to Robert Trujillo he should go over and protect him from strangers. He did, then immediately beckoned me back to join them both, Robert talking about when he joined the band in 1996, and how I was there in Japan.

"He was only a kid when I met him," Ozzy said to Robert, and grinned. Just a kid. A fan. Then a roadie, and for the last two decades, a ligger. Here, though, at his last show, I was all of those things and more. In this private moment between us, I felt like his friend.

SEVENTEEN DAYS LATER, AT 12:17 P.M., I was in New Orleans when Lynn rang on WhatsApp. Her name flashed on my phone, and I jumped up to move into the living room beside the router for better Wi-Fi reception.

"Hallo!" I said, excited to hear from her.

"Where are you?" she asked. I told her. "Good, you're at home. I'm calling with the worst possible news."

And she said that Ozzy was dead.

AFTER A FEW HORRIBLE DAYS IN Louisiana I couldn't take it anymore and booked a flight to London. I wanted to feel useful and be with everyone. We could all be together again in England—a reunion none of us expected or wanted.

In the days leading up to it, on multiple occasions we slipped up, so used to being with each other as part of another world, and instead of saying "the funeral" or "the service," we called it "the gig," or "the show." Ozzy would have laughed at that, one final intimate performance.

My daughter turned eighteen the day he was buried. She was born because of Ozzy—if I had not been in London for his birthday party in 1995, I wouldn't have met her American mother. I canceled my flight to North Carolina I'd booked to celebrate with her. One last time, I was forced to reschedule a trip because of an unexpected Ozzy obligation.

I'm not going to write about that week—the Osbournes have lived in the public eye, but they deserve to grieve in private. However, I'll tell you two things that happened.

On the morning of the burial, I was shook awake at 6 a.m. by a hotel security guard. I was asleep in my underwear in the corridor, nestled against a fire exit door.

"Sir, can we help you find your way back to your room?" he asked.

"Yes please, that would be great, thank you," I replied, fighting to get off the floor.

I guess I got up during the night to pee, and opened the door to the hall instead of the bathroom. I'd had a couple of beers, though certainly not enough to get blackout drunk—but I had hardly slept in five days, was jet-lagged, emotionally overwrought . . . it all must have been too much.

I told Jack what happened. "You did a Dad!" he said, and laughed. Ozzy was notorious for getting hammered, then sleepwalking in hotels, ending up in the lobby or the wrong room. At least I was wearing underwear. I often sleep naked, and I imagined getting arrested for indecent exposure and missing Ozzy's funeral because I was in jail. I would have regretted it forever. Ozzy would have loved it, I've no doubt.

Then, around forty hours after the service, Jack came into the kitchen at Welders House, where I was emptying the dishwasher. Of Ozzy's kids, I've always been closest to him, and we kept in touch even when we went years not seeing each other.

He said, "Stephen, I'd like to do something for you. Can I write a foreword for your book?"

Less than two days after the burial, he was thinking about helping others. That's the Osbourne way. That's how his mum is. And how his dad was, even the last time I saw him.

THE PHONE DINGED IN MY HOTEL room. A summons to Ozzy Osbourne's penthouse suite.

It was 10:36 a.m. on the day after the final show capping a mind-boggling fifty-seven-year career. I was packing up, getting ready to check out, at the end of one of the best weeks of my life. It was a text from Melinda: "Ozzy wants to see you before they leave, so maybe come up at 11:30 or so."

I was as shocked as I had been forty years earlier, when Ozzy invited me and my parents to breakfast the day after Rock in Rio. I busied myself stuffing my case, not stopping to think about it. I knew it would overwhelm me. In the lobby, Lynn was having tea with a friend. I stopped and put my hand on her shoulder.

"He wants to see me. Will you come?" I asked, my lip trembling. She looked at me, stood, and held my hand as we went to his room. We knocked and were ushered inside.

"Ozzy—look who it is. This guy worked his arse off yesterday," said Sharon, still in her pajamas.

I cried the whole time I was with him. I don't know why. I suppose I felt fifteen again, honored that even though he was surrounded by a galaxy of rock stars and his family and friends and God knows who else, he thought about me.

"Stephen, stop it. You're going to get me going if you don't," said Kelly, hugging me.

Ozzy was on his iPad. He feigned to whack me around the head, as if to slap some sense into me, but he knocked over his tablet instead. I'd texted Melinda asking her to snap a candid photo of us together, and she took a bunch. I'm so grateful she did, the moment captured forever, our final meeting, four decades and six months after that first picture together in the hotel bar in Copacabana.

Ozzy and I embraced and I sobbed on his tracksuit top. He turned back to his screen, and I knew he was embarrassed by my childish blubbering. I said goodbye.

"Call if you ever need anything," he said. "We've known each other a long time, Stephen Rea."

ACKNOWLEDGMENTS: GRUNT & GROPE

WRITING IS A SOLITARY endeavor, but I am lucky to have friends and family who bring me joy and laughter when I'm not at my desk pretending to work.

So for the high-energy set opener, those who provide never-ending hospitality in London and its environs: Joe and Louise Thompson, Steve and Rachel Scully, David Feldstein, Roger Lowry, and Gurbir Dhillon. For their gracious help with a different kind of hospitality, my fellow Chelsea glory hunters Ian Seymour, Paul Mason, Neil Barnett, and Nick Beasant.

For their friendship, and providing a room when I'm too cheap to spring for a hotel: Tony Tomelden and Stephanie Coleman, Gordon and Dawn Sheals, Stephen and Pauline Patterson, Jackson and Catherine Collins, Alan Megahey, Jonathan Hird, Darren Bolton.

In Northern Ireland, my schoolmates Conrad Smyth, Matt Crozier, Neil McKeown, Neil Warburton, Doug Ferguson, Jason Patterson, and Blair Harvey. And to Sharon "Helen" Miles, Stephen Cullen, and Julie Smyth. A shout-out before the drum solo to those who rocked with me—Brian White, Stephen Wright, and Cormac Neeson.

In December 2019, my friend Neil Billingham visited from England, and he asked if I had an idea for my next book. I said I wanted to write about my relationship with the Osbournes, but had never found time. It was a daunting project, a story spanning decades with researching and transcribing and cross-checking. He wasn't an Ozzy fan, but insisted I should write it. He was the impetus. Thank you, mate. RIP.

In my adopted home of New Orleans, where would I be without Finn McCool's

Pub owners Sean and Carmel Kennedy, and the players who make it worth getting up on Sundays at 7 a.m. Sometimes. The pub and club have given me so much, as well as friends like Paul Daley, Adrian Simpson, Jeremy Dwyer, Joe Ryan, Jesse Stewart, Julien Meyer, Andy Smith, and Benji Haswell.

And to this lot who don't play football: Tom and Patricia Schoenbrun, Sam and Joe Guichet, Cat and Will Bishop, Christine Harvey, Dina and Bill Perrault, Paige Patriarca, Katherine Gurley, Ray Ziegler, Aidan Gill, Bert Swafford and Mary Kelly-Swafford, Kevin and Erin Muggivan, Jamie Midgley, and Michael Whalen. Roy Qualls for those AA loads, and Mary McCarthy and Brad Walton for feline dinner duty.

To the writers who return to classes time and again. This sort of mid-set sentence is the one that is for you because I am often a bit proud of some of your writing! (See what I did there?) Petrina Amacker, Marcia Bigelow, Jenelle Boucher, Chaya Conrad, Sara Cusimano, Samantha Frost, Rachel Henderson, Marissa Hogan, Tana Joelle, Catherine Levendis, Laura Michaud, Amy Porche, Anne Reed, Ash Rouen, Cathy Schieffelin, Bill Tice, and Ginger Vehaskari, among others.

To my extended family on both sides of the Atlantic: Carol and Jim Magill, Humberto Tavares, Sandra Conlane, Anne, William and Rachel Rea, Jo and Chris Wright, John and Tamara Ford, Barrett Ford and Maerin Laskey Ford, and Lindsay and Andrew Buscnlcncr. As I hope I made clear, I owe my parents, Billy and Linda, so much. But I'll mention it again, in case you got distracted watching the guitar tech stage left.

Let me take a moment to introduce the road crew, whose hard work behind the scenes made this possible. In grateful recognition of their professionalism, expertise, and patience, the quartet who did the important stuff to bring this book to life—Sam Chidley, Kevin Dupzyk, Rob Sternitzky, and Sean Manning. And thanks to the whole Simon & Schuster team, who fought for me to have the time and space to tell the story the right way after circumstances overtook us and gave it a new ending. Mia Robertson, John Paul Jones, Lauren Gomez, Allison Har-zvi, Wendy Blum, Irene Kheradi, Priscilla Painton, Stephen Bedford, Larry Hughes, Alia Derriey, Mike Nardullo, and Amanda Mulholland, you have my never-ending gratitude.

Time for the big set closer, the "Crazy Train" of acknowledgments. So, in the great wide, wide world of Ozzyland . . . first and foremost, the wonderful, incredible Lynn Seager-Putterford. In 1985 at Live Aid she got me Sabbath's autographs, at their (first) final performance thirty-two years later, she scooped up the commemorative confetti and sent me a packet. This book is down to you. And thanks to Paul Dale. Hot on her heels are Michael Guarracino, and his wife, Denny Sarason.

Michael has worked for Sharon for more than thirty years, and I'm thankful for that, and for his friendship. And to the three Johnny-come-latelies of Team Osbourne: John Fenton, Melinda Varga, and a digitally added Dave Moscato.

To Martha Heckman and Greg Price for thinking about me, whether it's sending swag or saving space on the mixer. I still drink tea from one of Ozzy's special mugs Martha gave me. To Keith Willey, a relationship I treasure. To the nicest bassists in rock, Mike Inez and Robert Trujillo. To Colin Newman, with thanks for his repeated generosity. To those ex–Ozzy people not mentioned by name, please know I am grateful for your help and friendship down the years.

And once again, to Ozzy, Sharon, Aimee, Kelly, Jack, and Louis for welcoming me into the Land of Ozz.

AND FINALLY, "PARANOID." The greatest of them all.

The first draft of this book was knocked out during COVID, when for months on end I was closeted with Nicola and Elicia. I could not have wished for better cellmates to spend quarantine with. I love you both so much.

Elicia—you are the most supportive wife imaginable. I am so lucky to have you, as you frequently remind me. But as we both know, you're worth it. And not just because of your sexy bum.

Nicola—you make me proud every day. Enjoy life. See the world. No skipping classes to tour with a rock band.

Thank you and good night. Stop by the merchandise stall on your way out.